MIND, MEMORY AND QUANTUM ENTANGLEMENT

The Estate Agent Who Thought He Was Einstein

Nick Greaves

2019

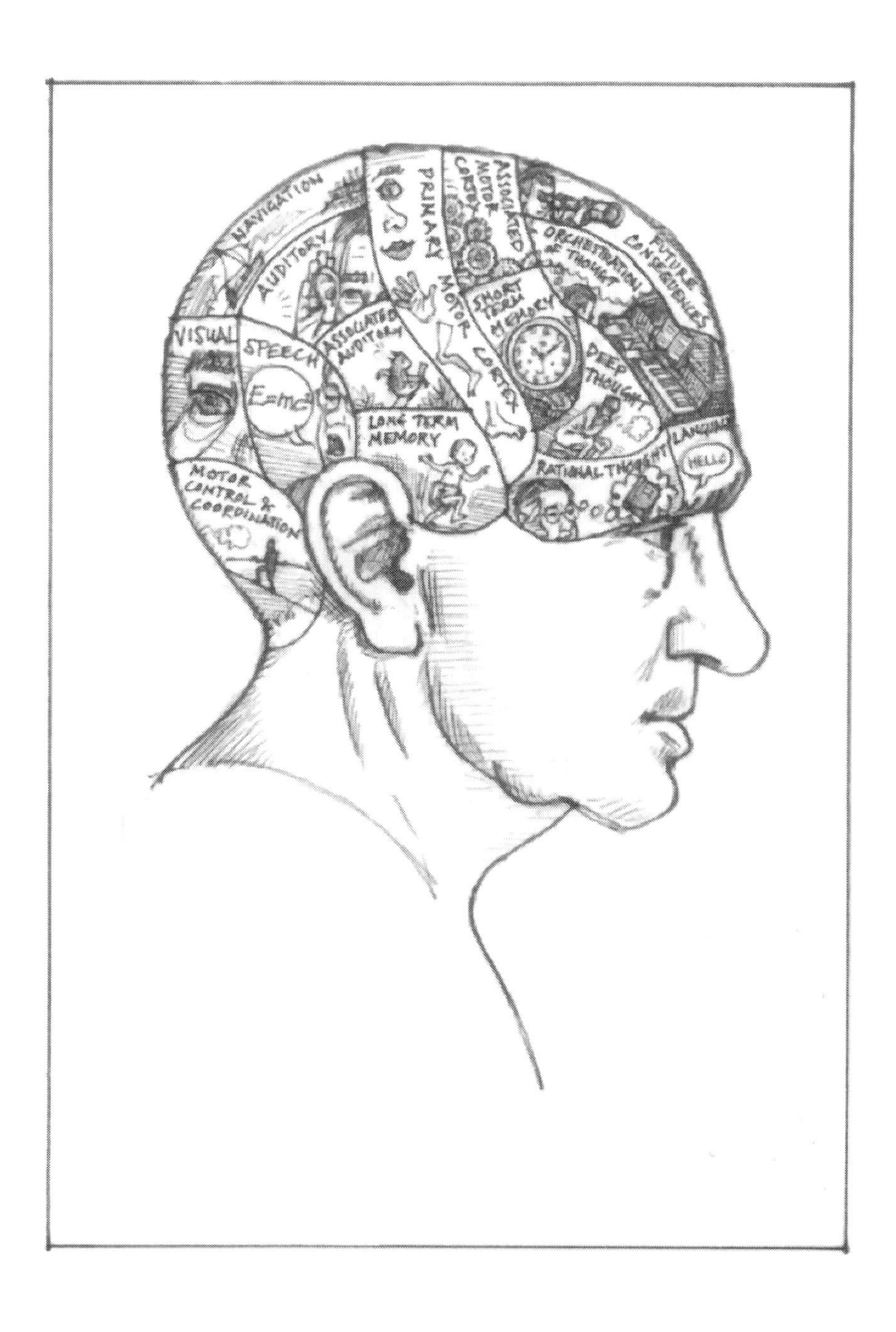
NAVIGATION
AUDITORY
PRIMARY MOTOR CORTEX
ASSOCIATED MOTOR CORTEX
ORCHESTRATION OF THOUGHT
FUTURE CONSEQUENCES
VISUAL
SPEECH
E=mc
ASSOCIATED AUDITORY
SHORT TERM MEMORY
DEEP THOUGHT
LONG TERM MEMORY
RATIONAL THOUGHT
HELLO
MOTOR CONTROL & COORDINATION

MIND, MEMORY AND QUANTUM ENTANGLEMENT

The estate agent who thought he was Einstein

Printed in the United States of America

Mind, Memory and Quantum Entanglement

ISBN-13: 9781712069776 (Pbk)

Acknowledgments

I owe a debt of gratitude to a number of individuals who have encouraged me to do something about my fixation that there must be a relatively simple answer, at least in principle, to form a basis of explanation for the mechanism behind memory. Having seen at firsthand how Alzheimer's disease and loss of memory is able to destroy the finest minds, I made the assumption many years ago that much of the workings of the mind would fall into place once the problem of memory had been resolved. I therefore need to thank anybody who has listened with apparent interest when I have attempted to explain with my usual minimal coherence what is involved in my hypothesis and why I considered it so crucial. Not that many people have managed to do this, without glazing over after a few minutes, quite understandably, but to those who did and those who managed at least to appear fascinated, I am much obliged.

Amongst the few who had the patience to encourage me in writing, if not in person, to continue and push forward with publication, regardless of the futility of being taken seriously in such an ambitious quest, I owe gratitude to the following: Arthur Koestler, Karl Pribram, Henry Margenau, John Beloff, Rupert Sheldrake, Arthur Chester, Goetz Oertel, Larry Dossey, Bob Laughlin, and Shelli Joye.

Of friends who do not specialise in the subject of the mind but who have either been enthusiastic, or at least encouragingly amused by my obsessional interest and musings on the subject, I have to thank in particular Stephen Fry, Simon Boler, Chris Leeming, Rob Hartford,

Susan Glasspool and also to Graham Philpot for the illustrations. Members of my immediate family who have been resignedly patient with this perennial distraction, not to mention nonplussed over so many years, have also to be thanked, especially my wife Angela, who having heard my muttering arcane discussions with myself for decades, suggested the book's title would be catchier if it was 'The estate agent who thought he was Einstein.'

Introduction

This book is an autobiographical account of how the author, attempting to make a living out commercial property development from the late 1960s, was diverted into the pursuit of something rather different: an answer to the mechanism behind thought. It is written in the first person singular rather than attempt a dry academic explanation of a subject lacking any agreed solution. My hypothesis has been developed on and off since 1978, and has received support sporadically since then, especially recently when one of its central themes correlates well with recent crucial experimental research on quantum entanglement.

Despite the huge advances made in science in technology over the 150 years, there is one field of investigation that has defied all attempts to ascertain the mechanism behind mind and memory. There have been useful advances in what parts of the brain control different various activities, and an impressive amount of analysis of how electrochemical currents pass between the components that make up the brain, via neurons, synapses, axons and dendrites, but how these manage to bring about memory and thought, is not known. There are theories on how parts of the brain might be involved, but the experts, and especially the philosophers seem unable to agree on much.

For reasons which are described later in this book, I first became fascinated in the subject of mind and memory in a manner that can hardly be described as orthodox, and ditto the answers I derived almost haphazardly over a number of years. Since this initially occurred well outside the usual way in which academia and research operate, I decided that my best course of action to explain my conclusions was to describe in this book the mental procedures involved, usually governed by what I was doing with my life at the time. When I first experienced strong curiosity to learn what was known about the mind, I had assumed that something positive was already in place about the mechanism behind memory. This was in the late 1970s, and I soon realised this was a mistake.

Although we can store information electronically on very small volumes of material, we do not know how this is done in the mind. I assumed that memory represented the mainspring process behind thought, and it seemed to me such a crucial issue to be resolved, that I became involved in the subject, not as an academic, but in my spare time. This was done whilst carrying out a nine to five office employment in order to make a living which was necessary to bring up a family in the sort of middle-class background and material circumstances that I had enjoyed. Having absorbed much spare time reading relevant material over the years from the perceptive work of others, my various conclusions seemed capable of being pieced together to become an explanation for some aspects of memory. In the late 1970s these received some qualified support from one or two sources of authority even though such observations were made in a loose conjectural manner. I was encouraged that they had the makings of a more comprehensive hypothesis to explain a mechanism behind memory in principle.

It has taken me from 1978 to 2019 to reach the stage where I might have enough subjective clarity to be able to describe in some detail my version of the workings of the mind with the possibility that a non-specialist readership might be to be able to grasp the essence of my various conclusions made over the last four decades in fits and starts. This has been helped by the work of specialist well qualified others whose results have reinforced some of my conjectures over that time, and most recently, by the research and advances in quantum entanglement.

For all we know, the answer might well be sitting there before our very eyes and which would appear at once immediately apparent if we had not been led a little astray by a few existing mistaken assumptions. This has often been the case in the past. My proposals might be no more than flights of self-delusion, but I have some support from a few individuals who are sources of authority, past and present.

This is a highly speculative exercise but separate parts of it and the assumptions I have had to make are reinforced by some papers of the most highly qualified physicists over the years: Erwin Schrodinger, John Wheeler, Richard Feynman, David Bohm, John Bell, and Heisenberg to mention the most prominent. This leaves out the bio scientists on whose subject I have less knowledge but I have strong qualified support from one or two quarters in this discipline, and in particular from Rupert Sheldrake whose conclusions are remarkably similar to mine albeit from a very different approach.

My proposals do not require mathematical ability, and the basic premise of similar structures or images resonating down through time, should not be too hard for anybody to conceive, although the problem then is to decide at what level to pitch my argument to explain the supporting reasons for such a system.

I provide a new self-organisational principle for the operation of memory. I do this via an explanation of what I describe as Duplication Theory, (more accurately a hypothesis but referred to as DT for brevity in future). It has further possible explanations in similar terms for a number of other phenomena which hitherto have been inexplicable. For instance, that of how vision might be processed, and how we see objects in the external world projected in hologram form as interference patterns created by the firing of synapses between the neurons in our brains.

Science usually progresses in what is often described as a bottom up progress conducted by experiments which, if successful, advance knowledge of the subject under investigation in small theoretical steps forward in academia and in laboratories for proof by practical work. Instead I work in a top down manner which involves my reading as much as is known about a subject, and then test in my mind series of 'what if' situations. These are more or less mental images based on what is known and then I make some assumptions as to what combinations of varying circumstances might possibly lead to a result.

The first two chapters are autobiographical. I find it easier to explain what were initially very subjective conclusions with a description of the way in which ideas come and go haphazardly, and which then lead to eventual fruition. The most immediate and direct subject for investigation is one's own mind. I have attached as appendices some truncated versions of a few of my papers that explain critical
aspects of DT in more detail.

In 1982 I came across a book first published in 1981 by biochemist Rupert Sheldrake whose proposals for what he called morphic resonance outraged a large section of his fellow academics. He demonstrated by examples of animal and human behaviour in nature, how there has to be a system whereby information resonates down through time to later generations, despite no explanation existed for such a process. His proposals are very similar to mine, and from 1982 I started to take my conjectures more seriously.

In the last three or four years, advances in research on quantum computers and entanglement have demonstrated strong similarities with some crucial aspects of duplication theory that I never anticipated existed in 1978 when I first started out. I cannot believe that this is mere coincidence. This is connected with the significance of randomness which forms a major role in my description of the operation of memory.

There is a mathematical proof which has only recently come to my attention, the Free Energy principle proposed by Professor Karl Friston FRS of UCL. This shows that the brain has a self-organisational function which results in some remarkably similar conclusions to those of Duplication Theory.

Contents

Family Background & Life in the Sixties: 1943 to 1970

When I was instructed at school on the basics of the special theory of relativity by the chemistry master (not actually then part of the A level syllabus) I had difficulty in grasping its principles and why it was so important. It was much later when I read Einstein's personal account of how and why he came to make his conclusions and what was happening in his life at the time, that my interest was really aroused and I was much better able to grasp the theory and its possible consequences. I was more absorbed by the personal details of his life at the time and for me the most fascinating thing about his conclusions was not necessarily the actual breakthroughs and their rationales, but rather the way in which the originating mind operated to produce such a radical new paradigm. Was it pure brilliant intuition, or was it gifted and maybe just plain lucky guesswork?

It was Arthur Koestler's first book on the creative process of the mind, *The Sleepwalkers*, which I read in my early twenties that started me to think about such matters. My first employment in 1968, after studying the tedious subject of law at university, was in Canada as a negotiator for a substantial UK based Property development Company MEPC Canadian Properties Ltd. One of my English flat mates, Russell, had a copy and evinced some surprise I had not heard of Koestler so I made good my apparent ignorance. I knew nothing about the mind and learned to my amazement that neither did anyone else: well not in any certain terms. Koestler's book followed the lives of Copernicus, Kepler and Galileo to show how science went forward haphazardly in fits and starts, more in the manner of sleepwalking than an orderly progress. Quite fascinating and I then read all his following books on the mind and the paranormal, of which a fair number followed over the years. On top of that I had always read as much science fiction as I could get my hands on, some of which were trite enough but some books by authors such as Alfred Bester, Theodore Sturgeon, Olaf Stapledon, and Arthur C Clarke to identify just a few, were gripping and visionary enough to see way beyond their time.

So that was where my curiosity remained in stasis for the next three or four years when I returned to London to work as a surveyor for a couple of large firms of commercial estate agents based in the West End from 1970 onwards for another seven years. I was a partner's assistant working on huge office and shop developments, the largest of which from memory was about 250,000 sq.ft. of shop and office (or it might have been 750,000 sq.ft. but memory fails me) along the length of Victoria Street to the Army and Navy Stores. Part of the scheme opened up a piazza in front of the Roman catholic Westminster cathedral for the first ever times so that it could be seen from Victoria Street, but so little had been spent on the Victorian exterior that the developer client Arnold Silverstone, later elevated to Lord Ashdown for services to the Conservative party, gave the catholic church adequate funds to have the front elevation exterior scaffolded and cleaned up so that the appearance of his scheme would not be downgraded.

It was later in 1976 that I decided to resign temporarily from the world of business in order to write a novel, but that book was never completed. Instead I spent long hours, both frustrating and enjoyable at the same time, in the wonderful reading room of the British Museum on and off for two years, to be amazed to learn that nobody had the first idea of any validity of the mechanism of memory and as a result, having the audacity to come up with an answer of sorts. At which point, I became very involved with the subject and the operation of the mind in general after which it took me little time to realise it was perhaps the most fascinating problem remaining to be solved. I suppose I knew it was an impossibly ambitious quest, and I would be foolish to even consider getting involved, but I had nothing to lose with time on my hands for a while before I ran out of money and would have to return to work. So why should I not wrestle with a problem that I found so totally involving? I had nothing else to do and with some glimmerings of a possible scenario based on a resonance through time effect derived from the plot of a novel on which I was working, why should I not continue to tinker with my ideas? Furthermore, I was in one of the few libraries in the world that could provide access to anything in the English language that had ever been written, what more suitable vineyard in which to toil could be found? Instant information via Wikipedia in those days was still thirty-five years distant. Besides which it was a wonderful place in which to spend the day working for a few hours, then wandering around those amazing halls of exhibits and information, and then back to my comfortably accoutered desk again, in my own time and at my own pleasure. This was very pleasant: not at all like the competition of life in the office.

Having given an outline of my life up to my early thirties, when I decide to break away from my predictable life style as a member of the middle classes, I shall now regress to give a little more detail of how I reached a stage where I broke away from the normal life style in which I had been brought up. In order give some foundation to the way in which the unlikely progression from the capitalist world of properly dealing led to an obsessive interest in such a very different subject, I shall now describe my background in more detail, which might at first sight have little to do with the central issue of this book. But the best and most direct material we have for research into a mechanism for memory, at least until some more progress is made experimentally, is the subjective workings of our own minds as we cannot yet see into those of anybody else other than by guess work and hypothesis. Then I shall later describe some principles and assumptions that I found attractive, as much from observation and gut feeling as anything else, but combined with some knowledge from my ensuing study of physics, absorbed in the BM reading room from a few wonderfully perceptive scientists, some from a number of decades ago.

Although at school I was usually near the top of the class in everything but maths where I was middling, I had an unfortunate tendency to panic and seize up under the compulsion of exam conditions, and would under perform. I was put in for a scholarship from my prep school Brambletye in West Sussex, and my head master was very disappointed to receive a letter from Radley College stating that Greaves should not have been submitted for a scholarship, but of course he would be accepted. My first term at Radley I was put into the second from bottom form 4.3 for the first two embarrassing weeks and then suddenly promoted to 4.1. The next term at the start of the new academic year, I was promoted into classical shell (regarded in those days as superior to shell1) since I found Latin easy enough, but having made good friends in 4.1, and had no desire to start on Greek, I asked to be moved down shell 1, where I would not have to learn Greek but do a little more work relevant to the 20th century such as chemistry and physics. I still like to believe I was the only boy in that school ever to ask to be moved down a class.

The reason I later decided on property as a career was that initially I had no idea of what I wanted to do with myself. Having studied maths, science and physics at school with English literature thrown in my last year of repeat A levels to see whether they might be improved to S levels, alas my results from that later year were worse than the previous year. I had rather lost interest and thus failed to achieve an expected place at Peterhouse, Cambridge, presumably because under pressure I made another hash of the prelim exam I took at that time, and I dare say my interview technique was not exactly impressive. I also had no convincing notion of what I wanted to study, and no doubt such lack of enthusiasm did not seem that convincing to the interviewing tutor. I seem to recall I had indicated a desire to study law or economics: I cannot now recall which. Maybe it was because I knew nothing about either, and realising that I ought to go to university, should perhaps try something other than that which I had already covered. Science had no appeal for me, with an image of wandering about the science block in a scruffy white lab coat, which how I saw things then, and neither did languages or history seem absorbing. I had found the extra English literature A level exam in my last year's remarkably light work, but had no desire to have to study Beowolf at university.

My father had left school to go into the family furniture business with his two brothers before the war. His father had offered to pay for his university education, since he was academically competent, but he said he wanted to get on and work to develop with his brothers an expanding and successful business. Both my parents urged me to get a degree. My older brother had gone to art school to do furniture design and then gone into the family firm as expected.

So, what to do? My grandfather had started business manufacturing furniture in Clapton, North London, in the first decade of the twentieth century, which had been successful and grown to be the second largest furniture manufacturer in the UK by the start of the Second World War, employing something less than 2000 employees at its height. My father was the second of three sons and one youngest daughter. All the boys were in the firm, Greaves & Thomas 'Master craftsmen and cabinet makers' whose profitable specialty was in making sofas which converted into beds, the patent for which my grandfather agreed with the inventors, the Seng company of Chicago. In 1938 my father and his younger brother Oliver volunteered and were later commissioned to join the Royal West Kent regiment, otherwise known as the Buffs. My father, thank goodness, was transferred from infantry to train with the 15th Scots division as very mobile light artillery: quick firing Bofors guns mounted on top of lorries, rather than trailed behind, so that they could advance rapidly to the front line, knock out an observation post, perhaps in a church spire. This would be done by father and his batman carrying a radio transmitter advancing forward into no man's and then directing his rapid firing bofors to fire a few ranging shots onto the observation post target, and then scarper when the German mortars had identified the position of his guns, and who would open fire with mortars. Father and his gun crews would rapidly scuttle back out of range as soon as the observation point had been knocked out.

In short, he had a front-line seat viewing the action for much of the war without incurring much risk of hand to hand fighting. He landed in Normandy on D day plus five, and was involved in very fierce fighting in the taking of Caen which took far too long, and then worked through Holland, the

Reichswald forest and the into Germany across the Rhine to finish up not far from Bremen. On the way his battalion was involved with the Americans and the liberation of Celle, the satellite concentration camp of Belsen Bergen. He never said much about the latter experience other than it was not very pleasant and that the allies rounded up all the local population in the area above the age of fifteen to march them through the camps so they could not deny its existence before it was later burned to the ground due to avoid the risk of typhus spreading. His younger brother Oliver was sent to Syria and was shot in an infantry charge against the Vichy French in a last attempt to take a strongpoint hill outside Damascus but died of wounds a few hours later. He did not live long enough to learn the irony that the following day the French forces agreed an armistice, but his father, my grandfather, must have been aware, and he died within the year from a heart attack.

My father returned from the war to his wife and two sons to run the family business with his older brother Hugh, and within a few years decided to float the company on the London stock exchange as a PLC, apparently to enable death duties to be paid. The London factories in Clapton were sold and the business moved to Harlow new town and my family moved from the green suburban reaches of Esher in Surrey (where fascinatingly Robert Maxwell lived in the house next door for some years, some of accounts of which would provide an interesting insight on his later career, but that ought to wait for another separate narrative), to a small farm in Hertfordshire between Rickmansworth and Watford. Apparently on his return from the war my father was seriously inclined to take up a quiet life, sell the business and retire to a farm in deep country. The Greaves family had been hill farmers in the Peak district outside Sheffield from the conquest until my times four great grandfather joined the army as a second lieutenant (without purchase) in the Grenadier Guards to fight at Waterloo and then retired to live in Harrow on the Hill. My father enjoyed fishing and shooting and was an enthusiastic gardener, and perhaps would have done better to do that than persevere on in a difficult business, very much at risk in the hands of the stop-go credit restrictions of the fifties and sixties. The big furniture retailers made far better financial gains out of hire purchase terms selling three-piece suites to young marrieds than they ever made out of their actual sales of furniture.

Even so my family seemed more affluent than most in those decades as the owners of a then successful business, and I was sent to very good and well-chosen schools, Brambletye and Radley, and was never given any grounds to worry about how well the future might provide for me and my two brothers. I initially worked hard at school, more to avoid trouble than out of interest in any particular subject, and although I was always near or at the top in form work and was put in the scholarship class as I explained above, I lacked any vestige of a proper strategic approach to answering the required questions in exams. It was assumed I would get into Cambridge, but when I failed, I was suddenly left with what is now known as a gap year before I could find somewhere else.

After I had left school, I recall very well my first serious encounter with a member of the opposite sex in summer 1962. She was the daughter of old friends of my parents whom I knew from earlier holidays on the Camel estuary in Cornwall. With only brothers and a boarding school education, I had little experience of girls until I was almost 19, despite my mother's best intentions and introductions to suitable candidates in the infuriating way so many middle-class mothers would push sons forward in the late 1950s. My mother once sent invitations to my two study companions in term time to a party to be held for me at the age of sixteen in the forthcoming holidays. This was to be held jointly with a girl I had never met, but whose mother was very nice apparently. I do not think I had ever felt so embarrassed before that time, and what's more, possibly not since.

But back to the sand hills, golf links and surfing on the north coast of Cornwall opposite Padstow the other side of the estuary, when this splendidly attractive, amiable, and athletic young woman had spent the previous year in Paris and then Florence on some sort of art course. She returned with Emilio, a small dapper Italian in tow, before preparing to go to art school at the Regent Street Poly as it was then. I hardly recognised her on her return from Italy that summer in Cornwall, with a confident manner and fashionably long straight dark red hair which the previous year had been in a short bob slightly curled to presumably conforming to the way most mothers of that generation considered fashionable, but by no means as alluring as straight long shiny dark red hair was to my generation.

So having been brought up with brothers with minimal social contact with girls, at the age of nineteen I was taken firmly in hand and suddenly learned a fair amount in a short space of time in the sand dunes of the Camel estuary, she having obviously gained some useful experience in Italy and France the previous year. This was a complete surprise for me and a great distraction to the serious business of building a future career. The affair, such as it was, rather changed my perspective on life and lasted a couple of years until I was twenty-one. Before that time my existence was entirely governed by family life and I had no relationships or dependencies on anyone else, which I assumed was normal. Then suddenly there is this other person out of the blue who seemed to be very concerned about where you were and what you were doing, which had never happened before to any marked extent, beyond my parents, and an auntie or two.

If you were out of contact for more than a week then there was this exchange of written communication, letters the like of which I had never dreamed I would enjoy drafting other than through obligation, and this was well before the age of instant electronic communication. This was no doubt due to the allure of this new experience of physical contact which opened up a range of emotions and novel sensations which often rendered me breathless and bereft of common sense. This knocked me sideways, all the more so since they were reciprocated by the other party: completely unanticipated that such a thing could happen. This was wonderful, entirely unexpected and went on with some passion and further exchange of reams of letters, for two absorbing years until the summer of 1964 when I was at university and she was at art school, the Central school of arts and crafts, in Holborn when I had decided to drive to Greece for a summer holiday with my oldest childhood friend William who used to live next door in Esher.

I had failed to ask Gini if she wanted to come along, thinking that a threesome might be awkward, not realising that this was a cardinal error. By the time I returned four or five weeks later she had been taken up with a suave young barrister who also was on holiday with his family in Cornwall, someone five years older than me and very much more experienced. That was that, although she let me down in as much of a sympathetic way as might be managed, for which in retrospect I am grateful, since I now know we were far too young to become a permanent fixture, and as her mother, whom I liked and who used to make me laugh, once commented to her daughter that she really ought to be going out with someone older with more experience because Nick was very young and would inevitably be inclined to sow wild oats before settling down.

Of course, she was right, although I did not know that at the time, and the break up hit me very hard. My weight went down to well under ten stone when it was usually about eleven and half, and I grew very irritated by my mother, aunts and grandmother all reminding me that there were plenty more fish in the sea, when the one that had just slipped away from me was pretty wonderful, and had convinced me for a couple of years that I was the centre of her universe, reinforced by two long letters a week when I was away in Dublin during my first year at university. The older generation were doubtless not wrong, but that was no comfort at the time, and I suppose that this was the first time I had ever experienced a major shock and set back in what had to then been an easy and trouble-free life.

I include a description of this episode not only because it was part of growing up but also because it was a turning point for me. I have always been grateful to Gini for her introduction of my middles class bourgeois existence to the bohemian way of life, to become envious of its style, the delights of which have held me entranced ever since, even though my involvement has been somewhat indirect. The effect it had on me changed my outlook and the sort of friends whom I later found congenial. It was just so seductive to inhale the aroma of turpentine and linseed oil wafting from the fine arts department as I stepped into entrance hall of the Regent Street Poly, and later the Central school of art, to wait for Gini and her wonderfully scruffy and colourful colleagues as they streamed noisily out from the various classes at the end of the working day. During 1963 she shared a room in an empty house in Cheyne Gardens just off the Kings Road with

Lynda who was in her first year studying painting at Chelsea Art School. The building was waiting to be done over by the Cadogan Estate just before the expiry of a former long lease, whereupon wonderfully varied, louche even, members of Chelsea life had move in on a very informal short-term basis. It was effectively a squat before the term had been invented. The social life there was diverse and exciting enough for a member of the respectable bourgeoisie such as myself.

Flat Mate Lynda was charming, attractive and much later moved to Spain to become the muse of a celebrated member of the pre-war Bloomsbury set, Gerald Brennan year or so later the two girls both moved to 24 Gunter Grove near the World's End in Chelsea where an elderly retired academic and mathematician, Richard Cooke, had a large house with a huge studio at the rear for his artist wife, some years since deceased. He then let four bedrooms and two beds in the studio off to young women students, and Gini and Lynda ended up in the large and airy studio, wonderful in summer but freezing in winter with only overhead, entirely inadequate, gas fired heaters. The rent per head was only twenty-four shillings per week (plus milk) which was very little even then but there were conditions attached. No boyfriends were allowed to stay the night: fair enough and flagrantly ignored, since Richard lived in the self-contained basement flat. But each of the six girls had to eat an evening meal, once a week, with him at a little Italian restaurant in the Fulham Road, and then play a game of Bezique back at the flat for an hour or so, with absolutely no other strings attached other than the sake of their company, and certainly no hanky panky. He was a very pleasant old academic, about 80 and I reckon he had life organised very well. He would leave for summer holiday for a month or so each summer when wonderful parties were given by the girls, well attended by exotic art school product in the capacious studio.

But to return to my last term at school in summer 1962, and the fraught question of my further education, having failed Cambridge my housemaster discussed with me where else to try and he suggested that some of the new redbricks such as Keele were very worthwhile and progressive. I had no idea where Keele was, never mind that it existed, and responded that a friend of mine had said that Trinity Dublin was similar in many ways to Oxbridge, albeit as they were a few decades ago, and I was thinking of applying there. He coughed apprehensively, scratched his chin, pondered for a moment and commented that it had the reputation of being little more than a cheerful backwater. The moment I heard that, I was committed. I sent a photo, my A level results and an application to study law for want of anything more exciting, and was accepted within a few weeks without interview or exam to start the following year in September 1963. I have to say at that time I was not looking for academic excellence but instead for a few years off before I would have to start serious work for a living, anticipating student life in the middle sixties to be not much different to those halcyon days depicted in the novels of Evelyn Waugh, John Betjeman et al left over from the nineteen twenties. This was more or less how it turned out.

Then I was sent to Salzburg to learn German to fill the intervening year, a sort of gap year before such things were invented. Haus Wartenburg was a genteel jugendheim with about a dozen other young musicians and students staying there run, by a rather fierce Austrian widow, Tante Lottie, or Baronin Charlotte von Wachter. I had no knowledge of this at the time, and certainly my parents would have been horrified that her late husband Otto, had played an interesting role in the war as governor of Krakow and later the district of Galicia (see Wikipedia). A fair amount has been written in the press recently and programs on BBC television and also a book in which he is featured about his role in the war. The three months I spent in Salzburg that Spring was pleasant enough and I learned to ski a bit, and also to drink a bit, but little of the German language was absorbed. That being so, and with precious little previous knowledge of classical music, I left a few months later with a strong appreciation of Mozart: hard to avoid in that city.

Until the late 1960s it still was regarded as a mortal sin for Catholics to attend the august university of Trinity College Dublin without papal dispensation, due to its being founded by Elizabeth the first. Things are very different today, but back then I did the minimum of work to obtain a third class honours degree in law, never having much ambition to practise other than it might be a useful fall back in extremis to know something about the subject. The first essay I ever had to write I just copied a few comments from various judges on an appeal case, agreed with one of them and commented that the dissenting judgements were ill founded. All this requiring minimal mental effort, and to my amazement I received an alpha minus, only one point behind the alpha scorer who later in life transpired to be the first woman president of Ireland. I was surprised at the little amount of thought I had to spend on the task in hand. On top of that, it occurred to me the whole business of law seemed to be something of convenient fudge depending on the ability to express a point of view convincingly rather than be concerned with finer points of ethics and justice.

Of course I now know much better that the law has to be a blunt instrument in order to operate at all, and that moral justice is not what it sets out to achieve but that it is just a framework that has to exist to give stability to society so that its members can live relatively in peace with each other and not risk oppression or excessive suffering. Fifty years later having spent a life mainly in commerce, I now see the law as a system that often does not bring about justice but is essential for the retention of a stable society in which others might develop new initiatives to help increase the level of understanding and improvement of the human condition. But fifty years ago, in the confident ignorance of youth, I knew little of this, and still today I am convinced that the law places far too much emphasis on the skill of rhetoric and use of words. I have little idea of how this might be changed, but I did not find it compelling enough for me as a student to start thinking about how this might be brought about. I now conclude that solving problems of the mind's operation is probably easier, and what is more, when once completed, my conclusion is that with perfect understanding, the need for law, courts and lawyers will fall away, but needless to say, such rationales will be substantiated later in the text.

So, four years later, in my last year at university, I did not know quite what to do. My parents thought I ought perhaps to join one of the Inns of Court in case I should decide to become a barrister and paid £100 for me in my third year to become a member of the Inner Temple. This involved sitting through a number of dinners of that organisation that was a requisite before any exams could be taken. A bizarre entrance ritual to an ancient profession but diverting enough to give me a taste of practice at the bar before eventually falling back on the family business, or so I thought. However, the latter alternative disappeared two weeks before my final exams in September 1967 when I was back in Trinity revising, or in some cases going through the syllabus for the very first time. A couple of weeks before the first day of exams an acquaintance, far more worldly-wise than myself, asked me why the shares of Greaves and Thomas PLC had suddenly doubled from half a crown to five bob to which my response was a surprised "Have they?"

I had no idea that the family business had been making a loss for the previous couple of years, which on checking I found it had, and that a take overbid had been launched by another furniture manufacturer run by a systems engineer who managed to keep his work force and machines working 24 hours per day. That meant I suddenly had to start to think about my future rather more seriously than I had to date. Indeed, it might have been helpful as an incentive to greater study if this information had been made manifest a week or two before I took my final exams. My father was honourable and the rules of the stock exchange did not allow him to take advantage of such prior knowledge even with his family, to whom he had passed some shares to each of his sons.

It took me quite some months to decide what to do after my third class degree in law came through, and I have to say that my thoughts at that time were very much taken up with a Swedish girl whom I had met the previous year 1966 on holiday once again in Cornwall where she had been acting as an au pair for friends of my parents. She was doing an extended teacher training course and I went to spend a fortnight with her in Stockholm in Easter 1967 and then in June she had come over to Ireland during that last summer term and toured the West to Mayo and Connemara with me, and then back to Cornwall for the family summer holiday on the Camel estuary. So taken by her was I after a few fallow years since my loss of the art student, that I had inevitably allowed myself to cut short the time I had allowed for revision before the final exams in September. But even so, in the 1960s anybody with a degree of any sort was able to find employment without the heavy competition for professional or lucrative employment that the graduates of today have to endure, so all that remained was for me to decide what it was I wanted to do.

I really had no idea, but I knew that with the family fortunes suddenly at low ebb, I had better choose a career that would allow me to amass capital so that I might be able to continue to exist in the style to which my upbringing had led me to be accustomed. It was apparent that such value as there was in the family business was due to the four acre site of the factory in Harlow. The value of commercial and industrial properties had taken off into a major property boom during the sixties so I decided that I would become a chartered surveyor and to attempt to regain some capital which might then allow me to decide at leisure what I really wanted to do with my life. My father's oldest friend from before the war, Jack Hawkes, was a commercial chartered surveyor and had done very well out of developing the largest shopping centre in Guildford, amongst other schemes. He was also a director of one of the largest public property companies in London, together with branch offices in Canada.

This was intriguing since I had been pressed by a good friend from Trinity, Simon, to come over to America where he was having an interesting time in Montreal and New York. For a couple of earlier summer holidays, I had travelled to join him and other friends to Ibiza, and this was before that island had become well known for discos, yachts and expensive hotels. In those early days that island was more a haunt for young European and American hippies, than the affluent bourgeoisie, and living costs there were minimal. Discotheques had not yet been invented and the nearest equivalent was one juke box in a bar, the Oveja Negra, in the old town, although tower blocks of apartments had already started to cluster around San Antonio to encompass package tours some miles to the North.

Simon had an awesome reputation in his student days as an object of desire for many members of the opposite sex due to his smooth appearance and confident, teasing manner. He had met the amazingly attractive singer Nico on the island and formed a relationship with her that summer and after completing his finals, had followed her out to New York where she had become very much involved with Warhol's factory and the Velvet Underground. He had written suggesting I should join him in USA where life was good, and with the help of my father's old friend who was a director of a this substantial property company, MEPC, I had managed to arrange employment with the Canadian branch's head office in Toronto, but by the time I had arrived there in March 1968 Simon had moved on further South and then onto his native Australia. I was never sure what had happened but he said that her increasing heroin habit had not helped. On top of that, or so I much later read, the other members of the Velvet Underground, were in competition for her favours.

But that was only part of the reason I had ended up in Canada and it was not a bad introduction to the world of property development. I remained there for a couple of years, ending up in the office in Vancouver which had a view of the Pacific Ocean on one side and the snow-capped Rockies on the other. This was alright but I missed the diversity of life in England with the added interest of Europe so close at hand, not to mention the absence of my friend from Stockholm with whom I had continued anxiously to correspond on a very regular basis, and who took time off from her studies to stay some weeks touring the West Coast with me in Summer 1969. I finally decided I preferred life in Europe and finished up by touring round the West coast of the States, staying en route some time in Anniston, Alabama with this old childhood friend, William with whom I had spent too much time in on holiday in Greece in 1964. He was now a journalist with the Sunday Times on a sort of year's exchange, the owner of the local paper and TV station having previously worked in UK with the Times.

Attitudes towards the problem below the surface in that part of the South did not seem much different from the way it had been presented in some Hollywood films from the nineteen thirties: quite fascinating and a little worrying. William did a daily round of visits to the police station, the morgue and the courts before starting work day drafting copy, and I went with him. The charming local chief of police, not being accustomed to visitors from the UK, offered to drive us both around the town giving us a commentary on the local action. There was black American walking down a smart suburban street the right side of the tracks. The chief halted his cruiser, rolled down the window and asked what he was doing in this part of town. I was surprised, but even more so on return to the police station when we were chatting in the office and an officer rushed in, grabbed a repeating shot gun off the rack on the wall with the words, "I am going to get me a sonofabitch" and then rushed out. I had to assume this was in jest.

By April 1970 I was back at home with my parents a few miles north up the A11 from Saffron Walden, and had little trouble in finding employment with one of the largest firms of chartered surveyors in their project management department in Bruton Street in the West End. I was able to persuade another friend from student days to be able sleep in her flat in Notting Hill in a cupboard under the eaves off the sitting room whilst I started to search for a flat to buy for myself. Before the end of that year I had found and bought a scruffy and very cheap basement flat at the junction of Elgin Crescent and Ladbroke Grove, Notting Dale rather than Hill, but with access to the attractive communal gardens behind the crescent. It seemed to me I was now well set up to face the future, and when the Swede from Stockholm evinced an intention to move to find work in London, having just completed her surprisingly long and intensive course of teacher training, I grew apprehensive. The prospect of possibly having to settle down to domesticity in my middle twenties was not how I saw things just yet and we fell apart. This I regretted very much within the year, not having been able to find a replacement anywhere near as stimulating. It took me less than a year to realise that I had made another cardinal error but by that time she had found Nils, another teacher in Stockholm. It was too late for any serious rapprochement, such is the impetuosity and misjudgment of youth, especially as this was for me a continuing source of regret for years to come, although sporadic correspondence was resumed after a while on her proud announcement and a photograph of the recent arrival of another wonderful Scandinavian blonde, her daughter.

Office Work in London and Beyond: 1970 to 1977

I found work that summer with one of the largest firms of commercial surveyors in the West End of London, Richard Ellis, and over the next few years I went to work from nine thirty to five in a thick 16 ounce pinstripe suit, winter and summer, with two weeks holiday a year, and tried to impress my superiors that I was a worthwhile employee. At least I was in the West End office rather than the head office in the city where the staff had to wear white shirts and wear bowlers. In Bruton Street we were allowed to wear coloured shirts: hooray. I did not find many like-minded individuals with whom I could easily socialise when out of the office, but instead resorted to old family and university friends. I did not care much for the surveyor in the development department with whom I worked alongside and who had been in the office since he left school and indeed knew much more about the business than I did, which was aggravating. Within 18 months I had moved to another similar West End firm for an increase in salary to £2500 pa up from £1750. I was assistant to a partner who was managing the development of about a quarter of a mile of Victoria Street, and a few other large office development schemes dotted about the country. My life was fairly humdrum in the office for the next half dozen years working under a surveyor in his late thirties who had just been brought into the partnership, and with whom I had little in common. It was as though I was just serving out my time doing what I was told whilst learning something about the business and the conduct of office politics.

In short it was my life outside the office with old friends who came and went and with whom I shared my flat in Elgin

Crescent, W11. It was the diverse socialising that went on with all that, and which now sticks in my memory. In the middle seventies Notting Hill suddenly started to seem to change month by month in a flood of skips, scaffolding and builders' merchants' vans, converting itself from a broken-down slum into a fashionable quarter for the young and trendy. During this time, I experimented a little with hallucinogenic substances which did not mix that well with office life, but I will return to that subject later in the script since it played a diverting part in the later development of my thesis on the operation of memory.

I shared my flat with a number of friends, old and new, and continued to try to find replacements for my former Swedish inamorata but signally failed to come up with anybody who came near the mark, despite a fair amount of not very serious and failed attempts to do so. The last possible candidate in 1974 before I met my future wife had left a husband in South Africa to join me in London. This was what I was given to think, but she only managed to stay with me a week or two after her fleeing her home. I therefore concluded that I had been used to provide a temporary base in the UK before she settled down to a new academic career studying for a doctorate in immunology in London which she had been able to arrange when I had first met her the previous summer. At least that is how it seemed to me at the time. Very rapidly she moved in with someone who appeared to be living in the house of a well-known minor TV soap star. This was something of a dent to my pride and self-assurance, and I fell apart for about a week unable to work before I managed to recover.

So, all this was an adequately interesting time but I was not that happy working in this second firm, and further more I had not summoned up the enthusiasm and energy to take the surveyors exams without which I could not become a partner in a chartered firm. This was not yet a problem but would be some years ahead, and I knew I would have grit my teeth and swot hard for the qualification by taking what was known as the direct final, although having another degree already, I was exempted from the two initial years' exams. Either that or do something else, but I had had just enough of taking exams. Early in 1976 I had asked my partner if my salary could be increased to £4000 on review at the year end and he indicated that should not be a problem. Later that year the market fell into depression following the escalation of fuel prices as a result of the earlier Yom Kippur war, and towards the end of the year I was told that there would be no salary increases that December. Being aware of the size of the fees that just the one Victoria Street on which I was working had brought in from letting the offices to BP and the government, I was exasperated.

Two days after Christmas 1975, a couple of months after my thirty second birthday, I had married Angela, formerly of Camberwell Art School, and now a freelance woven textile designer, who shared a large flat leased from the Church Commissioners at a remarkably low regulated rent in Sussex Gardens close to Lancaster gate tube station off Hyde Park. She worked on a large loom in the sitting room, and shared the flat with George the poet, her brother Malcolm, an oil broker, who was in the process of buying a flat in Clapham, and her old friend Viv, who was another ex art student, very versatile and could turn her hand to almost anything. Angela announced she was pregnant that summer of 1976 and realised I had some serious decisions to make.

It had earlier occurred to me that I could move in permanently to Sussex Gardens and let my Notting Hill basement flat, or possibly sell it and move to the country and become a provincial estate agent and not have to commute many miles to work which my father and other family members had always done. Furthermore, I could afford to resign my job, claim the dole for a year quite legally and together with the rent from Elgin Crescent, we could live comfortably enough for a year or two. This would allow me to study full time for a few months to pass the wretched surveyor's final exams, and then I could take time off to write the novel that I had always not only wanted to do, but felt I might be wasting my life if I did not make a serious attempt to do so.

I had always spent more time reading than most other people and friends I had come across, that and listening to music, very often both at the same time. As already mentioned, having made a nonsense of my maths 'A' level paper in my penultimate year at school, when I repeated the A levels to maybe convert them to S level next year, I dropped maths and did English literature instead. It was so much easier than studying physics and chemistry, less intellectually taxing, and to my amazement I found poetry, especially that by Keats and Coleridge, more stimulating than I had thought possible. This came as a surprise since I had never previously been much taken by verse compared with prose. My reading material had mainly been science fiction in my late teens with a few modern popular novelists thrown in. At university my interests widened into more of the classics, perhaps just to keep up with one's peers, and having spent a great deal of my time writing to various young women over the years especially when I was overseas, I had begun to enjoy the drafting of letters, as well as their receipt.

So, to my family's horror, I offered my resignation with effect from Christmas day 1976, and when my partner under whom I worked asked to which firm I was moving, I said I was not moving anywhere but had decided to live abroad for some time in order to write a book. He blinked, registered some surprise and his reaction was to wonder how they would contact me if they wanted to know something, if for example they could not find required information from my files. I said I had no idea, since I might be anywhere, destination not yet decided. I had failed to mention that I was intending to spend the next three months swotting for the surveyors' final exams which was just as well as it turned out. A few days later he came back to me and said that if I remained in the country for three months after Christmas so that they could contact me if necessary, then they would pay me full salary for those three months.

I was surprised to say the least since I had no idea that my participation was that crucial. Perhaps it was that he did not trust my records and filing to be the most ordered, but whatever it was, I was delighted to accept. To this day I still am undecided why this bonus was offered. If an employee moves to another firm in the same business then he has to act reasonably in the process lest his old employers might be inclined to give him a bad reference. Perhaps it was something else but it made my life much easier over the next couple of years. With the dole money and the rent from my flat in Notting Hill which was becoming smarter by the month, I was actually earning more for that first year than I had been when full time employed: wonderful.

So, I worked moderately hard for three months at Urban Land economics parts one and two, valuation part two and God knows what other arcane property subjects, all very tedious, and took my exams in March 1977, the last day of which coincided with the birth of my first son Augustus just before midnight. I was there with my wife for hours in the maternity ward of Westminster Hospital, revising between contractions for that last exam which started at 9 a.m. a few hours after I returned to the flat in Paddington. Coincidentally it was also the last day I was paid in full employment for quite some time: a memorable occasion in more ways than one. Needless to say, I did have to retake one exam to get a pass, but I forget whether it was the last one whose revision was interrupted by the arrival of number one son. So not much writing of novels was carried out in the next few weeks and it was pleasant enough not to have to worry about the office in that time of novel fatherhood to assist in general domestic chores. It was also a memorable interlude since after the first few weeks in London we decamped to the village of Seend in Wiltshire, where in the previous year four friends of my wife had raised funds to buy equal shares in a fine old but dilapidated Georgian manor house and out buildings, Seend House, to live together as a sort of middle class commune.

Three of the co-owners lived permanently elsewhere, one a bachelor architectural historian, Martin Meade who was working for the department of the Environment in the inspection of suitable properties to be listed, and the other co-owner was his sister and the third was another friend from Bath. From memory they had all managed to stump up £10,000 each for their quarter share of an elegant Georgian building with a gate house, and a wonderful view of unspoilt Wiltshire landscape receding into the distance from the rear elevation.

From memory there were at least eight bedrooms, and a number of these were permanently occupied by the fourth co-owners Karen, another weaver who used to work with my wife, and her husband, Graham (George the poet's brother), who had worked as barrister. He had ceased work in order to help look after his children who were at that time five in number but since she always produced twins, eventually finished up with nine, the odd number being caused presumably by a miscarriage. The walls were thick and relatively sound proof: just as well with young parents trying to condition very young infants to sleep through the night. The huge old coke fired boiler was stoked up only once per week, bath night for all, in the interests of economy, but the view of distant hills framed in the bath room window, viewed through clouds of steam when supine floating in the vast old roll top Victorian bath on a fine summer's evening, with the sun filtered through the leaves of copper beach just outside, was just heaven, all the more so being a weekly pleasure.

Out of the south facing rear windows was a small vineyard on the sloping garden below. The house was on a ridge and although the vine yard needed a great deal of work and pruning before it might start to produce in any quantity again. When I think back I did not realise then how wonderful it was to be able to spend a number of months there in the summer, with very little to worry about other than pass the time and being able to appreciate the joys of young parenthood with little responsibility and all the time in the world apparently to luxuriate through the long hot days. I do not think I was ever again able to appreciate such ease and mindless comfort. Some leisurely weeding and gardening took place, with communal meals with the other raucous and charming young family, and then with diverting friends from Bath and London coming down to spend weekends there.

I started to type a few pages of the novel but never really became that involved and was more taken up with the construction of balsa wood model gliders which I had first started to make at prep school two decades earlier, but now with the benefit of new radio controlled technology, not that expensive any longer, allowed flight without much fear of loss.

I would take off in the evenings to the downs to launch into windward facing slopes and make them soar almost effortlessly up and across the ridges, surprising local bird life, without having to crash land them provided there was enough gentle breeze stirring the leaves on the trees to do so.

London and the Reading of the BM: 1978 to 1979

Of course the summer idyll could not last for more than two or three months and on our return to London I started out trying get on with the novel on which I had begun with little result and enthusiasm thus far. It centred on a young man who was disappointed by a desultory life in London, nine to five in the office. Mostly this was inspired by personal experience and also by Joseph Heller's book 'Something Happened' which followed his better-known Catch 22, and was a diverting narrative about office life. I had progressed little more than 10,000 words or so with it in Seend, and back in London, I started off in a library in Swiss Cottage since they had typing booths but these were airless glazed boxes and it was not an inspiring place to work. I mentioned this to a friend John who had spent quite some time working on a film script for a film of Guy Fawkes and was trying to get someone to produce it. He told me at once the best place to write stuff was the reading room of the British Museum and I protested that to get a reader's ticket you had to be an academic doing serious research. He just laughed and said he would write a suitably impressive sounding reference and proposal for me to submit with a photograph, and in no time, I would be in there with all the other dusty old eccentrics and scholars.

So that is what I did, and as predicted, it was a wonderful place to pass the time in those solid old blue leather upholstered chairs in lengths of a numbered work stations in straight rows radiating out like wheel spokes from the central control with the circumference wall about 30 foot high stacked full with books. Above this the huge dome was separated by white and gold vaulting to blend into the light blue dome above. It was pretty scruffy in those days but that seemed to me to make all the more redolent of serious intellectual achievement and impressive studies. In short it was an inspired choice of workplace, even if there was nothing of any consequence to squeeze out of one's brain pan. There was one old boy who tottered around the perimeter shuffling about the books lining the walls to seemingly no purpose at all, and I assumed that he was tolerated by the librarians as a worthy but harmless old eccentric and generally part of the scenery.

I quickly learned to sit in the same desk every day, P67, from which I spent more time than necessary observing the working habits of others when stuck for useful activity, never mind inspiration. They might be researching and drafting material ready to broach a new paradigm, in the footsteps of Karl Marx for instance, or they might just be passing the time, seeking to put on paper something worthwhile and maybe even capable of publication. At midday I would buy a sandwich and sit on the front steps to the museum to watch the tourists and young women students milling about if the sun was shining, and if not, I would join midday lecture tours. To my surprise the best exponents in a couple of cases were led by actors whose faces were familiar from BBC TV soaps and dramas, their delivery being nothing if not dramatically impressive.

After a fair amount of time had been wasted savouring the delights of the BM I realised that I had no final ending to the plot line for the novel on which I had started. It started with a thinly disguised version of my own existence as a young disillusioned office worker giving everything up to launch out in a new direction, and then getting into scrapes in travelling abroad, somewhat in the manner of some of the hapless young men in the novels of Evelyn Waugh which had made me laugh, and yet were written in faultless English language whilst describing piercingly observed scenes of social embarrassment. My problem was that although I knew how to start the narrative through the simple expedient of personal experience (as indeed I am doing now) I had real idea of how it was going to end. So, after maybe 35 pages of fairly turgid stuff I gave up and instead decided to try something entirely different.

I had been impressed some years earlier by a couple of novels I had read involving an individual being transferred back in time. One was rather amazingly written by Daphne Du Maurier, 'The House on the Strand' and the other was by John Dickson Carr, the details of which I forget, but I was thinking along the lines the proponent would be somehow carried back through time four or five generations to fall for an attractive young woman who eventually becomes his own great times five grandmother. The result would be there was an interesting genetic mix by the time of the twentieth century, as his own forebear. I was rather pleased with the plot line although I had no fixed idea of how it would end, and this was well before the series of feature films that started with 'Back to the Future' although the plot line of the latter is not dissimilar to what I had in mind.

I had decided that the characters in the 18th century would have to speak in terms of speech and vernacular that were then prevalent. This would take a great deal of research and be time consuming, and in order to give the novel some sort of basis of possibility, I also decided attempt some sort of semi scientific rationale to justify for the jump back through time. This would require me to read a fair amount about modern physics and also some reading on the paranormal, ghosts and such like which perhaps might be invoked. So, I started on this as a diverting initial research project not expecting it to result in anything more than amateur science fiction.

However, the more I had earlier read about Heisenberg's Uncertainty Principle leading to quantum theory, the more I was drawn into attempting a pseudo-scientific justification of such a time jump event. For example, in pondering over the possible genuine existence of ghosts, whereas I was not at all sure that such things were no more than a figment of imagination conjured up by over excited individuals, I was not prepared to absolutely preclude their existence. It had occurred to me that sensitive individuals might possibly have some preternatural ability to sense certain striking events resonating down in one particular location so that they appear as some form of haunting connected with that one location. I did not believe or disbelieve such things, trying instead to keep an open mind. I had never experienced such a thing, but I knew some people who were convinced they had.

For instance my wife had an out of body experience, otherwise known as an OBE, when she had an operation for her wisdom teeth which went wrong and the local dentist with her doctor father thought they were in danger of losing her afterwards when at home she had been given an anti-coagulant to limit her bleeding gums, to which she proved to be allergic. She was able to recall to them afterwards the conversation they had word for word in the next-door room, whilst she seemed to be hovering above them, whilst unconscious. But she is absolutely not interested in such phenomena, and has no understanding of why I found it so fascinating, but then she is involved in the arts and design and instead reacts instantly to visual impressions. She does not really want to understand why and how she reacts that way: the reaction it causes at once is enough in itself. Thus, she has little interest in any such analysis of why and how. It seems I do not have this instant reaction to colour and appearance to any extent, and need to take time to react, but instead I absolutely want to understand why things happen and how, driven by pervasive curiosity it seems: two very different mindsets.

Reverting back to my historical novel and musing further about ways I might clothe haunting or time jumps in some sort of half reasonable rationale, I pursued a number of possible themes. One of these was that maybe it was not a strikingly awful event which impressed itself through time on one location but instead one exceptionally boring or tedious event, repeated over and over again in the same place. From my reading of the experiences of people who had apparently experienced and recorded such events, it seemed that very often there were vestigial forms of women wandering aimlessly down corridors or sitting forlornly at windows, waiting for their paramours to arrive and who presumably never turned up. Having experienced the loss of a young woman with whom I was heavily involved on more than one occasion, I was too aware of how similar obsessive thoughts could repeat themselves ad nauseam to the point of distraction: the injustice of it all, and how life would never be the same again, and why had it happened to me of all people.

They were the strongest emotions that I had ever felt to the point of desperation and near impending insanity on the most recent occasion so maybe it was this constant and obsessive repetition of similar thought patterns that might impress themselves on a specific location, a sort of resonance down through time. I did not really believe there was anything in it but I thought it was rather ingenious and not that unreasonable. What was more, as far as I knew it was really quite original not having ever read of a similar hypothesis, and I felt really pleased with myself. Perhaps it was the first time I had felt real pleasure in coming up with something different and original, incorrect or not.

When I had earlier been suffering from the inevitable writer's block on the first attempted novel, rather than just stop work, instead I took advantage of the best equipped library in Britain and read up a number of subjects about which I knew very little but would be of an improving nature and which would assist in my appearance of someone with a well-stocked mind, God help me. I started with subjects of subjective interest such as physics, quantum theory, theories of everything, and the history and philosophy of science. I also read some philosophy and found it heavy going with only one or two whose ideas caught my imagination: Spinoza, Leibniz and Schopenhauer as I recall. The latter followed from my earlier discovery of Arthur Koestler's books on the mind and consciousness. I also read about biochemistry and was amazed to find that so little was known about the operation of mind and memory. It had occurred to me that memory was an ability for the past to be brought forward into the present, but if I wanted a quasi-scientific explanation to reinforce my story line of jumping back through time, then maybe I should examine memory in more detail.

I had assumed a great deal was known about the mind's operation: wrong and almost nothing was a more accurate summary. I found this amazing and so absorbing that once started on the subject, I found I was taking in information at maybe three times the rate that I had managed when battering my reluctant brain with tedious old law studies. I was happy enough sitting in that venerable seat of learning just reading whatever caught my fancy with no imperatives or deadlines to satisfy. For the first time in my life I really enjoyed the process of learning, unprejudiced by external pressures.

It was also about this time that I had started to read about the Uncertainty Principle. It suddenly occurred to me I could perhaps adapt some of the latter into my conjecture that repetition of similar patterns of obsessive thought in the same location might resonate down though time, but I will go into this in more detail a little later, after I have first described one or two other assumptions I had made about some aspects of the function of the components of the brain.

I started to read whatever I could find about the nature of time, not that I succeeded in doing so on that subject in the middle seventies. I could see there was a minimum Planck interval of time just as there was a minimum interval of Planck length below which it was impossible to go, according to Max Planck. I was intrigued by the theory of quantum mechanics that his research had instigated from this observation derived in his epoch engendering paper in 1902. What I found fascinating was that never mind how little was known about time, other than it existed, neither was there any accepted theory of how memory operated, which was obviously bound up with the nature of time. There presumably had to be some mechanism where information in the form of specific thoughts could be transferred from the past to the present, albeit in relatively vestigial form, unless perhaps an individual had an ability of perfect recall which I had learned occasionally existed, when it might be a little more than vestigial.

I suppose I had assumed that there were theories that were reasonably credible but that the matter had not yet been proved absolutely: not a bit of it. There was nothing concrete I could find in explanation on memory, and I soon realised it was a tabula rasa in the same way that consciousness was.

Having read a little philosophy, I was aware of our short comings here, but had assumed there was less mystery of the mechanism behind memory: serious mistake. There were a few outline theories but nothing which seemed to me to hold water, or in any detail, that many others agreed upon.

The more I thought about it, the more I realised that if we know virtually nothing about the mechanism behind memory then how could anyone claim to know much about the operation of the mind. It seemed to me after a fair amount of reflection that memory was maybe about 75% of the mental processes involved in thought and that if once the riddle of memory was cracked open, then thought, consciousness and so many of the other problems that philosophers have wondered about for the last three millennia, would probably fall into place not much later. It occurred to me that the obverse of this was that most modern-day philosophers, unless they were intuitive geniuses like just a few of their forebears, were unlikely to come up with anything of much use, unless they also took a strong interest in neuro-science and/or physics. Of course, there had been a few philosophers in the past with superlative intuitive ability, who seemed to have come up with some observations of the workings of the mind well in advance of the understanding of medical science available in their lifetimes. Having said that there seemed to me a disappointing lack of such ability and accomplishment in the philosophy put forward over the last hundred years or so.

The subject of memory was indeed a tabula rasa, a great unknown, and as such it occurred to me it was open season for anybody to have a crack at coming up with answer of sorts, and that I might make something of my slight obsession with the theme of duplication of pattern and structure. During this time, I was still thinking along the lines of the novel where perhaps repetition of an obsessive thought would represent the duplication many times over of similar structures of patterns in the brain. After all, a particular obsessive thought would have to be produced by one particular sequence of firing neurons in identical structures time and time again in the brain. Such a duplication of similar or identical structures of thought might just possibly be visible to a sensitive individual at a later time, having made an impression on one particular location where that specific thought process had been duplicated constantly. Furthermore, such thought structures would doubtless be highly complex and highly ordered, given the physical complexity of the brain's billions of nerve endings and components. Perhaps it was also this degree of complexity and detail of repetition that enhanced any such resonance effect. It was certain that the construction of the human brain was the most complex structure yet known to exist in the universe.

By this time, I had also read enough to know that the brain consisted of vast masses of interconnected neurons, which are electrically excitable nerve cells, which receive and transmit information through electrical and chemical signals. There are synapses separating them, sort of gates, which fire when a certain level of charge is achieved to allow electrochemical currents to pass across the synapse to another neuron. There are also connections between the neurons made via axons and dendrites which were other variations of transferring electrochemical stimulation between neurons. The precise chemistry of this process I did not assimilate in detail but assumed that complex passage of these currents was generated in that part of the brain that dealt with cognition, and that this would have to be highly ordered to produce structured thought and memories.

It was also a certain fact the passage of these electrical currents would produce electromagnetic waves which would inevitably interfere with each other. If these electrical flows between neutrons were highly ordered as structured thoughts would need to be, then it was possible that this could result in the production of holograms, maybe highly detailed ones at that, which would effectively be projected from the brain. Holography requires the use of laser light and a holographic image could be pretty much indistinguishable from the actual subject viewed, so it occurred to me that there might also be a connection here with the way that vision or sight is generated, but I did not attempt to develop that possibility until later, memory and thought being my main concern at that time.

(A) Holograms and Holocepts

Thus, I made a large but not unreasonable assumption that such holograms would be ordered enough and radiated out beyond the brain in three dimensions to somehow be seen or interpreted as thoughts or memories, or a combination of both. I describe them as Holocepts, and they are what we experience immediately as vision or sight as a representation of the external world in line of sight when an individual's eyes are open. Or, as far as thought is concerned, this would be in a far more vestigial form as shadowy holographic images when incoming information is melded with memory to create and project out from the brain in a more indistinct form as thought.

An image is registered on the retinas, sent to brain (Fig 1), to be converted to electrochemical signals between firing neurons & dendrites. These produce structured EM waves by interference waves to project a visual image as a hologram in 3D outside the brain (Fig 2) as exact duplicates viewed.

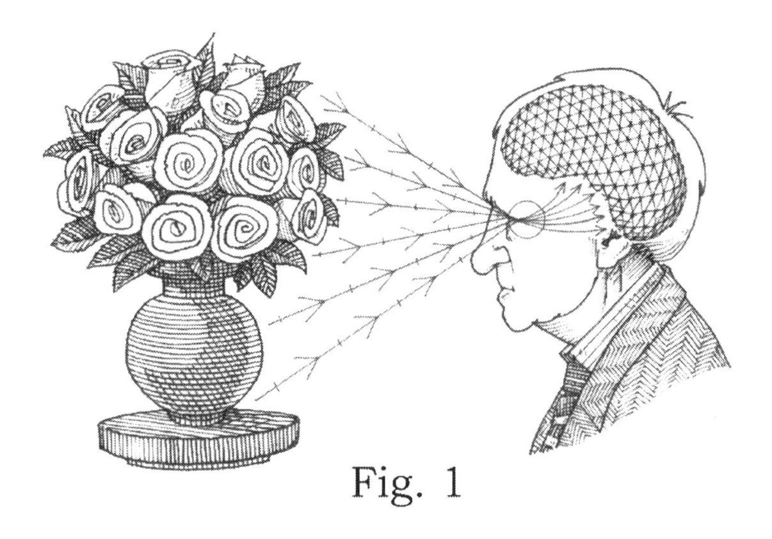

Fig. 1

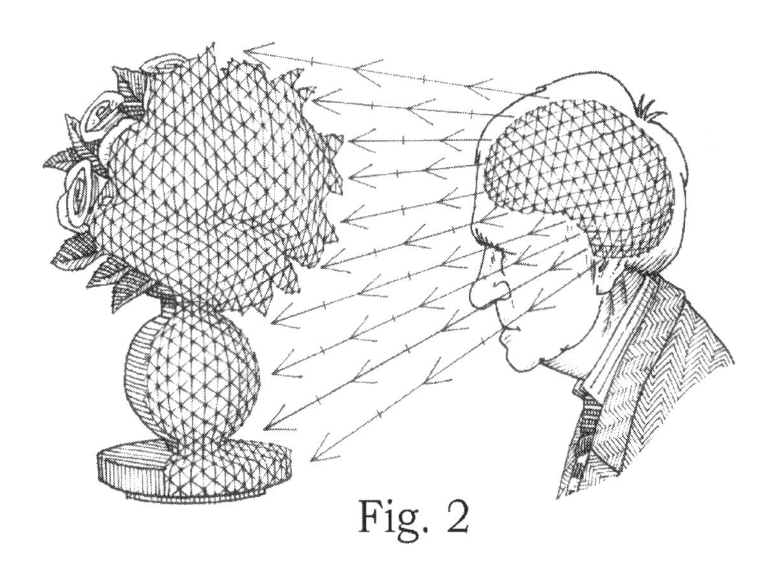

Fig. 2

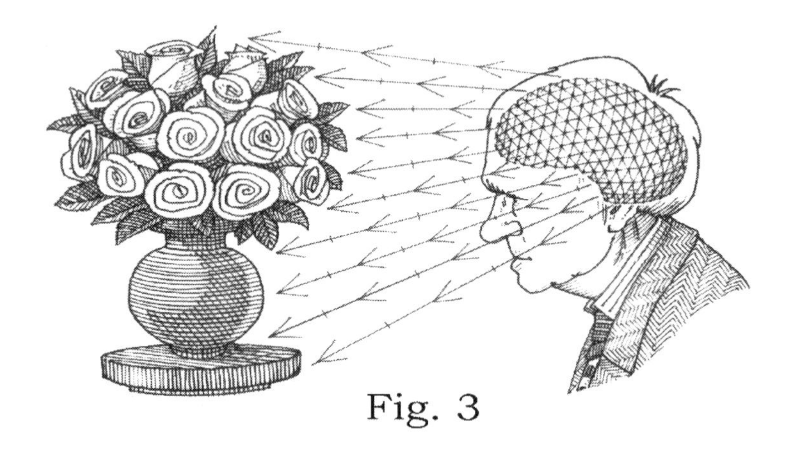

Fig. 3

Visual holocept of observed external circumstances projected out beyond brain.

Fig.4

Quite how these three dimensional very exact images might be experienced is another matter for which I will provide a degree of explanation later in the text, but my assumption that there will be interference fringes created by the complex passages of electrochemical passage between the neuron and synapses, cannot be doubted. Just how structured they might be is another matter but as I look at this keyboard in front of me typing away, there is certainly a great deal of order and structure in this vision or three-dimensional image that must be created from inside my head. It would seem very contrary to claim that the interference patterns that must have been set up by these so complex currents of electric charge of one sort or another within the brain are just producing arbitrary chaos. We experience ordered thought and vision which cannot be denied, and which is indeed controlling the way I transmit such thoughts and deliberations into document form as I now type these words in front of me. The latter has to be created by highly ordered processes in the brain.

So that is the first crucial assumption that I made in those days in the reading room that later became the foundations of Duplication Theory (hereinafter DT) when dovetailed in with five other conclusions I made during the course of 1978. I shall refer to this first assumption as section (A), which not surprisingly are followed by B, C, D, E & F in this and the next chapter. The next step (B) was connected with the significance of pattern form and order, but before I go further into that, I now schedule out the six stages for ease of future references, even though they might make little sense just yet. They are as follows.

A. Interference patterns from electrochemical flow to create Holographic projection from the brain.

B. The significance of pattern, order and structure as opposed to Chaos and entropy.

C. The significance of Singularity states which when newly ascertained cause laws of nature and physics to be reassessed.

D. Uncertainty and the impossibility of two structures being absolutely identical, but with very close approaches leading to unanticipated side effects.

E. The connection between hypnotic trance, mystic religions and emptying the mind, and its comparison with the possibility of neurons on the brain being capable of firing in random motion.

F. The melding of conclusions from the above into a self organisational hypothesis to be the basis of explanation of memory and some other phenomena.

(B) Pattern, Order and Structure

From my early twenties I had often speculated on what it was that made some things beautiful and others not. I wondered how much changing fashions created some arbitrary concept of good design, or whether beauty was governed by some fundamental law. I intuitively supported the latter, perhaps persuaded by what little I had read of the Golden Mean and the mathematical Fibonacci sequence that applies to the ways in which plants and organisms develop over time. On one particular occasion during a long night of insomnia, I had made notes on the considerations passing through my mind in the hope that something constructive might be derived. I will return to a description of this particular episode in more specific detail in section F in the next chapter for reasons that might become apparent, but initially I describe my absorption with the significance of structure and order as follows. For anything to stand out for its beauty, or even for that object to be perceived at all, it had to have an element of pattern in it. Reducing the problem to fundamentals, I considered a mass of particles. If they were arranged randomly, they would appear as a formless blob. If, however they were arranged so that their distances apart were equal, then at once a pattern would emerge with perceivable form through its ordered structure. I realised that pattern was little more than the duplication of equal intervals in space between similar points. Sophistications of structures could be perceived through harmonics of equal intervals, and further equal intervals in different directions.

I was also considering why it was that beauty brought pleasure: why there was such a thing as job satisfaction, and why worthwhile activity culminated in a pleasant sense of achievement. For this I realised that any activity had to be organised and had to bring about increasing degrees of order before this satisfying sense of achievement could be attained. Physical activity results from mental activity, and in order to develop thought, greater degrees of order have to be developed in the mind. Whether the subject is music, fine art, literature, science or philosophy, it is all the same: greater enjoyment of any subject is instigated by a greater understanding of its structure and organisation. I concluded that pattern and structure is synonymous with order and its perception out of what might formerly have been regarded as near chaos, produces this sense of satisfaction and achievement.

Since pattern and order could be reduced in fundamental terms to nothing more complex than the repetition of equal intervals in space, then I assumed there must be something very singular about this fact of repetition or duplication. I went on to conclude that that the function of intelligence was to arrange ordered patterns and structures in the mind, and once these structures were established, a greater understanding of any subject was possible. It seemed to me that without this ordering activity there would effectively be no existence at all, so that self-awareness and consciousness itself were confirmed and increased through this ordering process. Since ordering was the direct result of repetition, then the fact of existence had to somehow be closely connected with this phenomenon of duplication. I still have the notes I made at the time I had scribbled down, pages of them and although they seemed fairly incoherent by the cold light of day the following morning, I did not chuck them away. Then when I was seeking a plot line to render my jump back through time in my historical novel, the latter concepts of form and order recalled from that one night in 1972, suddenly seemed to be more relevant once I had better understood the implications of the possible holographic functions of the brain.

During that time, I was also trying to understand more about Einstein's break through research from 1905 to 1915, and considerations on some of what was involved gave rise to the next step in the formulation of DT.

(C) The Significance of Singularity States

I had read about Einstein's theories of special and general relativity, of which the special theory I found easy enough in the end to appreciate by the use of diagrams set out in the better sort of text books. I shall not attempt to explain that here but instead summarise its extraordinary results. Basically, Einstein concluded that nothing could move faster than the speed of light and that light was just one particular group of wave lengths of Electromagnetic (EM) radiation. However, what was amazing was what happened to an object (mass) when it started to approach the velocity of light. Its mass would start to increase radically with a close approach, its length would become foreshortened, and it rate of passing time would slow down. These were all fairly astonishing side effects in 1905 when the theory was first published, but are now taken for granted and implemented in all sorts of modern technology from astral navigation to telling the time accurately.

But it is not only light speed that is a quantity that is impossible to be attained: there are a number of other such absolutes which cannot be reached, such as absolute zero of temperature, resulting in the weird effects of superfluidity and superconductivity. I realised I could classify all such circumstances by the general term singularity states, and note that whenever a close approach is made to such an unachievable end, then the rules of nature and physics as we are familiar with them, have to be amended, and often very substantially. Neither does it just affect physical conditions but also theoretical ones as well such as that of the invention of infinity on which result Euclid's rules of geometry, and also the advances in maths by George Cantor, inventor of set theory, and others. It seems to me to be the case that as the rate of scientific progress accelerates, increasingly more singularity states are being revealed, and whenever this happens, a new vista of a small area of physics has to be amended, and sometimes quite a major reassessment as in the case of the special and general relativity theories. This was perhaps even more so perhaps with Max Planck's discovery in 1900 that it was impossible for matter or radiation to have smaller dimensions of time and space than certain micro dimensions which Planck had calculated, and again fall into what I describe as a singularity state.

As already mentioned the singularity of light speed is the most obvious example, but another lesser version is the way in which one particle of matter cannot occupy exactly the same space as another, perfect penetrability it can be called, but when they are forced under great pressure to occupy increasingly small dimensions, part of their mass is converted into radiation energy. This is predicted by a conclusion of Einstein's general theory of relativity which shows that energy is equal to the mass of an object times the square of the velocity of light, perhaps the best-known algebraic equation of all time, being so short and simple with astonishing results. The most striking and familiar practical example being the fusion process of the hydrogen bomb or atomic reactors to produce heat form radioactive solids. It is possible to regard black holes as a new singularity state, although perhaps there will be some explanation in future to make comprehensible what happens inside such entities, and what function they serve. Meanwhile their existence and the lack of any proper understanding of how and why they exist is an embarrassment to physicists or should be, but when once resolved, a large step forward will have been taken. This to me is a fine and current example of the way in which science progresses, or will be just as soon as more is ascertained about black Holes

It was also at that time I was reading about Heisenberg's Uncertainty principle, and this turned out to be the fourth of my basic considerations (D) which led to my being able to combine these separate conclusions into a basis of explanation for the operation of memory in principle. This I called Duplication theory for convenience, and then later realised how it could be applied to a few other allied phenomena. It seems to be an unrecognised general fact that whenever a new singularity state is ascertained, then the rule of physics will have to be amended, and the best current explanation of this is the quandary of black holes or possibly the disputed existence of the multiverse. Since this connection between singularity states and major advances in science does not seem to be acknowledged much, if at all, and to my mind is a paramount feature of my general thesis, I have attached *Appendix 1* which is an abbreviation of a paper I wrote in 2017. However, it also deals with one or two other issues which come out later in this book.

Further thoughts on Memory's operation: 1978 to 1979

By September 1978, I was so involved with my conjectures on the mind's operation that I had almost forgotten about the novel, and had started to research anything I could find that might reinforce the various vague conclusions I had reached thus far. The next step was perhaps the most crucial of the six subheadings that I indicated above, and some of the content might appear hard going for readers who know very little about some of the more technical content, so I will append a summary of them all at the end of this chapter in terms as straightforward as I can manage, in case the lengthy descriptions are lacking in clarity.

(D) Uncertainty and the impossibility of two identical structures, but with close approaches leading to unanticipated side effects.

I have to elaborate a little on the concept of uncertainty to show how it is interconnected with pattern, order and the significance of similar structures. Heisenberg's work, with that of Schrödinger and a few others in the 1930s, formed the basis of quantum theory. This hugely increased understanding of the characteristics of materials by the way in which electrons and nuclei combined in atoms and molecules. Not being able to understand the maths, I did not bother, but found I could usually just reduce the complex algebraic proofs down to a useful synopsis that could sometimes be found in a few initial paragraphs of verbal abstract or the summary conclusions at the end of the usual reams of figure work. For instance, my understanding of the crucial Uncertainty

Principle in a nutshell is as follows. It is impossible to be certain of the exact location of any particle. This is because all tiny particles are always in motion.

In slightly longer more specific form, my interpretation is as follows: Since every tiny particle down to molecular and atomic level is always in motion above absolute zero of temperature (which is what I describe as a singularity state, and which is something that can never be achieved) then it is impossible to ever be sure of the exact position of that particle. This is because it takes time for the light from that minuscule particle to reach the eye of the observer or the instrument involved, such distances being relatively astronomical on the scale of these tiny particles. This is exactly the same reason that we can never be sure of the location of a star, or even if it still exists, since the light takes years to reach us. It is all a question of relevant scales of distance and time. There are mathematical proofs and other ways of grasping why there is this uncertainty of any tiny particle in motion but this is the one that seems the most obvious to me and the easiest to describe.

So, having grasped at least some of the crucial implications of the Uncertainty Principle, it suddenly occurred to me I could perhaps adopt some of the latter into my conjecture from my novel that repetition of similar patterns of obsessive thought in the same location might resonate down though time. I reasoned as follows: if it was impossible to ever be sure of the precise location of a particle, then one could never be sure that one particle could ever occupy the same space as another at the same time. In short, we, as observers could never know if this had happened, and I reckoned that this was the same as saying that this could never happen. Thus, two particles containing mass could never occupy the same space at the same time, which we know from observation, but this was a theoretical result of the uncertainty theory. We might physically experience such impossibility via the senses but here was a scientific reason to reinforce physical experience, which can after all be delusional.

The logic here might seem not that convincing but is very similar to that which is involved with light speed and relativity. Nothing can ever travel faster than light, and one of the easy to visualise reasons for this is that if such an object was in excess of light speed, the light emitted from it could never reach anything else and thus such an object could not be detected by an observer. In other words, it cannot happen, and via the same line of reasoning, neither can two objects occupy the same space at the same time.

However, never mind the nice philosophical arguments, it is very well accepted that no solid objects with mass (known as fermions) can reach light speed, unlike photons which can transmit action by radiation and which have no mass. As already explained, I use the expression 'singularity state' to describe any condition that can never quite be physically attained although it can of course be described as a concept. Perhaps the best example of this is light speed being a singularity state for objects with mass, but as described in C above, what seems obvious but not yet well recognised, is that wherever a new singularity state is ascertained, the laws of nature as they are then understood, have to be amended. This sometimes results in a crashing reassessment of the rules of physics and nature. For instance we know that when two separate protons of hydrogen (and their accompanying neutrons) are forced together in the attempt to make them occupy the same space, as in a fusion bomb, there will come a moment when they fuse together to become a different element, Helium, whose nucleus has two protons. Without going into detail of the actual mechanics of the whole process involving neutrons, the mass of one molecule of the latter is slightly less than the combined mass of the two separate hydrogen atoms, and this extra mass being redundant after fusion, is converted into energy and radiated off with effective results too familiar since Hiroshima and Nagasaki in 1946. Because a single helium molecule is more stable in construction than a single hydrogen molecule, it requires less energy to hold it together as a single unit than the more volatile hydrogen molecule. The reduction in mass into radiation is known as the nuclear binding energy

In short when a close approach is made to the singularity state of two hydrogen molecules being able to occupy the same space at the same time, this leads to very surprising effects unanticipated much before the late 1930s. The reason I quote this example again is because I then started to wonder what would happen if a number of particles all at regular intervals apart in space, thus making a specific and perceivable structure, were considered instead of just one particular location in space. If the same uncertainty rationale was applied, an observer could never be sure of the precise dimensions of the structure, so that it would not be possible for another structure at a different time in the same location to be identical to the earlier version. All the constituent particles would be moving very slightly with respect to each other so it would be even more difficult for perfect duplication, and therefore a second later absolutely identical structure would be yet another singularity state. If so, it would be consistent with the rationale developed thus far to anticipate that unexpected side effects would result if close approaches were made to that end.

I speculated that perhaps as the later structure became closer and closer to duplicating the earlier original, they would effectively become the same object albeit at different times with exciting consequences. This seemed not impossible to me so I ran with it as a conjecture. It seemed to me that if the earlier structure were to change its shape, which it would have to do since its component particles will never cease their motion on an infinitesimal scale, then ex hypothesi, the later structure could tend to duplicate the motions of the earlier, especially if it is effectively the same object to infinitesimal dimensions.

At the time in 1978 I then made the conjecture that the unanticipated side effect might be that if there are two near identical structures in the same location but at different times, the later in time, rather than start to convert some of it mass into radiation as in fusion, will instead start to duplicate more exactly the structure of the earlier, as a resonance effect. The reason it will not tend to convert into radiation energy is that the constituent structure of earlier particles will have moved on, being ceaselessly in motion, being above absolute zero of temperature, yet another singularity state. Another very physical reason is of course that we never have observed a duplicate structure evaporating to convert a small part of itself into radiation, well not as far as I am aware. On the other hand, there is presumably a vestigial potential to initiate such a conversion and in the later structure in time this could be used instead to drive the change in formation of the latter to duplicate the motion of the earlier in time.

Now instead of squashing particles into just one point simultaneously, if we consider again a specific complex structure, then for the same reasons that perfect fusion is a singularity state, its perfect duplication is equally impossible, and possibly more so with more constituent particles involved, so that such a structure could never be perfectly replicated, either obviously in the same place at the same time, or even at some later time. (There is also the possibility that it would be equally impossible for that duplicate structure to exist in another location at any other time. This would complicate things too much to go into the implications of the latter possibility since it invokes questions of entanglement which will be dealt with in later chapters.)

So here we have a singularity state which is directly equivalent to the earlier rationale that two particles can never occupy the same space at the same time, both circumstances being direct inferences of the uncertainty principle. And as to the definition of the same location, this ought to be qualified. Since we are in an expanding universe the expression 'the same location' has to be relative to a structure's immediate surroundings in the same scale.

Since it is the most crucial bedrock point of DT, I rehearse again the arguments involved. This resonance through time effect resulting from a newly recognised singularity state may appear just too speculative to be taken seriously, but just suppose it is rational enough for even the incredulous to run with it for a moment for the sake of argument, then what else might we expect from this newly discovered singularity state? According to the rationale set out above in (C), when a close approach was made to perfect duplication of another structure earlier in time, we should anticipate that the rules of nature and physics as we are familiar with them should start to require amendment. In the case of a close approach light speed, we now know well that some astonishing side effects are registered: the mass of the object starts to increase, the time it experiences starts to slow down and its length becomes relativistically foreshortened. As already mentioned, the crucial quality of the singularity state is central to an understanding of how DT operates, which is why an abbreviated paper on the subject is attached as *Appendix 1*.

How might such bizarre side effects manifest themselves? It was not difficult for me to conjecture that if a structure in a particular location happens to have a very similar structure to another earlier in time in the same location, then there will be an increasing potential for that later structure to resonate with or duplicate the original's structure, especially if the latter was very complex. This would certainly be a radical variation on our understanding of the laws of nature, which might appear too glib for ready acceptance, for scientists working in a bottom up capacity. For myself working the other way round as top down, I saw that such a result might present a new principle as a basis to explain the brain's ability for recall, which is currently lacking, and given some tweaking and further research, I might be able to justify such a modus operandi.

Another way to put the conjecture is to state that as the later structure (which will comprise the components of an object) starts to become increasingly the same object as the original earlier one, that later version takes on more than just the identity as the original. It would be as if they two were ultimately the same thing the closer the approaches to quantum tolerance levels. Now this state of affairs is remarkably similar to what has been shown to happen in recent very exciting experiments to demonstrate quantum entanglement over distance, and over time as well, albeit experiments over time have not yet been much researched to date (early 2020) on a fairly minimal scale with photons and the way they spin. My conjecture is that the structures that are concerned here I assume will probably be holograms generated by the interference patterns projected from the neural networks of the brain, rather than actual physical of firing neuron structures which would presumably have mass. So, whether there is an element of feedback here in the case of memory to mediate the thoughts in the later brain structure is beyond me to currently come to a conclusion. This question is of some consequence to considerations of entanglement and to which I shall return in a later chapter. I just thought I would mention it now since I will later attempt to show how this transference of similar structures through time is also a quantum effect.

In any event if the unanticipated result of this duplication singularity is as above then such a side effect would be a splendidly easy and convenient modus operandi to show how an image formed in the brain, highly structured and complex as explained above in the form of a hologram, might be caused to resonate with the original version, provided it were indecipherably similar to the earlier thought structure. Furthermore, if there was little resistance of the later structure to move in any other direction, which it would be so if the mind concerned was in a fairly neutral and even trance state, then the easiest thing for this later structure to do would be to emulate the motions of the earlier in time. In short, here would be a primitive form of prefect recall transferring similar structures over time. There is however the principle of minimum energy which is a restatement of the second law of thermodynamics. This is that for a closed system, the internal energy will decrease and approach a minimum value at equilibrium. A closed system, is one which is connected to another, and cannot exchange matter (i.e. particles), but can other forms of energy (e.g. heat), with the other system. In a closed system, in which the entropy rather than the energy remains constant, then it follows from the first and second laws of thermodynamics that the energy of that system will drop to a minimum value at equilibrium, transferring its energy to the other system.

Effectively this means that such a system will revert to that of its most stable position. So, if the later mind was not thinking of much else other than the same thought that had occurred earlier, then the continuing sequence of motions of their system will continue to be duplicated, until some other thought perhaps from external sources causes the sequential flow to cease. Thus, if the later mind were otherwise or momentarily in trance state with its neurons firing randomly, then on following the introduction of a copy structure of firing neurons similar enough to cause a resonance with an earlier memory, then the latter would continue to duplicate the sequence of events recorded in the earlier mind. It could be a series of thoughts or it could also possibly be visual images, to account for the basis of a mechanism for perfect recall, also known as eidetic memory.

If it is assumed that this tendency of structure duplication is an additive effect, and I see no reason why it should not be, then the more complex the structure, the stronger the resonance effect will be. Since the brain is the most complex system of which we are aware, then it seems safe to assume that any such thought structure in the form of a hologram generated from the interference of electrochemical currents constantly coursing through the brain, would be not only highly detailed, but the most complex possible on that scale. The four headings thus far do not explain in any detail how memory might operate, other than indicate a possible means of transfer through time of similar structures. There needs to be one further section before I attempt to pull all these observations and conjectures together to assemble of more convincing picture, as follows.

(E) The connection between hypnotic trance, mystic religions and emptying the mind, and neurons in the brain firing randomly to emulate the trance state.

When I was a student in Dublin, I went with a number of friends to see a stage show by a professional hypnotist. I was staggered at what he was able to extract from volunteers called up on the stage, and hypnotised to act out little scenes and dramas. Three of us volunteered to be involved and we were turfed off fairly rapidly for not taking it seriously enough. This was a relief for me for I was very reluctant to put myself under the influence of a rather flashy performer. However, I was extremely impressed how a dozen or so volunteers from the audience were made to act out scenes according to his somewhat seedy instructions. Of course, the volunteers might have been a put-up job but judging by their ordinariness, but I thought not, as did my colleagues: the acting ability of such stooges would have had to have been very professional. This was reinforced by having watched previously one or two similar displays on well accredited television shows, and when I saw the same hypnotist at work in a show in Finsbury Park some years later, the wife of an old Dublin friend was one of the subjects hypnotised, and she was not a compromised volunteer, although her involvement on stage was less dramatic than most of the others on stage.

So, this episode made a huge impression on me and the day after the stage show in Dublin, I was tempted to give up tedious law and take up studies at once in the art of hypnosis. Of course, I did not, but the recollection remained with me like that of a recurring tooth ache which could not be ignored. It seemed to me that in trance, ordinary individuals were capable of accomplishing activities under instruction, but of which they would be incapable when fully conscious. I found it amazing that so little research had been done on the subject, and this was one of the subjects on which I read up in the BM a few years later. I had also been reading about Eastern mystic religions and the way in which yogins could accomplish most amazing feats, and there seemed to be a general principle that all mystics pursued, and that was the ability to empty the mind completely.

This was apparently not as easy as it might first appear and novitiates spent years in learning techniques that would help them to achieve a state of nirvana, Samadhi, or whatever each separate religion might describe it. But the ultimate intended result seemed always to be described in the same way as resulting in perfect bliss, with full understanding of everything in nature, very often by concentrating on some form of ritual or contemplation process. This not only applied to Eastern religions but also to a number of the early Christian mystics, so I wondered how it was that there seemed to be a common denominator of all these beliefs, and which seemed to be that of emptying the mind. From what I had read of the mystic religions, it was extremely difficult to empty the mind completely and techniques of meditation in its various forms can take years if not a whole life time to achieve with any degree of effectiveness. Then when it is achieved, it appears that an exalted state of consciousness is the result: perhaps a deeper understanding of existence and what Koestler describes as an oceanic feeling.

I knew that the neurons in the brain never ceased firing, including that part which controlled consciousness, but if the intention was to empty it, then the result would be a complete absence of memory and structured thought. This would have to mean that the neurons were firing completely randomly. That seemed such a simple answer that I was rapidly convinced to run with it and develop variations on this theme to see how I could link it with memory, or rather lack of it. Hypnotists all seemed to persuade their subjects to relax and empty their minds so perhaps that was what was happening when they fell into trance under such suggestion.

I had also reached some conclusions about the way in which the mind worked, initially from Arthur Koestler's book, 'The Act of Creation.' He suggests that the way intuition seems to work in the attempt to make some radical breakthrough such as those wrought by Copernicus, Kepler, Heisenberg and many others of the scientific illuminati is as follows. They wrestle with irresolvable problem to which they are convinced there has to be a simple answer, sometimes for weeks, months, or even years, trying all sorts of alternative possibilities fruitlessly. Then when they are out walking, or relaxing, an answer suddenly presents itself out of nowhere, almost fully fledged, just like that.

I wondered whether this sudden intuitive vision of the state of a particular part of nature as it properly was, might not have something to do with the mind being in semi neutral trance state. Suddenly, after a morass of possibilities has been considered endlessly hitherto, then perhaps the position of least resistance, as it were, just slips into place as the duplicate image of the actual external reality and continues to do so indicating how reality would continue to act in the inevitable sequence of events that would inevitably follow assuming there were no external further perturbation forces at play. The mental hologram formed by the mind duplicates the structure of the external world, and how it would then proceed to act and with what result, or at least that specific small part of it that has been under consideration.

What was it about the trance state with the mind empty that made it so susceptible to suddenly being able to understand a concept that had been apparently been irresolvable for weeks, months, even years beforehand? The various speculations I had about the uncertainty principle being connected with memory and its possible connection with form, order and duplication of structure had occurred to me in about May 1978 and I wrote a letter on this subject dated 25/05/78 to Arthur Koestler, describing in an execrably typed fashion my half formed conclusions on structure and order that had occurred to me earlier that April and May. He replied on 15/06/78 encouragingly manner *(appendix 2)*. I was surprised and delighted, although I had also heard back from Colin Wilson who had written a surprise best seller, The Outsider, who had also replied politely enough in January 1978. In July I had taken a temporary job with a small firm of house agents in Dalston in the East End of town with the senior partner hoping I could start a commercial department. That was a forlorn prospect and in five weeks I had left to rush back to the reading room when I settled down very pleased to be back in August.

By the end of September, I had read a great deal more and started to wonder how I might continue to develop this theme of the possible flexibility and adaptability of the mind in trance when its neurons were firing randomly. What was so singular about this business of randomness? In late 1978 it occurred to me that perfect random motion might be what I described as a singularity state. I had no idea at the time, but this later turned out to be a major turning point for me then and also many years later when I learned that quantum entanglement depends to a huge extent on the involvement of random systems, as I will show in later chapters. As mentioned in C above, I had earlier realised that there were a number of singular circumstances that could never be achieved, but yet close approaches could be made, and these are singularity states (light speed, absolute zero of temperature, etc). But if a very close approach to one of these singularity states was made, which was demonstrably possible in many cases, the rules of nature as we were familiar with them have to be amended to accommodate what was then observed to happen. In which case even a new paradigm might be in the offing, if the singularity state was one of consequence such as light speed, or perhaps there would be a lesser result such as super conductivity at near absolute zero of temperature.

That September it suddenly occurred to me that absolute randomness could be regarded as a singularity state since it must be impossible to achieve absolute perfection of disorder for the same reason that perfect duplicates of structure and order can never be achieved. I was at once delighted with this new apparent insight. If perfect randomness cannot be achieved, very close approaches can be made, for instance by random number generators, but it seems they can never attain absolute randomicity. If so, then by the hypothesis described above, perhaps some concurrent unanticipated effects might be anticipated. If the latter were somehow connected with the passage of time then that seemed to be not inconsistent with my rationale of resonance through time thus far conjectured. There was already my thesis as described above, that it was impossible to have two identical structures, but if close approaches were made to that singularity state, either at the same or different times, and then one might expect some unanticipated phenomenon to emerge. My conjecture of the interaction of similar structures through time would then be consistent with such a rationale.

The extraordinary mental abilities of individuals under trance, together with the assumption the latter was brought about by the neurons in the brain firing randomly, suggested to me the conclusions as follows. A mind in trance would be blank with no structure: just be a random mass of firing neurons. But if somehow a very accurate recollection of an earlier experience recorded in the mind was injected into the brain, this would be recreated as a specific structure of firing neurons. Whilst the mind was in trance with no other information coming in via the senses to interrupt the random chaos, then according to the minimum energy principle, *(see page 55)* this later mind should continue to duplicate the sequences seen and experiences by the earlier mind, a sort of echo effect, unless and until the trance state was broken by some outside interference: perhaps from an instruction from a hypnotist for example.

This would not be a model for every day working memory, but if such a hypothesis is the basis of a system whereby a thought structure from an earlier time can be evoked at a later date, then such a function would enhance the chances of survival for any sensate organism by helping it to avoid a repetition of dangerous circumstances encountered in the past. I found this all so fascinating that it was well worth persevering with such an enticing subject. By early 1978, I had effectively ceased work on the novel and its attempted quasi scientific explanation of a jump through time. Instead I just concentrated on reading as much as I could find in that inestimable store house of information as it then was, so I might perhaps find evidence to support the vestige of a hypothesis on memory that was stirring my enthusiasm.

So, I had an explanation of sorts in principle for the mechanism of perfect recall, also described as eidetic memory, of which many examples have been experienced, especially in trance state. It occurred to me that it might be possible for the mind to increase rapidity of recall by curtailing long sequences of perfect recall down to workable short extracts telescoped into a few microseconds. This would allow the involved individual to take whatever preventive action to bring about the best result to enhance his chances of survival. I have always thought that the basic purpose of memory is this function, survival of the fittest, albeit much sophisticated over the years. Such a system would require a physical store of a great number of memory structure molecules, probably in the form of DNA molecules, and these would act as short-term memory instigators to start a sequence of an earlier episode by resonance. I decided to call these engrams, a word borrowed from neuroscientist Karl Pribram whose work I will describe later. These engrams would be discarded as time passed unless they proved to be crucial to an individual's survival, or unless the incident of sequence to be memorised was repeated parrot fashion time and time again.

I had already read a little at that time that DNA molecules have huge storage capacity on the smallest scale, and that they had been already suggested as possibly part of the memory storage system in the brain, but without much of a modus operandi attached. In my thesis these engrams would be selected by the force of the impact of the original situation when they were first experienced, and then reinforced to become semi-permanent in the brain especially if circumstances were repeated a number of times. This would be especially so if such experiences were either likely to prejudice future continued existence on one hand, or on the other, likely to enhance the enjoyment of life. The duplication of such strong experiences would be dinted in to such short-term memory molecules to endure over time and not be scrapped as redundant. These engrams would serve long term to advise the best action experienced in the past evoking by resonance an earlier relevant and similar sequence to fit the circumstances.

All these notions came to me in the reading room in September and October 1978, whither for the first time in my life, I looked forward to getting to work every morning, itching to piece a few more pieces of the puzzle into place. Whether or not I could do anything of objective use with all these speculations I had no idea but I almost did not care, so enjoyable was the process whereby it was all my own work in the metaphor of the proverbial pavement artist. It was entirely original and even if it turned out to be completely off the wall, at least I was working with my mind on a subject that was central to existence, besides which everything else was secondary. In fact, it was also a very busy time for me out of the reading room since I had my flat on the market and had to clear up the awful state in which my minor celebrity tenant had left my basement flat but that will come out the next chapter.

(F) The extension of memory's operation as above into a self-organisational hypothesis for the basis of explanation for intuition and other phenomena.

Whilst speculating along these lines to explain memory, one other implication of the singularity of randomicity occurred to me along much the same lines. If a physicist for example had been attempting to work out an explanation for a specific observed result which involved a large number of separate components, the qualities of which were familiar enough, but it was not known what and how they were all joined together to give this observed result. The physicist might have toiled for months fruitlessly without result, maybe indeed a life time. But what is recorded to have happened on a number of quite well known instances, the physicist (or chemist, mathematician, poet, artist: it does not really matter which) will be walking in a forest, in the country, down a street to catch a bus or whatever, mind blank enough (or as my wife's family has been known to describes this state: thumb in bum and mind in neutral), and suddenly the answer comes to him in a flash, when the subject was not even being thought about. This is recorded to have happened to Heisenberg with his Uncertainty principle, Friedrich Kekule on the shape of the benzene ring, and there are many other similar examples, Henri Poincare, Karl Friedrich Gauss, and even Samuel Taylor Coleridge when drafting his poem Kubla Kahn in a semi dream state which was famously interrupted and ruined by the visit of a man from Porlock, scientists not having a monopoly on this creative process. Many such examples are assembled and well described in Arthur Koestler's admirable book The Act of Creation.

I assumed that such a scientist, when thinking about such problems, has a more or less mental image in his mind of all the constituents of the problem which he shuffles about waiting until all the variables can be melded together but presumably there are so many permutations and combinations, possibly many billions of them, with the correct answer just being one: that is in any event how my mind seems to work. Now if his mind is in random motion thinking about not very much of consequence, with the numerate/cognitive part of his mind not in use but firing randomly then he reverts for a moment to the problem, his mind has an increased potential to duplicate or resonate with what actually happens in the external world. The fact of near perfect duplication with the latter is sensed by the scientist's mind (or any other problem solver for that matter) due to the slightly increased potential that the two near duplicate entities have to convert a tiny amount of their rest mass into radiation energy as described in D above. How the scientist detects this, is usually by the feeling of pleasure he registers in at once sensing he has the correct answer: a feeling of aesthetic satisfaction and probably some sort of empowerment. If reality is very accurately reflected by his mental holographic image, then there will be a state of much increased potential to convert a few molecules of the latter back in to radiant energy as described above in nuclear fusion process and its equivalence to the perfect duplication effect. Perhaps the whole neural frame of the individual involved senses the approach of such a state of achievement. In any event, it seemed to me that this newly posited singularity state of perfect random motion was definitely connected with the brain's operation especially when it came to the beneficial effects of emptying the mind, further to its role in instigating memory sequences by physically stored short-term complex memory molecules or engrams.

Before I start the next chapter and get back to more narrative of what else I was doing to survive at this time, I mention with some slight trepidation an incident from the early 1970s which was in some ways a prelude to section B: the significance of pattern, order and structure as opposed to chaos and entropy. A friend of mine from Dublin, George, who was I assumed very numerate as he was working in the city with computers, was also interested in the workings of the mind about which we had a few useful discussions in the early seventies. In one of them he related that he had been experimenting with lysergic acid, the effects of which he had found fascinating, and he said he and a friend had gone to a restaurant after having ingested a reasonably strong dose. He had just ordered and when the soup arrived, he became transfixed by the pattern of vibration on its surface, which elicited the comment from him "Waiter, I say waiter, look here, there's a pattern in my soup." After which he had convulsed with laughter and almost fell under the table whilst believing it was the most significant thing he had ever seen or thought. Of course, a few days later, he could not describe why but I thought it was amusing enough to commit to memory.

This latter event might have been partly inspired by my memory of an evening of bizarre revelations from a few years earlier in about 1972 from an episode of hallucinogenic consumption that must have made an impression on me at the time. So, I dug up this old file from the early seventies with notes I had taken whilst trying to get through a bout of indulgence in lysergic acid. I had tried dope, marijuana, in my early twenties a few times but since I had never mastered the art of inhaling smoke into my lungs without choking, it never did much for me. My father and my brothers used to smoke cigarettes fairly heavily, although my siblings ceased the habit after a few years, but not my father. I had avoided all that until I was about twenty-two. I very much liked the aroma of French and Turkish cigarettes that a few others indulged in so I sampled the occasional Gauloise no doubt because it looked cool and allayed embarrassment at parties when not knowing what to talk about. But since I could not inhale dope without coughing, hardly cool, I never did, and I never much cared for the smell of the weed marijuana, the effect of which seemed to me much less immediate and effective than alcohol.

My friend Simon had returned from his travels around the world in the early 1970s and had brought with him from his short time in New York in pursuit of the captivating chanteuse Nico, some tiny purple pills of LSD, lysergic acid, which in this case was Owsely purple, very strong so that just half would do to start with, or so I was advised. I was nervous of it, but was assured it was something that should not be missed as an experience although it was better to try it in company with others, which initially I did once or twice. At the time I was living in Elgin Crescent, Notting Hill, and I forget which friend was occupying the second bedroom at the time, but one evening I was alone and I tried another dose by myself. The effect was amazingly powerful, so much so that I realised this was not something to be trifled with and not taken more than a few times. Nevertheless, the expression used to describe its effect at the time, mind blowing, was not an exaggeration and I decided to note down events or thoughts as they occurred to me, and I still have these, five A4 pages of hand written fairly lucid notes to begin with followed by 22 sides of small note paper with letter heading that happened to be close at hand, scribbled feverishly in pencil on both sides.

The hastily written sentences initially recorded the various physical sensations: breathless, dry mouth with constant need to salivate, time seeming to slow down so that on listening to music it was possible to listen to each individual note being drawn out, all this followed by a short bout of exhaustion, and a sweep of nausea downwards, and then back up again shaking with ecstasy. I started by listening to rock opera of Tommy through earphones, noting the shimmering of the carpet with patterns which were not really there, sofa looking saggy and then heaving with Tonbridge ware patterns. Bouts of paranoia and then ecstasy repeated, as I listened to a mixture of the Who on earphones, followed by more sedate classical music, by which time I was sweating rather much. So, when seeming to get out of control again, I attempted to reduce the paranoia by trying to analyse and record in writing what was going on in my mind. This had some sort of calming effect and seemed to work.

Two hours later things had calmed down and the sentences become a little more lucid, and I suddenly start to try to reason things out. There is a page missing at this stage which bridges the stages of the panic and exhilaration back down to attempted rationality but it seems by then I must have been listening to a Beatles album since I started to obsess on the words of one of their songs 'Oh that magical feeling, nowhere to go' and I began to comment on formless oblivion which might be the fundamental reason for life and perhaps the song writer was grasping in some way at the reason for existence. This led me to wonder and respond that in order to stave off the bottomless perdition of oblivion, it would be better to create things in the form of pattern and order since that would be a presupposition of our existence, and to quote from the scribbled script:

"Therefore, out of random motion by molecules, form, matter, whatever you like, suddenly and arbitrarily motion or position is duplicated. Motion though is position with regards to time, Jesus and now we're back to time which again is only measurable by duplication or pattern. Everything has to be relative to something else in order to be measured, time included, therefore time, as space and/or shape must have been brought into existence by again duplication—I'm losing energy now and acid is wearing off—I can smell sweat and feel the on creeping of normalcy and the deflating loss of enlightenment-- doubtless subjective but I'll have to try again. Possibly the music has something to do with the stimulation of certain trains of thought, sets a pattern flowing which is too much for my tiring mind now; back to pattern. Presupposing duplication can be recognised, there it is, a pattern which is recognisable, possible to register, to compartmentalise, to make a note of and to comment on etc. With pattern form is vindicated, confirmed and given existence. Therefore, we are happy with form as pattern as we must exist. Conversely to exist there must be pattern. Now I have to check this, never mind the boggling fundamentals which exhaust me. What about pattern? It is pleasing- architecture (yes) music (yes)- a tune is such simply because it duplicates gradations of frequencies with which the ear and hence the brain becomes familiar through repetition. Why should we enjoy sophistication which is making existence more complicated by hiding its pattern, but it is still there for the few that can discern, and this makes them content, though why pleasure should be found in excluding others from it, I cannot think about now, but there must be a reason."

The scribbled script goes on like this for another fourteen sides of A6 paper, analysing the significance of form and order to bring the universe as we know it into existence until I retired to bed just before 4 a.m. The next day I realised that it would most likely be a load of old cobblers if I bothered to read the content of last night's ravings. This I did not bother to do for quite some time, as I recall, to avoid serious embarrassment, having decided to lay off such hypnagogic experiments. However, I must have checked it over at some later time because I did not throw it into the WPB, and it later became the first entry in the file, which I started to build up from my time in the BM six years later. Presumably I must have been prompted into reading it through again since it had some relevance to my novel's plot, and assisted greatly in later building up my notion of the significance of similar structures having the ability in certain circumstances to resonate through time from the past. Indeed, it is why I eventually decided to describe my proposal as duplication theory, which is hardly the most elegant of titles when resonance theory might have been better, but that never occurred to me at the time.

Since these six sections represent a major part of DT, I have summarised below each section as a sort of convenient aide memoire for those who might wish to piece together my assumptions and rationale thus far in a sequential manner. Maybe for those who have been submerged into too much hypothetical argument and postulates and who might be tempted to give up, then this will just spell out briefly the ground rules of the my proposals as simply as I can manage to show how information might be transferred through time, never mind the qualifying support and detail.

SUMMARIES OF ABOVE 6 SECTIONS

Section A: Interference patterns from electrochemical flow to create Holographic projection from the brain.

Remarkably little is known about the operation of the brain although its components have been identified, and labelled for many decades. The main nerve centres, the neurons are interconnected via specialised connections called synapses and from the cell bodies of these neurons also flow other connections called dendrites and axons. Electrochemical currents flow along these networks between neurons at all times. Part of the brain automatically controls all the physical attributes of existence, breathing, pumping blood, digesting food, muscle control etc. and another cognitive part deals with thought, memory and the other senses. These hugely complex passage of electrical currents between these cells will create electromagnetic waves and these will inevitably interfere with each other and the assumption is that the result will be so complex and highly ordered that holographic images, described as holocepts will be created. These will produce three dimensional images of the external world as vision and also more vestigial such images to serve as memory and thought, possibly when two or more such images are mixed together. These holograms are projected from the brain of an individual, and how they are registered and observed will be described elsewhere starting from page 93.

Section B: The significance of pattern, order and structure as opposed to Chaos and entropy.

If in a swirling mass of its component particles in a liquid or gas has order suddenly imposed on to part of that chaos, then at once a pattern or structure will become perceptible. Such visual order is nothing more at the most fundamental level than the distances between separate particles or other objects becoming the same or possibly regular harmonics of these same distances. For beauty to be perceived, then there have to be degrees of order in the construction of any object, or indeed in harmonics of sound in music. This gives sensations of satisfaction and pleasure when registered by individuals of some degree of intelligence and understanding. Again, this ultimately depends on the fact of repetition or duplication of similar intervals in space, and also in time for music. Greater enjoyment of any subject is instigated by a greater understanding of its structure and organisation, and structure is basically created by duplication of similar intervals in space and time. I conclude that pattern and structure is synonymous with order and its perception, out of what might formerly have been regarded as near chaos, produces this sense of satisfaction and achievement: existence where nothing formerly existed.

Section C: Significance of Singularity States

Singularity states are circumstances that can never be achieved but to which close approaches can be made. The best example is light speed, but there are many others such as absolute zero of temperature, and the Planck minimum quantum dimensions of intervals of space and of time space. This also applies to concepts such as infinity, but what is common to all such states is that although they can never be attained, close approaches can be made, and which when achieved, the rules of nature and physics as we are familiar with them start to change. The closer the approach is made the more increasingly weird the new effects become: for instance, as super fluidity and conductivity close to absolute zero of temperature, and time dilation, mass increase and length diminution close to light speed.

Section D: Uncertainty and the impossibility of two identical structures, but with close approaches leading to unanticipated side effects.

Heisenberg's uncertainty principle states that a particle may have position or it may have velocity but it cannot have both. I see this simply as follows. Since all particles are in motion by the time the light from a particle has reached the eye of the observer, it will have moved on resulting in the observer never being sure of its position. One result of this is that we can never be sure that two particles will occupy the same space at the same time which would make it an unattainable singularity state. However close approaches can be made to perfect penetrability as in the fusion of two hydrogen atoms into one of helium and when this happens from the application of huge pressure, the mass of the two protons of helium is less than that of the two hydrogen protons and the difference is converted into radiation energy. The best example of this is the hydrogen or fusion bomb. This was a result Einstein's well-known proof that mass can be converted to vast quantities of energy according to the equation that energy equals mass times the speed of light squared. This was not anticipated before 1915, and a fine example for me of a close approach to a singularity state changing the laws of nature as we are familiar with them.

For the same reasons, it is equally impossible to be sure of the precise positions of a number of particles comprising a structure, so that it would be impossible to have an identical structure in that same location at a later time, in which case here is another singularity state, and ex hypothesi one should expect another equivalent and entirely new side effect on an approach to perfect duplication of a similar structures. The most immediate answer might be to postulate that a small amount of the mass of the later similar structure in time will increase the potential of a minuscule amount of the mass of its constituent particles to start to convert into radiation energy, as in the fusion process. This would be consistent with what happens in the fusion process above. But the latter is done under conditions of huge pressure, whereas the particles of the later structure are free to move at large anywhere. There is however the principle of minimum energy which is a restatement of the second law of thermodynamics. This states the energy of closed system energy will tend move to its most stable state of minimum energy. The implication of this is that the similar later structure, rather than convert part of its mass to energy, will instead move its constituent particles to duplicate the motions of the original structure, their being in constant motion.

Another way of resolving the crucial question of the nature of this unexpected effect is to consider that two complex structures which are almost indecipherably the same to almost quantum levels. I speculated that perhaps as the later became increasingly close to duplicating the earlier original, they effectively become the same object albeit with the later duplicating the actions of the earlier as the easiest thing to do to reduce energy levels rather than convert to radiation energy. The latter never actually happens since due to the uncertainty principle; two structures can never be identical being constantly in motion. The result is that the structure of the later in time will continue to duplicate the motions of the earlier in time: a resonance through time effect, so that information can be transferred from one time to the present time, or indeed any other time at all, providing the locations in which this is done are relatively the same. In other words, a later thought structure in the brain can be evoked at later date, the essence of mechanism behind memory. This is a quantum effect which subject will be qualified in more detail later in the text.

Because the universe is expanding, the words an event in 'same location' is impossible and has to be qualified by being the same location relative to its immediate surroundings and general circumstances.

E: The connection between hypnotic trance, mystic religions and emptying the mind, and neurons in the brain firing randomly to emulate the trance state.

Subjects under hypnotic trance have abilities of recall and other characteristics well above those exhibited in their everyday conscious and ordinary working lives. Many eastern mystic religions are based on the ability to empty the minds of the adherents in order to achieve a contemplative state of calm and understanding of existence. The neurons in the brain never cease firing, including the parts that control cognition and thought, so if individuals have been put in hypnotic trance with instructions to empty their minds, the neurons will be firing randomly without any semblance of structure. But perfect randomness is impossible to attain so this is yet another singularity state, and ex hypothesi from C above, as close approaches are made towards it, then unexpected side effects will become increasingly apparent. A mind in trance with information being excluded by instruction from a hypnotist or self-induced by chanting or some other self-discipline, is capable of perfect recall and other capabilities not usually characteristic of that individual. This further clarifies the modus operandi of perfect recall or long-term eidetic memory.

DNA molecules have huge capacity for storing information and are thought to be closely connected to memory. Short term memory instigators or engrams similar to DNA molecules are stored physically in the brain whose function would be to resonate with a current situation observed or experienced externally. This would then instigate a resonance with similar past experience, which would be curtailed down to very short sequences allowing the individual to anticipate the best course of actins to enhance survival. The engrams are effectively the mechanism for short term memory. These physical short-term memory engrams are discarded with passing time, unless they are repeated frequently or created initially under circumstances of great stimulation.

F: The extension of memory's operation as above into a self-organisational hypothesis for the basis of explanation for intuition and other phenomena.

Events in the external world are viewed to create a duplicate in the mind/brain of the observer projected in the form of a holographic image. There are many examples of individuals in the history of science working with problems that involve a certain number of variables which can only be combined in a specific way to produce a resolution which is viable. But the amount of permutations and combinations of the various quantities involved invariably seem insuperably immense, having often toiled on them far too long without any sign of success. Months later, with the mind of the researcher in neutral, when relaxing and thinking of not much at all, suddenly the answer appears as if out of nowhere, resolving the problem instantly in an unanticipated moment. Such instances were experienced by Heisenberg with his Uncertainty principle, Friedrich Kekule on the shape of the benzene ring, and with many other similar examples from Henri Poincare, Karl Friedrich Gauss, and even Samuel Taylor Coleridge when drafting his poem Kubla Kahn.

In such circumstances the cognitive part of a researcher's mind has been wrestling with the problem in a logical manner attempting to fit the variables like a jig saw into an acceptable order without result. But when an individual's mind is thinking in a relaxed manner about nothing much in particular, firing neutrally, and momentarily considers this major problem, then there is suddenly an increased potential for the actual structure of the problem as it occurs in the real world to resonate and form a duplicate image in the mind of the researcher. The latter will know it is correct from the pleasure at once sensed. Possibly this is due an increased potential of the mental image to convert minuscule elements of its structure into radiation energy, which presumably does not happen but is detected as pleasure from an increased potential for such an event.

Leaving London and Gaining Support: 1979

By the end of September 1978 I had drafted most of the principles described above in very rough terms and also a whole other section that evolved from the consideration of what might happen when identical intervals in time are considered, rather than intervals in space. I have not mentioned this hitherto even though it first occurred to me in September of that year. Having explained the radical part of the theory dealing with transfer of structures through time, I will deal with my more standard version of the way in which electromagnetic energy and information is transmitted across space at light speed in a later chapter. It is very supportive of the content described to date as a remarkably simple corollary effect. However, there is already a well-known theory for the transmission of electromagnetic (EM) energy, albeit not perfect with some gaps and serious inconsistencies therein, but too much of this more technical detail might obscure things at this stage, and risk tedium.

When it comes to sources of inspiration, I have already mentioned the nonpolitical books of Arthur Koestler whom I first read in the late 1960s, The Sleepwalkers being the first and for me the most crucial followed by 'The Act of Creation, and then 'The Ghost in the Machine'. I wrote to him with a very badly typed draft of my rather vague proposals in May 1978 to which he replied and later when I sent him later when my ideas were better expressed in a draft of 50 typed pages in January 1979 he replied on 20/02/79 (see *appendix* 3) and I was pleased to see that he thought my proposals might have something in common with the work of eminent physicist David Bohm, whose book I had already bought although I could not make much headway with it given the complexity of the mathematical proofs and what he called the implicate order. Nevertheless, I was encouraged to continue with my deliberations, but was running out of money with a wife and small son to support.

So back to the narrative account of how my family and I were managing to exist without employment. From early 1978, the property market had begun to improve, and I had started to apply for jobs in commercial agency and development, that were beginning to be advertised in the pages of the property press. The few prospective employers by whom I was summoned to interviews were usually nonplussed by someone having resigned from a safe position in a respectable nine to five job, especially in the wonderfully stimulating business of property. Frankly they were a little incredulous, and perhaps they were right. One or two had the intelligence to be more interested in the subject of the book I was trying to write than my prospects for the job they were offering. Anyway, the first job I was offered after about forty abortive applications, was to open a new commercial agency office in the city for a firm with an office in Dalston, the East End of London. The firm had quite an established name in the business, but it transpired that it was a branch of a larger firm which had split away some years before from the head office in the West End.

This all struck me as a little odd, but it was a job, and maybe a challenging one, to open a new city office, so I signed on during the first week in July. After three weeks, the city office had not come into being, and the whole affair seemed to be a figment in the imagination of my employer, and meanwhile, there I was sitting doing nothing in a pinstripe suit in a funny little office in the East End, so that job ended through mutual agreement by the first week in August, and I returned with great relief to the reading room. I had never left it mentally, since my head was full of the implications of my ideas, and how I could develop them further. Having again tasted and been reminded of the futility of office life, those next few months in the British Museum, were enormously productive, I was so relieved and delighted to be back in those august halls.

Towards the end of 1978 I had been out of the office for nearly two years, the last year of which I had let my flat in Elgin Crescent to the former manager of Jimi Hendrix and The Who, amongst others, Kit Lambert, who had been very successful and made large sums of money, but ran into trouble with drugs and mismanagement generally. The trouble was that my tenant was something of a professional wrecker. He had had fallen on awkward times and had been made a ward of the court of protection. The reasons for all this are all clearly explained in an absorbing book on the Lambert family by Andrew Motion (see also Wikipedia). His father was Constant Lambert, another fascinating individual, a leading figure in the world of music before the second World War, and his grandfather George Lambert, a painter who gained eminence in Australia. By the time he moved into my flat, his affairs were governed by an old friend of his, the charming Daria Schouvaloff, who paid the rent and with whom I consulted over all the formalities of the lease. To quote from the book:

"Kit needed the Court because he was incapable of looking after himself -incapable of even reading the papers of admission- but he wanted its protection without the deprivations that this entailed. Initially these deprivations did not seem too painful. Daria was able to supplement the £150 a week that he received from Polydor, who were prepared to give her Kit's dues because she was, as receiver, a director of his companies. She also 'did an amazing deal', she says, with Kit's bank, writing off his debt of £165,000 as against

£16,000; sold his burnt-out house for £20,000; and found him a flat in Elgin Crescent off Ladbroke Grove in Notting Hill. Kit's response was to set about turning his clean, smartly painted new flat into a 'pigsty'."

When I first met him, I had no idea who he was, except that he was something to do with the record industry, and that although he was a ward of court, there was no problem with lack of funds to pay the rent. I liked him, but did not have much to do with him except when summoned to clean out blocked drains, or to placate the disturbed neighbours who lived on the floors above him. I was advised by his cleaning lady not to call before midday, since one never knew what or who one might still find in bed. He kept a great Dane and a Labrador who between them, used the spare bedroom as a whelping box, and the state of was unspeakable. All the surfaces of the furniture seemed to be covered by a film of white dust, the nature of which I had grave suspicions. The lady in the top flat upstairs told me that there were often large limousines parking outside the flats with pop stars in glittering suits paying homage to the denizen of the basement flat. On one occasion, my tenant had been seen chasing a totally naked lady down the pavement, cracking a bull whip, screaming with laughter, but I suppose these stories might have been embellished in the telling. Certainly, the one I liked best was the story of Kit Lambert, wrecker king and inspiration of the Who's destructive act on stage, and who when staying at a luxury high rise hotel in Australia, phoned to complain to room service that his colour television was not working. The desk said that they would send someone up right away to attend to it, but their guest said not to bother, he had already sent it down to them, and he had. He had chucked it out of the window twenty stories down to the swimming pool below.

My tenant was certainly not dull, and I enjoyed dining out on stories about him, but it was worrying enough, all the same. The flat was being totally wrecked, and it represented my sole source of worldly wealth and income. I did not dare upset my wife by telling her exactly the state it was in. Daria Schouvaloff told me not to worry, Kit's estate would pay all the damages, and we ended up both trying to persuade him to leave. I wanted to sell the flat, and buy something in the country, and she was becoming seriously concerned that Kit would fall to sleep again, drugged up and smoking a cigarette, setting fire to the bed, and then the house, as he had apparently done once already. She was worried that if this happened, then the flats upstairs would also burn down, possibly with loss of life, and she might be held responsible. Initially he refused to budge, and the flat began to take on the derelict appearance of its tenant, but by early October 1978 Kit had removed himself and it was no easy task to get the official solicitor to reimburse the cost of the extensive dilapidations. I no doubt settled for far too little in order to get the flat on the market and sold as soon as possible. The considerate Daria who looked after Kit's affairs was horrified when I showed her an inventory of a claim for breakages and dilapidations claim to the official Solicitor who had taken over Kit's affairs. She was concerned I should do better than my figures: much better. "Mr. Greaves, Copeland Spode sauce boats and dinner plates are worth ten times the figure you have claimed."

Well I had indeed been given them by my parents as their second-best collection when they retired to Cornwall, but I knew nothing about such values. What I did know was that the official solicitor was in no hurry to negotiate and I needed reimbursement as soon as possible. The money had just about run out and having not had an easy time getting work in London we had decided to live in the country if possible, and in order to avoid the tedium of commuting I would become a commercial surveyor in some commercial centre in the South East countryside. By November 1978 I had been offered and accepted a job in an old fashioned professional firm of chartered surveyors in Reading, where all four partners were staunch members of the local rotary clubs, although at the time I had no idea of the implications of this and the way business was done in the provinces. Had I known, I might have done better to remain in London, but the prospect of country life and a proper garden was too attractive. Furthermore, I was more concerned that I should have the time to be able to continue to work on my theory, rather than spend hours commuting every day: such a grey existence.

In the reading room for three uninterrupted months to the end of November 1978 I had developed my deliberations further by starting to wonder what might happen when patterns of equal intervals in time, or similar actions were considered, as opposed to intervals in space. I found the possibilities so exciting here that I had given up on the time transference novel earlier that year to concentrate full time on relevant research which centred on the way in which electromagnetic radiation (light and/or radio waves) was transmitted: a large subject full of unknowns to a much greater level than when I had been taught physics at school. Since there is already an explanation for this which is generally held to be acceptable, I will not spend too much time on detail here. However, there are major problems with our current understanding of the way in which energy and information is transferred.

I was at this final stage of developing the barebones of my thesis when I was also starting my new job in November

1978 as a commercial agency negotiator with a firm of chartered surveyors in Reading, Dunster and Morton, which the then senior partner mentioned jocularly that he had once received a letter addressed to Dimster and Moron, which was the best of a list of malapropisms he had received over the years, which wry comment I found encouraging. They were very respectable, and although I had never regarded myself as aggressively quick on the uptake as some of my contemporaries had been in the West End in London, I found some of their attitudes to the dealing of property wonderfully old fashioned. Indeed, this was refreshing for me initially but later on was to prove frustrating. I was made an associate partner within a year and a full partner a little later.

Initially I commuted backwards from my wife's Sussex Gardens flat about 200 yards walk from Paddington station straight to Reading in twenty minutes, nothing if not convenient and during those first few months an old flat mate and fellow law student of mine from TCD, Eugene Lambe, did most of the redecoration and clearing up of the Elgin Crescent, part of which the official solicitor reimbursed after pressure had been applied in consideration of the ravaging effects of Kit Lambert. Eugene was the finest conversationalist I had then ever met, and never exceeded by anybody else of my acquaintance since. Such a statement requires a few qualifying comments. In my second year I shared the top half of a house in Dun Laoghaire just outside Dublin on the coast, with three others, David, Robin and Eugene, all due to go into law although Eugene and I never made it.

Eugene was older than us having been a civil servant in Ulster for a few years, by which time he had saved some money which was rapidly consumed in the Bailey, a popular pub in Duke Street, close to Trinity (a.k.a. TCD for ease of reference). By that time I had a minivan and every night in order to get Eugene home the five miles to the house in Crosthwaite Park, I would have to back it up as close to the front door of the pub, open the back doors and then Dave and I would go in, grab him ignoring his mumbled protests, pull him out to manhandle him into the back of the van, with much clanking of bottles of beer and half pint glasses secreted in his coat pockets. He was so affable and amusing that people never stopped buying him drinks and many of the celebrities passing through Dublin would end up for a drink in the Bailey, so that by the end of our first year his circle of acquaintance was remarkable.

This could not go for ever since he was not turning up for lectures, with the evidence of drink having been taken becoming obvious. It became apparent that the university authorities were used to dealing with such problems especially if they were talented students. So much was he valued as a conversationalist and good company that he was presented with a sort of scholarship which they paid for. This was a drying out course at St. Patrick's Hospital of mental health patients. I do not know what it is like now but then it was pretty primitive.

Towards the end of our or second year when we visited him, it seemed to be more like an asylum than a hospital. Eugene was a vegetarian before it ever became fashionable, and because St. Patrick's had never had to deal with such a diet, we had to take him in lettuce and suitable other veg. The cure in those days seemed to be to wean the patient off the alcohol presumably fairly slowly by keeping him inside and then when the cure seemed to be taking, inject him with some drug which would render him immediately ill to the point of vomiting if he took a drink. Then they would start to let him out. Trinity paid for all this but he was in there for some months and let out in stages as I recall, so that he lost a year's study which he had to repeat. After that he more or less stayed sober, but the habit of drink never left him although it was under control, and in the end I think that TCD gave him a degree a couple of years after we left to speed him benevolently on his way, or so I was given to understand because by that time I was in Canada.

Eugene was physically strong and worked a fair amount as a builder. After some time travelling in Europe and amusing new circles of acquaintances and friends, he moved to London took up residence in a house which he was helping to convert into flats above a book shop in Long Acre, which was then on the verge of becoming fashionable. His friend the book dealer gave him the use of a room whilst he was working there and he became a sort of concierge to the mainly gay community who ended up buying or renting the upper floor flats. He moved effortlessly into a bohemian life of the arts centring on the French House pub in Dean Street, Soho, and made an income carrying our painting and decorating for friends. He also had produced a son, Orlando who was about five when he was working on my Elgin Crescent flat in 1978, and if he ever gets to read this book or anybody knows Orlando whose Canadian mother took him to Australia, then I would be delighted if he would contact me. I last saw him at his father's funeral in the Catholic Church in Soho in maybe 2004, together with his three uncles, the brothers of Eugene, all in the British army, and at that time were apparently all colonels.

He had died of a sudden heart attack on the dance floor at Madame Jojo's, a well-known Soho night club, on transvestite night. I was told that the ravishing red head lady in the pew in front of me was his partner on the dance floor when he collapsed, but I was far too upset to enquire further. There were a number of contemporaries from TCD whom I had not seen for decades, all in rather tight-fitting old suits they had nearly outgrown, as my wife observed. That is probably too much information about Eugene but for one last incident. I had been invited by Rupert Sheldrake to a book launch in 2012 for his latest book 'the Science Delusion' in a fine house in West London in which modern paintings of quality were collected on every wall. There in the middle of all that colour and talent was a portrait by David Hockney of Dr. Eugene Lamb drawn in Lucca. I could not get over that chance viewing of my old china and occasional companion at law lectures, and was amazed and delighted to see that posterity had awarded him a doctorate, which he would certainly have deserved as a wit and raconteur.

Back to my more mundane life commuting to Reading, and working as a provincial estate agent. The fee income was not exactly overwhelming but I thought that if I could get my agency department moving, then in a rapidly expanding town such as Reading, regarded as the Golden triangle outside London with easy access to Heathrow, things could only get better. I started to house hunt at once since I was commuting backwards from London to Reading by train. Actually, Paddington station was only four minutes' walk from my wife's Sussex Gardens flat, so the journey could take as little as 25 minutes door to door but the idyll of family life in a country cottage was not to be denied. Within five months I had found and bought a house in a hamlet on top of Remenham Hill, Number five Upper Culham, about a mile outside and across the river from Henley on Thames. Greenfields in all directions, and a wonderfully hospitable pub, the Flower Pot Hotel, close to the river at Aston, less than a mile away. This came about when I was valuing a shop in Henley, and took the opportunity at lunch to do a bit of house hunting around the outskirts of the town.

I came across the Flower Pot by chance and was attracted by guinea fowl wandering around the slightly scruffy pub garden and was then served by Fred the genial and charming elderly proprietor. I was later to learn that he and the Flower Pot were well known to a surprising number of former customers that I might meet elsewhere in the most unlikely places around the world. I decided to buy a house within striking distance of Fred and the Flower pot, full of wizened old regulars and stuffed pike in glass cases, and this came about, not long afterwards.

The theory was that I would have more time under such a relaxed provincial regime to concentrate of getting my thesis of Duplication Theory published in some form or another, and this was now for me more of a driving force than was the making of millions in property development. After 12 years in the business I was almost able to admit that I was not a risk taker by inclination, nor easily capable of taking quick and crucial decisions necessary as an entrepreneur. I felt bound to describe all the risks to a client in making a purchase, as well as the possible advantages of possibly making a huge profit, and the former always seemed more real to me than the latter, especially because it was somebody else's money involved and not mine. I always wanted time to agonise and reflect on decisions rather than take them at the drop of a hat. Thus, I was probably unlikely to restore the family fortunes and the lifestyle in which I had been brought up, but which was now evaporating after the loss of the family business in 1967.

Having said that, with five years of London experience I was certainly able enough to identify and point out all the possible risks and advantages to provincial clients of the possible acquisition of a property in a balanced manner. It would then be their decision whether to buy it or not and I reckoned I was competent enough in this role and over the next few years and I assisted a number of shrewd clients who trusted my judgment, to double their money or much better over a very few years. I did well enough to be able, just about, to educate three sons in private day schools but it was something a struggle, compared to the way in which I had been brought up in the best of boarding schools (aka public schools) since the age of seven. But to succeed really well in a career, I now know that one has to believe in the task at hand implicitly and devote oneself to its achievement. Dealing in property and its development was not my first concern, and it is a business which often brings out the atavistic worst in people who might otherwise be pleasant enough.

But one has to battle on with decisions one has taken in order to provide for a young family, and besides, by then I had in the background this belief that I might have come up with something of consequence, and which, if proved to be so, would compensate for my lack of any significant commercial success and fulfilment in my working life nine to five. I was only too well aware that there was a big if here. First my hypothesis had to be valid, second, it had to be proved so in my lifetime, and third, someone else might take the credit since I had not managed to get anything properly published. The raising of children, three boys in my case, is a time-consuming occupation. My parents also raised three boys, as did my father's parents (my third son's third name is accordingly Tertius), and as I now realise, my father and mother had devoted themselves to the task, and that was what I obviously had to do at this time.

I lived in this semidetached agricultural labourers cottage, somewhat extended, at Upper Culham on top of Remenham Hill above Henley on Thames from 1979 to 1984, after I had sold the Notting Hill flat. On our first day there on a fine July morning, my wife remarked to the postman how wonderful the day was and the view, and he replied encouragingly “Yes but bleak in winter.” During that time I developed a few applications of the theory related to the way in which it might also possibly be applied to explain certain aspects of the way in which the electrons revolved about the nucleus of an atom in a way that had to be described by quantum physics as a wave of probability, and which always had seemed a bit imprecise to be satisfactory. Instead I saw this probability in terms of DT so that if very similar orbits were repeated at very high frequency many times over, then this would produce a repetition through time as well as through space. This might cause a sort of scattering or partial disembodiment of the electrons so that it would not be possible to be sure exactly where they were.

This still remains a question in physics which has not been resolved or agreed between the experts. Under the current state of the laws of probability such an electron might possibly be anywhere else in the universe but the probability is vanishingly small with increasing distance. I am confident nobody has yet suggested that such the impossibility of knowing where such an electron might be located is also compounded by the possibility that it might be located at other times as well. I also conceived that the more complex a structure of molecules in an object was, the more it would tend to want to remain in one place, resonating with itself through time in the same one location. I reckoned that this would produce a resistance to that structure or object moved to another location. It occurred to me that this might be another possible way of defining inertia but I took it no further at that time, although I did however develop this notion later in 2010 to write a paper on the link between gravity and inertia described in more detail later and attached as *appendix 10*. There were other possible spin off implications from the basic theory, but did no more than mention them in passing in a longish paper, the first draft of which I had completed by January 1979 in an atrociously typed paper of about 50 pages, to which extra chapters were added over the next couple of years or two as things occurred to me.

I had little idea of what to do with the 1979 paper so I sent off indifferently typed copies that year to a few luminaries whom I knew were interested in the mind's operation. Arthur Koestler and Colin Wilson as already mentioned were encouraging with some inevitable qualifications. I also wrote to Karl Pribram professor of psychology and psychiatry at Yale and then at Stanford for many years, and who had similar ideas to mine about the brain creating holographic images registered as thought and memories. He replied enthusiastically (see *appendix 4*) as did a few others expressing some qualified interest and encouragement but I could not think of much else to do to take things further. I cannot now recall whether I had derived my proposals for holographic projections from the brain before I read about his work, but regardless of that, I took great comfort from his research work on that subject and the fact that he later began to work with distinguished physicist David Bohm. Pribram had discovered three dimensional electric fields within the space of the dendritic webs of the cerebral cortex, and that they were similar to the way in which holographic fields in three dimensions were created.

He also discovered experimentally that memories were not stored in a single neuron or in a specific location but rather but rather were spread over the entire neural network, whereafter Pribram proposed the hypothesis that memory might take the form of interference patterns that resemble laser produced holograms. David Bohm presented his ideas of holomovement and implicate and explicate orders in a book in 1980. Pribram became aware of Bohm's work in 1975 and realized that, since a hologram could store information within patterns of interference and then recreate that information when activated, this could serve as a strong metaphor for brain function. Together, and together they developed the holonomic brain theory (see Wikipedia), which as far as I can see is quite similar in a number of ways to Duplication Theory

Arthur Koestler commented in his letter that my proposals should be of interest to eminent American academic David Bohm who specialised in quantum theory, so having his book and but not being able to understand enough the physics of it at that time, pursued that possible course of action no further, although today Bohm's quantum work seems to be held in the highest regard today as one of the best answers to the unresolved basic problem of how electrons fired through two separate slits can be in two places at the same time to produce interference fringes on a screen. Besides, I was working full time in the office with a young family keeping us both very busy, as Angela had also started to work teaching on woven textiles two days per week at the London College of Furniture. As every parent knows, bringing up young families is a demanding business, and although I did some spare time work on further research, not much was done until 1983, when major support suddenly arrived for me in the form of my reading a book by a young bio scientist, Dr. Rupert Sheldrake.

Support from an Unexpected Source: 1992

Friends of ours, Gerald and Clico Kingsbury, who lived in style in a rather well appointed house next door but two to ours, knew that I was writing about memory and the powers of the mind and an author friend of theirs, Andro Linklater, mentioned that he had read an article about someone in Harpers and Queen who seemed to have written a book very similar in content to that which I seemed to be working on, and had I heard about that? I had not but when I did, I was gob smacked. His book was titled 'A New Science of Life: the nature of formative causation' and was more of an academic paper than a popular science book, although it had many helpful illustrations and was much less starchy and tedious than a formal paper setting out a new thesis of how certain genetic characteristics are transferred over generations which could not be explained by current understanding.

The latter could only be explained by some as yet unrecognised rule of nature which governed how characteristics were passed down over time, since there was nothing in science that currently explained such ability, even though it was certainly there for all to see, but not explained by any current arguments in biochemistry or biology. The book also explained how the author's theory of causative formation proposed that there were "morphogenetic fields associated with previous similar systems: the morphogenetic fields of all past systems become present to any subsequent similar system: the structures of past systems affect subsequent similar systems by a cumulative influence which acts across both space *and* time." He describes this effect as morphic resonance. He also qualifies it later in the book by saying "It will be assumed on the ground of simplicity that morphic resonance takes place only from the past." He uses morphic resonance to explain a large number of problems which are otherwise unanswered by current beliefs in the biological sciences, such as memory, the inheritance of form and behaviour.

The approach was completely different from mine but the conclusions and anticipated results were remarkably the same. I could not get over the similarities of our two completely separate theses. One by a double first in biochemistry at Oxford followed by a year at Harvard on a Knox Scholarship (which my second son Felix by nice coincidence was awarded in the middle 1980s in medicine), and the other by an estate agent who had done some part time study for a couple of years and had come up with a very rough hypothesis. This latter had been presented in an amateur way but there was no question of the similarity of conclusions. They both dealt with the way in which information could be transferred across time to explain a number of otherwise inexplicable phenomena, via a system of resonance. My DT proposed a mechanism for this resonance which Rupert's did not, but then neither of us were physicists, so that I was inevitably on shaky ground, especially so lacking any relevant academic background.

I did not know what to think. Never mind that but I just felt enormous relief that at last I had something to tell friends and family who had looked askance at my two years out of office resulting only in a madcap theory, but which now had some backing from a source that was already causing conflicting comments in academia and even the popular press. Was this the break through that I had been waiting for, or was it just happenstance and irrelevant coincidence signifying nothing? The only way to find out was to write which I did and an extract of his reply dated 18/03/83 is attached (*Appendix 5: Extracts from Author's letter dated 11/03/83 and Sheldrake's reply dated 18/03/83).* I was hugely encouraged and even more so when I introduced myself to him at some conference on mind and consciousness run by the very competent David Lorimer, the mainspring force of the Scientific and Medical Network which I had recently joined, an organisation who arranged conferences and lectures on matters of the mind's operation and purpose.

By 1983 I had been working in Reading for five years, and I was pretty much jaundiced that I would get anybody to take my rather indifferently typed paper seriously, and suddenly out of the blue Rupert had arrived, for me at least, deus ex machina. Rupert's first 1981 book caused such a storm of protest from the more conservative elements of the scientific community, so that his book became something of a scandalous cause celebre, especially so since it sold very well indeed: most unusual considering it was more of a serious academic exercise than best seller material. It was given publicity in the national press with competitions arranged on crosswords that a section of the public who regularly solved crosswords (cruciverbalists apparently) would not see one in the Telegraph the day it came out, but would do it the day after, with a time limit, and the results compared with those of a similar section of such enthusiasts who did it the first day.

Rupert's thesis was that the results on the second day would be better than the answers from the earlier contestants on the day of publication. I persuaded the experiment to be carried out by sixth formers at Abingdon School where my sons were educated and since the cross section of those involved was very evenly matched, the results were apparently very useful in providing a convincing result. I cannot recall the precise result but there was a definite improvement of result on the second day. There were other similar public involvement tests, but his books would have to be consulted for such detail together with his explanation of why there has to be this resonance through time effect for the genetics of inheritance and a fair number of other phenomena to exist. Attached as *Appendix 6* is a brief summary of Sheldrake's morphic resonance, extracted from his first book.

One reason I was so pleased at the advent of Rupert's morphic resonance was that I thought, good, all I have to do is now wait for him to get his message across, and he is so articulate in debate, so competent, so well informed and even better, witty in the development of his supporting arguments, that I just wait for him to convince the scientific establishment that his hypothesis of morphic resonance has to be part of nature. Once that happens, they will start to look for an explanation for the mechanism behind this transfer of information through time, since this was lacking in terms of a physical theory in explanation, as Rupert freely admitted, but showed by many examples and observation that there has to be such a resonance effect. Once a majority of biochemist academics were adequately impressed by Rupert's rationale, they would start to seek a theory behind the observed effects. At this juncture, Nicholas Greaves armed with his Duplication theory fully fledged would enter stage left with flourishes: there we are Gentlemen, unless of course someone else has come up with an alternative and more exact theorem.

So far of course, the first assumption of the scientific establishment being converted has not happened, which leaves me in the shadows nursing my theory, or more accurately, hypothesis. I am still waiting to see what happens, whilst Rupert far more publicly battles on with slowly increasing degrees of credibility over the decades. The more recent advances in epigenetics, a new field of study, support his work, but it is beyond my competence to attempt an explanation, knowing little about the life sciences. When I first met him at a conference and later discussed matters of state in his house in Newark on Tyne, I recall he said something along the lines that although there was reaction against his proposals currently, the scientific community existed in order to pursue truth and to explain nature increasingly accurately (or words to that effect) and since they were all struggling to the same ends, they would come to see that his proposals had to be along the right lines in order to explain certain inexplicable aspects of the way biochemists and biologists and to understand how organisms develop over time for which there was no current answer. I remember saying, or at least thinking, I was not so sure about that and expressing some doubts about his impression of human nature, mine being based on a very different world.

Having worked in property for about a decade by then, I had great experience of human frailty when the stakes were large, as they usually were for most ordinary people in property deals, and I reckoned that human nature was not very reasonable when it came self-advancement of others over one's own interest. Thirty-five years or so later, I have seen little reason to change my views on human behaviour generally. Having said that, there are now signs that some expert theorists consider that the mind's operation is likely to be governed by a mechanism governed by quantum rules, which is an outcome anticipated by DT. But it was not until 2015 that I first started to attempt to understand in outline a few salient points of quantum entanglement, and this is not an easy subject even for the experts. I still do not have a clear grasp of the mathematics of the inequality theorem of John Bell which has become established over the last couple of decades. This ground breaking theorem shows how this entanglement process transfers, or more accurately correlates, information instantly across space and also time as well. In order to demonstrate experimentally such astonishing results, the instruments involved have to be capable of acting completely randomly, which was very gratifying for me since the ability of the brain to fire randomly in trance was a central element of DT's operation of mind and memory. This will be dealt with later in the text.

There were a few other sources of support from that time. The first was from Art Chester, a laser physicist who was employed at that time by HRL laboratories LLC (formerly Hughes Aerospace), and who later became president. HRL operated from a large research centre in Malibu working for the US government on Star Wars research, Boeing, GM and other major clients. In 1981 Art had published in the Journal of Psychoenergetics a paper written over years in his spare time 'A physical theory of Psi based on Similarity'. The complete original document was about two inches thick of algebraic formulae and equations none of which I could grasp but the short version in the journal made it fairly clear that his conclusions were very similar to mine and Rupert's on the way that information was transferred through time via resonance of similar structures. I met Art on one of his business trips to London some years later, and we were happy to agree on most things, although, like Rupert he had reservations about the second part of my thesis describing the way in which EM radiation carried information across space. "The existing explanation seems good enough so why bother with another one" was the gist of his comment. But I was delighted with his support generally, from an individual working the highest point of practical implementation of theoretical physics *(Appendix 7 copy extracts from letter dated 12/01/84)*. I had also sent a copy of an early paper to written to Professor Henry Margenau of Yale University's physics department, and he was quite supportive which I found very encouraging. *(Appendix 8: copy letter dated 18/03/83)*

The other source of support was from an old friend of my wife, Stephen, the grandson of C.B. Fry, scholar and athlete who was once allegedly offered but wisely refused the throne of Albania after the First World War. Stephen had actually studied physics at Oxford but never completed the course being caught up in too many other exciting activities, a full account of which itself would form an extraordinary narrative. Just one I will mention as an example: in the early 1970s he stood for election for the GLC under his own initiative as the 'Abolish the GLC' party which, mirabile narru, he did not win. No surprise there but two years later, the GLC was gone as had Stephen. He had departed for a brief holiday in the Azores having made a little property killing, and instead of returning to London had decided to continue on to Brazil, where he married and lived for the next 20 years.

He was always politically active and still is, now back in the UK, pursuing worthy but occasionally lost causes with great initiative. The most flamboyant of these was that on one occasion during the early 1970s, in the attempt to stop the development of the playing fields of St. Pauls' School at Hammersmith, and he had persuaded Margret Thatcher to support his private bill but on the day of the vote she was not in the chamber and the motion failed. He had also later heckled at a meeting of a select committee in parliament. For this offence he was the first person for 150 years to be locked up for one night in the private gaol of the palace of Westminster. Anyway, Stephen occasionally gives presentations of duplication theory and his particular version of it to esoteric meetings of philosopher and physicists, which ability I lack when it comes to verbal articulacy. I have a reliable tendency to dry up and become almost incoherent when confronted by an audience and a possible barrage of questions at the end. It seems I cannot operate at all well under pressure but need time to organise the wording of my rationale and then preferably describe it via the written word. If I have a particular understanding of some issue that I can expound and clarify, then there is so much teeming through my mind with all the variables involved that I can hardly separate them out, there and then, into an instant coherent verbal explication.

So, from 1983 and the advent of Rupert on the scene, I made very little progress with my own thesis but waited for Rupert to pull off a convincing proof that would astonish and dumfound the critics. This has not happened yet he has built up a loyal following and has given many stirring and intriguing lectures and presentations of morphic resonance and causative formation and the way it would change and explain so many unknowns in the world of the life sciences, once established. One only has to look up Rupert Sheldrake on YouTube to see many citations he has been given: a few hundred thousand last time I checked. He has also put out a new book every six or seven years, some of which dealt fairly exclusively with paranormal and other inexplicable phenomena such as telepathy and precognition, and the evidence from specific experiments to show how they must exist. I have always found this side of the mind's potential fascinating ever since I first encountered hypnotism in the flesh. But I have also tended to exclude any such discussion from my writings. If I wish to gain the attention of the physicists, then I reckoned it better to avoid this contentious subject, especially as a non-academic putting up proposals in the highly complex world of the mind's operation, a tabula rasa not to be tinkered with by amateurs. Furthermore, the world of ESP and the paranormal does have great attraction for the lunatic fringe, and given my lack of academic credentials, I need to avoid being be classified as such. His more recent book 'The Science Delusion' summarises his previous proposals and criticises the way in which science is now too often progressed as scientific materialism and too dogmatic.

Meanwhile back to 1983, and having been encouraged by the publicity and sales of Rupert's first book, and the consternation it caused in the press and acid comment by a large section of the academic community, I ought to get something a little more formal and comprehensive out in print. I started to draft a long paper completed in 1985 (51,000 words on 92 pages of A4), and paid my secretary in the office to type it on her spare time. That done I had little idea of what to do with it and from memory probably did nothing, being before the advent of E mail and then who would want to read an account by someone who had a theory about the workings of the mind, based on principles of physics without any adequate credentials, especially it being a subject which nobody had yet attempted with any more than superficial success. I had little experience of the usual formal academic way of setting out such papers so the first seven pages were an initial informal introduction and synopsis and motivation for attempting such an ambitious task despite my lack of academic experience.

This was followed by a description of a number of principles of physics together with a few assumptions of how they might act together to produce the transfer across time of holographic images projected out from the brain, with similar results to those described by Sheldrake. It also described how and why electromagnetic radiation was transferred across space at light speed, as a corollary effect, and as an addition to current belief patterns which do not give fully adequate answers to the all the mechanisms involved.

On glancing through this 1985 paper again for the first time in about thirty years, it has reminded me of a few possible conclusions about which I had since forgotten, which is gratifying, and as a result I have put a copy on the Research Gate and Academia.edu websites in mid July 2018. Some content needs to be ignored and some modified in the light of recent research but it useful for me to see how my mind was working then, which after all is the subject to hand, and no doubt my mind was working more efficiently then than it is today 30 years later. At that time my proposals were then based mainly on Heisenberg's Uncertainty Principle and my interpretation of some of its possible consequences, and some assumptions about the effects of random motion: I knew effectively nothing about quantum entanglement (QE), and at that time had little thought of a possible link. I now know from recent further study of QE as mentioned above, that there are some striking similarities in the way that the experiments on QE have to be carried implementing similar assumptions to those required by Duplication Theory (DT).

So, I never did much with this first exercise, even though it was the only way forward that I could divine other than by going back to university. I considered the latter occasionally but never for more than a few moments. I could not possibly afford it with three sons to educate, the last of whom, Henry, was born in 1984. For the next decade and a half, I did not do much with it other than tinker to make some amendments and correspond sporadically with Rupert and a few other individuals who had views on the subject not that different from mine, not that there were many of the latter. In those early days before E mail became widespread I would post letters to various people whom I considered might just be interested and a fair number would reply saying they would look into my proposals when they had a spare moment and I would usually not hear back, and the few that did might make some encouraging comments on my interest in the subject but would not be enthused enough to do anything more.

Today it is so easy for amateur theorists to approach eminent sources of academic authority by E mail with a copy of their theory attached and/or a reference their own websites, that I anticipate that such eminent scientists, especially those specialising in the mind, are much plagued by this, and tend not to respond at all. Indeed, I have noticed that very well-known academics have a tendency to avoid publishing their email addresses. Thus for the amateur outsider it is just as hard to put over a new approach to an unresolved problem as it ever was: probably worse due to the increase in access by instant electronic communication, although Wikipedia means there is instant access to information that formerly could only be easily accessed in very few large specialist libraries. That is a huge boon and convenience to anyone working outside established academia especially if a subject is a tabula rasa.

Being jaundiced having worked in property for a couple of decades I was surprised that in some ways it seemed not that different in the world of academia, where I reckoned that human nature was surprisingly unreliable when it came the self-advancement of one individual's proposals over those of another, with often both sides ignoring might seem to be obvious flaws in their respective rationales. Thirty-five years or so later, I am still resting my case on my version of human behaviour, both on property deals and what my friend Art Chester describes as the inertia of beliefs on which subject, he has written a paper, the maths of which means little to me, but his written conclusions do. These are that if a certain belief is held by many, so that the originating thought structure in so many separate brains is similar and duplicated many times over, this will have the effect of reinforcing such a belief, even though it might be incorrect and not an accurate description of what happens in the external world. This seemed to me a very apt description for the way in which erroneous ideas and belief structures can develop for a while, only to wither and disintegrate eventually.

The one thing I did manage to complete in busy years of young parenthood was that David Lorimer was kind enough to publish a brief synopsis of my Duplication Theory in the journal of the Scientific and Medical Network for October 1988, but that was as much publication of my proposals in the public domain as I managed for quite some time. Rupert and I corresponded sporadically and had a few meetings and discussions over the years, and we agreed that our separate hypotheses of the way that similar structures resonated down through time had a great deal in common. However, he was not at all sure that my corollary argument that similar actions (intervals in time) also resonated in the same way to explain transmission of Electromagnetic waves through space at light speed. Some years later he did come to agree that there most likely was a connection of some sort between EM radiation and his morphic resonance, and I will now revisit this part of DT back to 1978 which I have omitted to do thus far to avoid complicating the more crucial part that deals with memory.

I see from notes taken in the last week of September 1978 that having constructed a hypothesis of sorts from the consideration of similar intervals in space between particles, I must have realised that the other major continuum in which we exist is the passage of time. What would happen if there was a collection of similar or equal intervals in time? If such a thing could be imagined to exist, then perhaps there would be some singular side effects if close approaches were made to perfect duplications of such intervals. It did not exactly come in a flash of inspiration because the answer was crushingly obvious, once the right question had been asked. I realised that the passage of a steady electric current down a conductor was nothing more that large numbers of electrons passing any arbitrary point at very equal intervals of time. Furthermore, I knew that one crucial quality of an electron is that it will be indecipherably the same as the next electron: absolutely identical in fact as far as I knew other than its location and its velocity. I also knew that the motion of such electrons along a conductor caused a field to be created in its immediate proximity that would cause any other conductor consisting of electrons or other charged particles to experience a force to set them in motion, in accordance with the laws observed and first set out by Michael Faraday in 1831.

It was a very short step to see that if the passage of electrons was not steady but regularly back and forth to become a regularly alternating current, then here was yet another degree of duplication. This might be expected ex hypothesi to produce an increased resonance effect as a further duplication of the regular rate of change of acceleration, further to the existing duplication of identical events (intervals in time) of a steady electrical current. This should reinforce the possibility of some unexpected side effects as anticipated in section C in chapter 3 above on Singularities. But that is exactly what happened all that time ago when the Faraday discovered the rules of electromagnetic induction which were later quantified mathematically by James Clerk Maxwell into his equations which in turn evolved into modern field theory. The existence of such an electromagnetic field of force may be old hat today but then it was astounding, and very well qualified as an unexpected side effect. It suddenly occurred to me that here was an alternative answer to the way in which action or energy could be transmitted across space at light speed, and if highly structured as well, it could transmit information which ability the modern world relies on today and takes for granted. But when it was first discovered it was an astonishing, almost magical ability.

An interval of time being repeated is effectively a repetition of similar events and a steady alternating current is a fine example huge numbers of electrons, all identical, duplicating the same action time and time again, and it might be reasonable to suppose that if the rate of repetition is increased, then any side effects produced would be increased, assuming such an effect is additive, or more complex as mentioned in the duplication of structures to resonate with other similar structures through time as mentioned section C above. But again, this is what we find in Electromagnetism: the higher the frequency of the wave (or repetition of similar events, the stronger is the effect of the transmission of action/energy through space at light speed.

So this precipitated out in my mind surprisingly rapidly on a hot day in the reading room on 27th September 1978, as I see now from my notes, and I was so pleased with myself at the ease of reaching such a simple conclusion that I recall very well queuing in the heat for the underground at Tottenham Court Road with all the commuters returning home in their normal glazed state at the end of a long working day. I was elated and they were obviously not. I remember thinking that here was I, having maybe resolved a major problem, and here were they oblivious of this amazing possibility, rubbing shoulders with me. I wonder whether they could feel the buzz of adrenaline that was flowing through, and of course they could not, which quite surprised me. I was not concerned by this indifference, and in fact I rather liked it. If I had worked out this answer which gave me such intense satisfaction, all by myself, untutored by anybody else, coming from a normal middle-class background, bright enough in some ways but nothing exceptional, then all these people surrounding me were also capable of doing the same thing and deriving the same satisfaction. I found the thought that they might be able to share in my elation very comforting. As I have commented already, I was then still absolutely naive in the ways of the world of ideas, concepts and academic prowess.

The result of all this was that within the next couple of months I was able to fill in the basic framework of DT as far as I could at that time. Having said that, progress in research on the quantum world has required me to amend some of my assertions although the latter have reinforced my rationale more strongly in other directions than I had ever thought possible. It was also just as well I had those last two months of October and November in the reading room since by the end of November I was fully employed again as a surveyor. In those two months I was spurred with more enthusiasm than I had ever experienced into reading as much as I could about physics generally, the transmission of electromagnetism and about the problems that still dogged the current theory, which were far more complex than I had previously realised. I read a number of further books by physicists to see what support I might gather up in relation to the mind's operation, of which there were not that many then current but a fair number from earlier decades from some old sources of authority. Those that I recall made the most impression on me, mainly from books written by themselves rather than their papers with mathematical theory which I could not follow, were: such as Newton, Ernst Mach, Max Planck, Albert Einstein, J.W. Dunne, Arthur Eddington, Erwin Schrodinger, Werner

Heisenberg, Henry Margenau, James Wheeler, and Richard Feynman. But it was the books by Erwin Schrödinger I found most reinforcing. A quote from his short book 'What is Life' (1944) is amazingly supportive on the subject of repetition, duplication and order which he calls negative entropy as oppose to the increasing chaos of entropy:

> What then is that precious something contained in our food which keeps us from death? That is easily answered. Every process, event, happening --call it what you will; in a word, everything that is going on in nature means an increase of the entropy of that part of the world where it is going on. Thus, a living organism continually increases its entropy -or, as you may say, produces positive entropy -- and thus tends to approach the dangerous state of maximum entropy which is death. It can only keep aloof from it, i.e. alive, by continually drawing from its environment negative entropy which is something very positive, as we shall see. Or, to put it less paradoxically, the essential thing in metabolism is that the organism succeeds in freeing itself from all the entropy it could not help producing while it was alive............ How would we express in terms of the statistical theory the marvellous faculty of a living organism, by which it delays the decay into thermodynamic equilibrium (death)? We said before: 'It feeds on negative entropy' attracting as it were, a stream of negative entropy upon itself, to compensate the energy increase it produces by living and thus to maintain itself on a stationary and fairly low entropy level.

The above passages might serve to give some idea of the concept of negative entropy as it applies to life, and serve to show how it is nothing much more than an increase in the order, the pattern, and hence the degree of duplication in a material object. The next series of quotations from Schrodinger explain in more detail the significance of pattern and order.

> In the following stages of a higher organism the copies are multiplied, that is true. But to what extent? Something like 10 to the power of 14 (ten thousand billion) in a grown mammal, I understand. What is that! Only a millionth of the number of molecules in one cubic inch of air......... and look at the way they are actually distributed. Every cell harbours just one of them (or two if we bear in mind diploidy). Since we know the power this central office has in the isolated cell, do not they resemble the stations of local government dispersed through body, communicating with each other with the greatest of ease, thanks to the code which is common to them all. Well, this is a fantastic description, perhaps less becoming to a scientist than a poet. However, it needs no poetical imagination but only clear and sober scientific reflection to recognise that we are here obviously faced with events whose regular and lawful unfolding is guided by a mechanism entirely different from the 'probability mechanism' of physics. For it is a simple fact of observation that the guiding principle in every cell is embodied in a single atomic association existing in only one (and sometimes two) copies - and a fact of observation that it results in producing events which are a paragon of orderliness. Whether we find it astonishing or whether we find it quite plausible that a small but highly organised group of atoms be capable of acting in this manner, the situation is unprecedented. It is unknown anywhere else except in living matter...........

> It appears that there are two different 'mechanisms' by which orderly events can be produced: the 'statistical mechanism' which produces 'order from disorder', and the new one producing 'order for order'. To the unprejudiced mind. the second principle appears to be much simpler, much more plausible. No doubt it is. That is why the physicists were so proud to have fallen in with the other one, the 'order from disorder' principle, which is actually followed in nature, and which alone conveys an understanding of the great line of natural events, in the first place, of their irreversibility. But we cannot expect that the 'Laws of Physics' derived from it suffice straightaway to explain the behaviour of living matter, whose most striking features are visibly based to a large extent on the 'order from order' principle......... We must therefore not be discouraged by the difficulty of interpreting life by the ordinary laws of physics. For that is just what is to be expected from the knowledge we have gained of the structure of living matter. We must be prepared to find a new type of physical law prevailing in it. Or, are we to term it a nonphysical law? No, I do not think that. For the new principle that is involved is a genuinely physical one: it is in my opinion nothing more else than the principle of quantum theory over again. To explain this, we have to go to some length including a refinement, not to say an amendment, of an assertion previously made. namely that all physical laws are based on statistics.

I know it is something of a liberty to quote such a long extract from Schrodinger's book but he so clearly anticipates the necessity for an ordering system of negative entropy, which is exactly embodied in Duplication theory, that I could not resist it. Furthermore, it is written in a way that the layman can understand: he was a physicist, but not a biologist, and as one of the founding fathers of quantum theory, I can think of very few other authorities to whom I would rather look for approval than him. This extract passage of Schrodinger, given as part of a series of lectures at Trinity College Dublin in 1943, will be shown to be almost uncanny in the accuracy of its prediction, assuming a valid basis to DT becomes accepted.

I had typed an initial draft of my conclusions towards the end of that December, but it was about a year later that I was able to encapsulate the theory in a summary short form which was:

"Within a system of large numbers of similar particles in near perfect circumstances, then one specific pattern in space instigated into that otherwise random system, and its ensuing motions of its components, will tend to resonate or duplicate itself through all time in a specific location (or within similar systems elsewhere: the same locations relatively). Within the same system then a specific pattern in time- a repetition of similar events- will tend to resonate or duplicate itself at all other points in space at that one time, wherever other similar particles exist in free or random motion."

The theory can be more tersely stated in a very concise, albeit dense and somewhat incomprehensible summary as follows:

"Equal intervals in space -similar structures- tend to duplicate themselves through all time in one location. Equal intervals in time -similar actions- tend to duplicate themselves through all space at one time."

When I first came up with this last short definition, I was immensely pleased with it because it was so satisfyingly symmetrical. Notice that the words time and space are interchangeable without losing the sense at all. Over the next few years I came across evidence in support of this second part of DT that explained alternative versions of the way in which quantum jumps of electrons between their orbits (shells) within, for example, energised molecules of the gas neon caused electromagnetic energy to be emitted in the form of visible light. I had also read in those two months a book about the Absorber Theory by a mathematician P.C.W Davies, 'Space and time in the modern universe'. It was sufficiently fascinating for me to have made extensive notes at the time in 1979. It was published in 1945 by Feynman & Wheeler, two of the greatest physicists of the mid-20th century, when it caused interest but was too way out then to be taken very seriously. It backed up my version of the way that electromagnetic (EM) radiation is transferred across space without any need for a wave or particle in its transmission: in other words, action at a distance which was what my second part of DT inferred.

However, it was complex and I shall cover this in the next chapter although I mention now that today there are now distinct chinks on the horizon for the expert quantum theorists coming into accord with some general support for the transfer of information through time on a quantum basis. But it was not until 2015 that I started to attempt to understand in outline a few salient points of quantum entanglement, and this is not an easy subject for the experts, never mind the amateurs. I do not understand the maths of the crucial and central Bell's Inequality Theorem which is starting to change the shape of physics today but I managed to appreciate there were some recent experimental results on entanglement in which the involvement of randomness was crucial. This has recently proved gratifying for me since the ability of the brain to fire randomly in trance was a central element of DT's operation of mind and memory. I mention this now in case any readers well qualified in physics are wondering where all this is leading to and whether to bother further. As I have said before on a few occasions, some of this will be dealt with later in the text.

DT, Electromagnetism & the Expanding Universe

I continued to follow very attentively the progress of Rupert and the books he brought out every few years, and also attended a number of his public presentations and conferences. His confident podium manner and articulacy combined with humour always ensured a full house attendance and his delivery was always impressive. So much so that I suppose I continued to assume that he could not fail in the end to win through to make a strong impression on the authority figures of the academic world, although, surprise, surprise it was taking far longer than even I had pessimistically anticipated in 1985. This in turn deferred my chance of DT being taken seriously unless I could come up with some alternative approach to enable my views on the mechanism of morphic resonance to be taken seriously. His books and later interviews on the media made an impression alright but it seemed to me that established academia did not take very kindly being told that they might have to rethink so many of their preconceptions about the operation of the mind and the way in which information was passed down through time.

His first book sold very well, especially as it was a presented in the manner of a sober academic paper, and it is very rare for such material to sell in large numbers. But 1986 it had sold 300,000 copies, and presumably well over a million by today, so it seems to me that conservative members of academia might still be envious and derisive of this commercial success. In 1988 he published his second book 'The Presence of the Past', and again some of its content on the nature of time and his discussion on the speed of light possibly being variable presented me with a whole new topic for careful consideration, presentiments about which had been bothering me for some time. I had always wondered why light should be transmitted at apparently just one particular speed, which formed one of the most crucial constant figures of which the physicists were aware. Light speed controlled just about every factor in the world of electronics and cosmology so why should it apparently be at one particular velocity and not another? There was no answer other than it just was, which indicated to me that some very vital element of understanding was missing here.

Rupert put a strong case for the possibility that light speed was variable, and you would have to read his second book to appreciate his arguments, but they staggered me when I first read it in 1988. To me and everybody else who knew something about physics, light speed of 186,000 miles per second (approx.) was the most crucial constant there was, on which it seemed the whole subject was based. This is perhaps best summarised in Einstein's famous simple equation E equals MC squared. This simple statement indicates that the mass of an object times the square of light velocity (an enormous figure) equals the energy that might be liberated from that specific amount of mass. To demonstrate that light speed is variable and not a constant figure would mean a major reassessment of the laws of physics as they are currently understood.

This was the second amazingly thought-provoking proposal I registered from Rupert, further to our similar theories of resonance through time, and for this I was once again incredibly obliged. It helped to confirm for me the possible validity of a thesis which I have already mentioned in chapter 6, as the second complementary half of my Duplication theory. This is an alternative explanation of the way in which information is transferred across space by electromagnetic (EM) radiation, which effect has been very familiar to us for more than a hundred years, and my proposal for another alternative version is unlikely to be welcome and will not carry much initial credibility. Having said that, the current version is not that satisfactory: for a start EM waves go only one way from the present into the future, and do not seem to return. This is not symmetrical and is a serious theoretical problem for physicists, and an attempt was made to resolve the anomaly by a paper published 70 years ago known as the Absorber theory mentioned earlier, and which I shall describe below in more detail after the next couple of pages. However, before I get into the implications of this ingenious theory, I need to recap briefly the second corollary part of DT and how it justifies the radiation electromagnetic energy waves through space at light speed.

To rehearse briefly in this and the next paragraph, the first half of DT is based on the resonance of similar structures in space across time. In April 1978 I came to my initial to conjecture that according to the Uncertainty Principle it was impossible for two hypothetical points to occupy the same space at the same time. Thus, using the same rationale, it would be even more impossible for a structure of many such points to occupy the same location of a similar structure, in the same location, or elsewhere, or indeed at a later time. This is due to the fact that all such minuscule particles are in constant motion, thus making it impossible to ever be absolutely certain of the precise location of any of them. It should also be noted that any such similar structures are comprised of duplicated intervals in space between component particles.

But if a close approach was made at quantum levels for such a structure to be exactly duplicated, an impossible result and therefore a singularity state, then curious side effects will become increasingly apparent. My conjecture, as explained already, is that such similar structures will start to resonate or duplicate themselves across time. This would be an additive effect which would be enhanced by increasing degrees of complexity of the structures involved. I then applied the same reasoning to the duplication of similar intervals in time rather than in space, which would be impossible to duplicate with perfect accuracy to quantum levels: effectively another singularity state. To be consistent with the above existing rationale, it would be reasonable to anticipate that a close approach to this other singularity state this would deliver effects out of the ordinary. This is how I now see EM radiation spreading out through space spreading action in all directions.

The second part of DT shows how similar intervals in time, as opposed to space, resonate though out all space at one moment in time, which effect has been familiar to us for more than a century albeit a phenomenal effect when first discovered. How I came to make such conclusions was as follows. Having concluded in July 1978 that it was impossible to have one structure in space duplicated perfectly by another, with some interesting possible results, I started to wonder in late September of that Year, what would happen if similar structures in time rather than in space were considered. After all, it seemed to me that these were the two fundamental elements of continua in existence (continuum being such a useful general word): those of time and space, and both required consideration. At the risk of repetition, for the existence of similar or identical intervals in time, there have to be a number of similar or identical events taking place, since that is the only way for separate intervals in time to be created. Almost at once it occurred to me that an alternating current such as the standard fifty cycles per second of mains electrical power was nothing more than a very accurate repetition of similar passage back and forth of billions of identical electrons along a wire or conductor. Such similar actions in the case of AC current would be alternating at similar intervals in time. Not only that, but for any reasonable amount of AC current, there would be billions, if not trillions, of electrons involved, that would not only be similar, but almost indecipherably the same, all oscillating back and forth at very regular intervals.

On closer consideration it seemed that there could be no finer example of huge numbers of equally charged and dimensioned electrons all passing back and forth at equal intervals in time and if this were done to near singular degrees of accuracy from a source of AC, which it would, then by the conjecture already developed in DT, it would be reasonable to anticipate some curious side effects might start to become apparent. Of course, that is exactly what happens in that electromagnetic radiation spreads out in a wave like action in all directions from the conductor or charged wire, to cause a duplicate motion effect in any other conductor with free electrons within whether it is close at hand, or at a vast distance. In this second conductor the electrons will duplicate exactly the motion of the original electrons in exactly the same manner, albeit with a little less force. This is the very familiar effect of transmission of images and information though space at light speed by the radiation in all directions of electromagnetic waves. This might not today seem like such an amazing side effect, but it was when first discovered, and has radically changed the way we live for more than a century, but there are still a number of unsatisfactory anomalies connected to our current explanation of photons carrying transferring action over space at light speed, as briefly mentioned above.

Furthermore, I was able to reduce my existing definition of resonance through time effect down to its shortest form, and then when I reversed the words time and space, but otherwise repeated it, the new alternative definition of transfer of information/action via EM radiation, becomes apparent as now shown.

"**Equal intervals in one location** -similar structures- tend to duplicate themselves through all time at that **one location**. **Equal intervals in time** -similar actions- tend to duplicate themselves through all locations at that **one time.**"

It was so simple and aesthetically satisfying, I could not believe it was just a coincidence and of no significance when I first realised that the first definition was a corollary of the second. That is how it struck me then, as it still does today: quite extraordinary.

There is one crucial proviso: for this second part of DT to be implemented and made more plausible, it needs to be assumed that the shape of the universe is closed and finite. If so then a number of possibilities fall almost effortlessly into place. The implications are that the universe would have to be like a sphere expanding outwards, with a periphery beyond which there would have to be the biggest imaginable singularity of some other continuum not involving space or time, the possible implications of which are fascinating and will be developed below. This is not a currently fashionable interpretation of the shape of the universe even though it is by no means impossible and if the reader checks on Wikipedia, it will be seen that it is one of the three first posited by Freedman, and followed up by leMaitre, Robertson and Walker. In very simple terms the universe can either be spherical, with local geometrical curvature greater than 1, or hyperbolic with geometrical curvature less than one (near impossible to visualise), or it can be flat, in which case it would be infinite. There has been a great deal of quite contentious research with the WMAP probe and recently the Planck spacecraft to ascertain if there is a reliable answer to this problem of the shape of the universe, and the closed and finite version is not currently favoured but it is the one I prefer. I can visualise it and I was surprised when it fitted in very well with this second part of DT as well as the Absorber theory. The cosmologists of today seem to me just as fraught about the shape of the universe as they were in 1979 although a vast amount of research with satellites and telescopes has been carried out. They cannot decide whether there is just one universe or perhaps limitless numbers of them.

From notes drafted in idle moments in the office at 34 Kings Road, Reading, now a wine bar, in late 1979, I arrived at a number of possible conclusions which seemed to me diverting and consistent with DT and not impossible. They were nothing if not ingenious it seemed to me then, and still does today, but I did not take them that seriously at the time: there was no other backup evidence on which to do that. These were as follows. If the universe could indeed be regarded as a closed system, finite and bounded as a huge sphere expanding outwards at light speed, then that would satisfy my rationale for the way in which EM radiation was transferred across space at light speed. Beyond this spherical universe there would be not only nothing at all but rather a completely different continuum about which we could never know anything. The result would be that this effectively be the largest singularity state imaginable, which I called the singularim. And if so then all lesser time singularities within the universe, repetition of similar events, would ex hypothesi, tend to duplicate the actions of the largest event singularity in existence. This was surrounding them in all directions in the shape of the motion of the singular rim, so that any lesser time/event singularity in the form of EM radiation would balloon out in a sphere to duplicate the motion of the all-pervasive singularim.

Diagram A below shows the state of the universe well after the big bang with the assumption that the distribution of mass (star systems, galaxies and maybe dark matter) would be more concentrated near the periphery following the initial generative blast of the explosion with the mass of the galaxies more thinly distributed closer to the centre and expanding out at a progressively faster rate, in the manner of a bomb blast. The velocity of the galaxies close to the perimeter will be near light speed and that of the mass further towards the centre proportionately slower in general terms.

In further extrapolation of the consequence of such a scenario, diagram B gives a simple explanation of the consequences of how the effects of Einstein's special theory of relativity operates so that an AC source at half way out across the expanding sphere will have its transmitted wave fronts attracted out by the motion of singular rim in all directions in the shape of a spheroid from the view point of an observer outside the universe but in a perfect sphere as far as the AC source is concerned. I was pleased in having derived such a scenario which was not only easy to explain diagrammatically, but consistent with my own rationale. I thought there ought to be something plausible in it despite being so simplistic, and then I recalled what I had read sketchily a year beforehand about Richard Feynman and John Wheeler, and their Absorber Theory published in 1945, and read up on it again.

DIAGRAM A

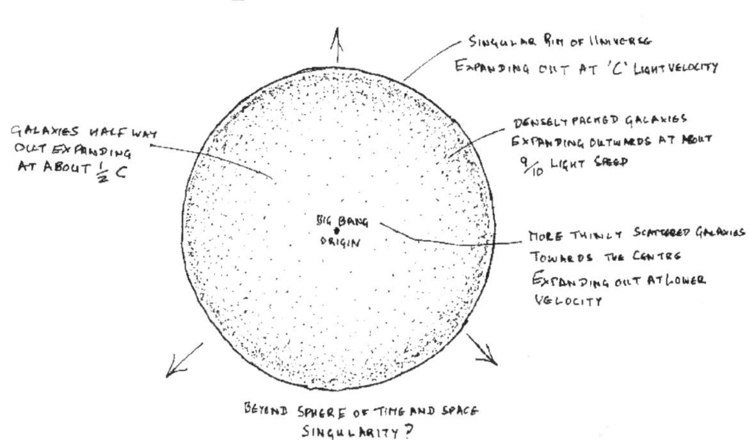

DIAGRAM B

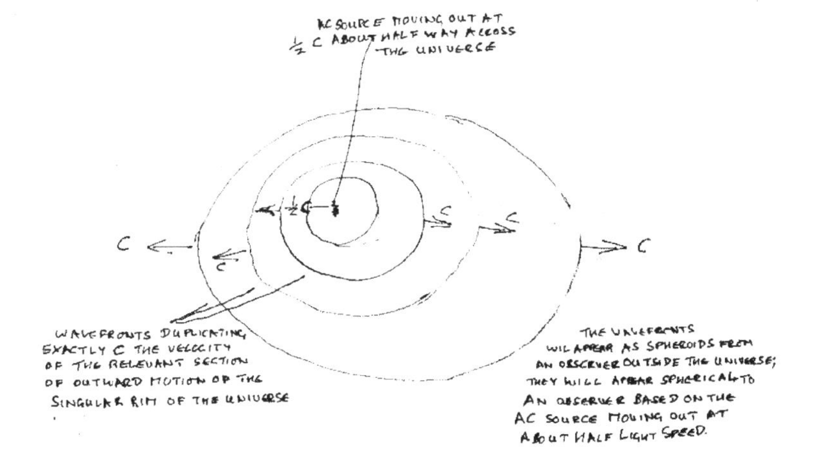

These initial conclusions first occurred to me in moments of office tedium in September 1979. By that time, I must have become accustomed enough to 9 to 5 office routine existence to allow me to slip into a semi hypnagogic state rather than estimate how many years purchase should one multiply the annual rent from a factory as a major factor contributing to its valuation. So much less engrossing than problems of existence. I still have scribbled notes from that time and because these give some indication of the way in which these ideas developed, which after all is the subject of this whole narrative on the mechanism of mind and memory, I now quote from them. They are not all that coherent and inconclusive in part but this was the first indication of one of the themes that is central to this book.

"Office thoughts, 20/9/79

1. Explanation of hierarchies at different levels.

2. Explanation of speed of light as being limited by expanding

rate of universe: instantaneity is governed by velocity of outside edge which is maximum speed of light.

3. Explanation of analogy of free will and determinism in that although in a cloud of particles, the motion of any one makes no difference to the whole so that each particle is free to do what it likes, the movement of the pattern of the whole is governed by rules of duplication theory which is determined by the position and circumstances of the external universe. So that considering a crowd of human intelligences, the antics of one, say a Napoleon, do not change in anyway the overall fate of the universe, and a world of human intelligence progresses according to DT governed by the rest of the universe and its eventual contraction, despite the v. radical behaviour of its individual constituents. I.e., we have individual free will but no overall freedom -our destiny is predetermined."

"Office Time. 2.30 p.m. Monday, 1/10/79.

Timeless sensation during perfect random motion of perfect samadhi meditation state occurs because the mind in neutral duplicates automatically or reflects the whole universe so that the mind or holocept of the mind becomes a replica of the expanding universe. But, the outer limit of the universe is expanding at the velocity of light (hence the limiting velocity for simultaneity of communication -NG to break this down for further explanation) so that the outer edge of the universe, indeed the greater part of it is timeless so that time stands still or at least passes very slowly. Therefore, the mind in random motion imitates this time stand still quality otherwise known as samadhi or perfect bliss; Viz. Blake's verses and most Eastern mystic quotes."

"Further thoughts at Office. 4.30 p.m. Thursday 4/10/79, post lunch with Halifax.

If speed of extreme edge of universe is limiting factor of velocity of light or simultaneity connecting different parts of space- then a distortion in space continuum, caused by a duplication in time, will radiate out from that point in all directions to match the velocity of the expanding universe. This accounts for the apparent anomaly that if a space ship travelling at nine tenths light velocity relative to earth emits a light or EM signal, that signal will travel to and away from earth at light Velocity C, regardless of the relative velocity of its source of origin. This is because that EM signal radiates out in all directions with limiting velocity of simultaneity according to the expansion velocity of the limits of the universe in all directions. The controlling factor is the velocity of expansion of the outer extreme edge of the universe. It is this distortion wave in space caused by the time duplication near singularity that is dragged outwards in space by the outward urge of the universe (entropy) and transmitted at this speed.

Myself, I am pleased enough with the above, struck me for no apparent reason in a moment of idleness after a large lunch. I can clarify this distortion thing further, I think. A distortion in time and in space is caused by a near singularity in opposite continuum. Time and space are very much the same thing. Space is growing outwards one way as is time-time will reverse when space starts to diminish and the velocity of light diminishes to zero and then back to a negative amount: success.

9.35 Thursday a.m. post coffee and Minster street sale success

A pattern in space will persist through time as we see through any solid substance which has form and whose constituent elementary particles are held together in a strict tight, probably well-ordered crystalline pattern through tight forces of electrostatic or covalent attraction. This is why objects hold their shape and endure. At the other end of scale, an event is a repetition in time which has no form and therefore cannot endure -its effect must therefore be felt simultaneously through the whole universe. It is important, this understanding of an event -it is all of time consequence with little or no space form about it so that by DT it will not endure.

As I read this last paragraph of old notes again today, incoherent and inconclusive as they are, I think I recognize a very early encroachment on to the problem that we now have today of attempting to reconcile the two worlds of classical and quantum physics. In 1979 I knew quantum mechanics existed but nothing more, although I had glanced through a book a year beforehand about Richard Feynman and John Wheeler, and their Absorber Theory published in 1945. I therefore decided to read up on it again.

It gives an ingenious answer which did away with the need for photons or electrons, also described as exchange particles, to convey action or energy through space at light speed. This alternative class of theory is also known as force at a distance which was then not generally much cared for as a notion but this concept is effectively similar to my proposals, which aspect I have not pushed that hard. However, what was hardly an acceptable notion in 1945, or 1979 for that matter, has taken on a different aspect today with quantum entanglement experiments having established that instant communication over large distances is possible. This has resulted in a great deal of reconsideration being necessary about force at a distance.

Current established traditional beliefs explain EM radiation being transmitted by photons through all space in a sphere emitted from the subject conductor or aerial, and when such photons meet another conductor, similar actions will be duplicated at the same frequency to resonate with the motions of the source electrons. However, there is a mathematical problem here in that an exercise called renormalization has to be applied to account for the current theory of quantum electrodynamics which was developed in the 1930s and shows how light and matter interact. This involved 'a collection of techniques in quantum field theory, the statistical mechanics of fields, and the theory of self-similar geometric structures, that are used to treat infinities arising in calculated quantities by altering values of quantities to compensate for effects of their self-interactions.' I have to say I do not understand the difficulties here, never mind how they were resolved but apparently in order to do this, this process of renormalization has to be applied. It was not much favoured by a number of the leading lights of physics. The brilliant Paul Dirac in 1975 commented:

'Most physicists are very satisfied with the situation. They say: 'Quantum electrodynamics is a good theory and we do not have to worry about it anymore.' I must say that I am very dissatisfied with the situation because this so-called 'good theory' does involve neglecting infinities which appear in its equations, ignoring them in an arbitrary way. This is just not sensible mathematics. Sensible mathematics involves disregarding a quantity when it is small – not neglecting it just because it is infinitely great and you do not want it!

Another important critic was Richard Feynman. Despite his crucial role in the development of quantum electrodynamics, in 1985 he wrote the following:

'The shell game that we play is technically called 'renormalization'. But no matter how clever the word, it is still what I would call a dippy process! Having to resort to such hocus-pocus has prevented us from proving that the theory of quantum electrodynamics is mathematically self-consistent. It's surprising that the theory still hasn't been proved self-consistent one way or the other by now; I suspect that renormalization is not mathematically legitimate."

In more general terms in the emission of EM radiation there is a problem with the current belief called quantum electrodynamics. This is that this outward radiated flow of action is not symmetrical and never seems to return back to the source and which for many physicists is unsatisfactory. One way of getting around this is just to say that accelerating a charged particle causes waves to be emitted into the future, but not into the past, but the original theory of its inventor Maxwell, the inventor of the electromagnetic field theory in 1862, was that electrodynamics has to be completely symmetrical in time.

Under the present understanding of electromagnetic fields, the radiated waves do not return and a result the two then top physicists Feynman and Wheeler came up in 1945 with an explanation to remedy this omission. They analysed what would happen if an accelerating charge emitted radiation equally into the past and future both. They found that if such an oscillating charged particle was placed inside an opaque box, then only waves (described as retarded) would be radiated into the future. Open the box and waves from the past (described as advanced) would reappear. This may not seem to be likely but in terms of pure physics it is easily possible which means that the electrons in the box vibrate in anticipation before the subsequent motion of the charged particle. I do not understand the physics involved but apparently it is quite possible theoretically via a mathematical proof and symmetry is preserved. To an inhabitant inside the box, the electrodynamic behaviour of the system is entirely in accordance with our everyday experience. The result of all this is that instead of having fields and waves of energy being transferred across space by photons or electrons, there instead is just direct action at a distance, not instantaneously but delayed action at light speed.

I find the mechanics of this hard to visualise and the mathematical proof I cannot manage at all, but it fits in very well with my understanding of the way in which the second part of DT explains radiation of action across space. The other crucial issue which struck me right between the eyes was that the absorber theory can only operate if the whole system was enclosed within an opaque box. But that was exactly how my universe within the singular rim would be. The latter was not only opaque but absolutely impenetrable and impassable. It occurred to me there could be no better description of the opaqueness intended by the authors, and curiously the excellent book by Dr. Davies describing the theory does not consider the possibility of a bounded and finite universe, but then things have moved on since 1977 when his book was published. I am also not sure how the cosmologists saw the shape of the observable universe forty years ago, but although still nothing is at all certain, there are a number of theories today, some of which I will mention herewith.

A number of assumptions have to be made initially that the universe is isotropic (uniform in all directions), and homogeneous (uniform in composition) and then General relativity explains that mass and energy bend the curvature of space-time and is used to determine what curvature the universe might possess. It turns out it can either be flat, or have positive curvature or negative curvature. If it turns out flat then everything is measured in Euclidean terms where triangles have 180 degrees. Or it can have positive curvature which results in the universe being a sphere, very easy to visualize, whereas if it had negative curvature then the universe would be hyperbolically shaped and not so easy visually. The FLRW metric mentioned above first instituted by Alexander Friedman in 1925, and endorsed by physicists Lemaitre, and then later Robertson and Walker, is the most commonly used model to explain various alternative ways of describing the universe, all using an exact solution of Einstein's field equations of general relativity.

The positive curvature version of the sphere is the simplest but not the most favoured currently. However, the cosmologists, more than in any other area of physics, seem to be least able to agree on anything, despite the millions be spent on huge new telescopes and satellites. In short, the subject is still very much up for grabs, and the simplest version seems the most likely to me: Occam's razor again. This is now doubly so since it supports my conjecture being in line with the Absorber theory which in turn adds credibility to the second part of DT which does away with the need for photons or particles which is non local and force at a distance, and therefore presumably is a quantum effect. Such considerations if correct would have deep implications for the nature of the passage of time which will need to be reassessed, an attempt at which will be made in a later chapter in the text (see also appendix 11).

In summary, the second part of DT that shows how EM transmission is entirely mediated by the rate of expansion of this singular rim, and that the small singularities of each repetition of huge quantities of similar or identical intervals in time (i.e. Events) cause a shiver in the fabric of space time which will duplicate the action of the largest similar event, which is the outward expansion of the singular rim. Having thought about this modus operandi for the last 40 years, it seems so simple and basic that I understand why it might seem just too ridiculous to be taken seriously when we already have a complex system of exchange particles and photons which does the job apparently well enough. However well enough is by no means perfect and there are some serious mathematical flaws in the current system, which can only be rationalised by what seem to me to be mathematical fudges as mentioned above, and also more generally, that it lacks symmetry.

The two complementary sides of DT as I saw them by the end of 1979 still represent the backbone DT as originally conceived after I had been working in Reading for a year. From then on over the next few years I wrote to a number of physicists during 1979 as a result. I received letters which were not too dismissive, and in some cases downright encouraging from the following luminaries.

Arthur Koestler (February) Harold Puthoff of SRI international, California (February); Dr. Tom Witten, physicist of Ann Arbor University, Michigan (April); Professor John Taylor of King's College, London (April); Karl Pribram, neuroscientist of Stanford University, California (July); Henry Margenau, Emeritus professor of Physics and Philosophy (November); Professor Brian Josephson (Nobel laureate), physicist of Cambridge (December), and especially John Beloff of Edinburgh University with whom I corresponded at length over many years. When Arthur Koestler died in 1983, he left about a million pounds for the promotion of research into the paranormal through the founding of a chair in parapsychology at a university in Britain. The trustees of the estate had great difficulty finding a university willing to establish such a chair. Oxford, Cambridge, and others were approached and would to accept the funds but not to use all of them exclusively for such a chair. Eventually the trustees reached agreement with John Beloff of Edinburgh University to set up a chair in accordance with Koestler's request, and this now exists as the KPU (Koestler parapsychology Unit). So, this was encouraging enough at the time and I still spent most of my spare moments, absorbed in the implications of my ideas, trying to rationalise a number of inconsistencies, especially those to do with the transmission of electromagnetic energy and time duplication.

After my first long 1985 paper was typed by the admirable Moira from the office in her spare time, I was not quite sure of the next step I should be taking. As a result, I did not do that much positive for the next couple of decades other than correspond at some length with a few other enthusiasts for Rupert's work, and attend a few conferences which might contain the odd physicist talking about the operation of the mind. I read any book or journal I could find that looked at all relevant to my material and I would write occasionally to the authors of such books with a synopsis of my conclusions attached but usually evoking limited interested response. Not many academics enjoy suggestions by an outsider that the way they understood the physical world needed serious reappraisal if they were going to make any further constructive and useful progress. I understood this well enough and the fact that my hypothesis involved time transfer smacking more of a novel by H.G. Wells than hard science, tended to be usually treated in a polite response of condescension and vague encouragement, which after time had passed, ceased to come as any surprise.

I had come to realise that the ownership of intellectual property and the proposals reinforcing such concepts was as competitive as the urge to acquire real property and resulting gains. Perhaps worse in some ways because success in business is measured very easily by financial gain which will take but a few years to manifest itself, whereas history shows that very often the advance of knowledge and understanding can take decades to become accepted, every often in the teeth of fierce opposition from fellow academics with their own established belief structures and reputations to protect. The latter did not affect me too much since I was as what is often known as an independent researcher and effectively invisible below the level of the academic windscreen. This has one useful if contrary advantage in that I could write whatever occurred to me about my subject, letting my imagination run loose, untrammeled by what others might think, and without fear that I would lose reputation and possibly prejudice future advancement by not toeing the line of established research.

EM Radiation and Correlation with Other Effects

It has been about 35 years since Rupert Sheldrake published his first book. This event served to double my faltering faith in my own work and allowed me to develop the following rationale. One of the reasons that so little is known about the operation of mind and brain, despite the huge steps forward since the 1930s and the development of quantum theory, is that physics is labouring under a belief structure which is probably flawed by one or two fundamental issues.

At least that is my subjective view. One candidate that comes immediately to mind is the nature of gravitation and how and why it works. We can measure the force between separate masses that attracts them together, but why this should occur is not explained other than it just does. Another fundamental question springing to mind is about light speed. Why is it measured to be at one apparently invariable constant velocity, and why does it happen to be at that one particular figure of about 186,000 miles per second? Again, there is no answer other than it just does. Why does nobody ever seem to wonder or to ask question about these two particular and frankly bizarre facts, take them or leave them. This blind acceptance without query or even much interest seems to be something of a cop out, and suggests that it is a subject aching to be investigated, or so it seems to me.

When in August 1978 I had developed my theme of why it was impossible to have perfectly identical structures at different times in the same location, I also realised that it would be equally impossible to have two identical structures at different locations, at the same time. This was according to the Uncertainty principle for reasons already rehearsed, but that as close approaches were made to a singularity state, which this was, the result would also bring about side effects formerly unanticipated. Why this should be so was for no reason that I could initially divine other than from observation, it always seemed to happen in such circumstances. I had also realised that one had to consider more carefully the definition of 'same location' since in a universe expanding out as a result of the big bang; you could never be in the same location in absolute terms. So, I qualified this by stating that the same location had to be with reference to a body's constituents in the same relevant scale. This would allow the creative process of a thought structure from within the brain to produce this resonance effect for memory to operate within a particular brain the location of which would be constantly on the move as the individual concerned moves about. So, for a moving centre of complex actions, such as the brain, the 'same location' needs to be amended:

"Within a system of large numbers of similar particles in near perfect circumstances, then one specific pattern in space instigated into that otherwise random system, will tend to resonate or duplicate itself through all time in a specific location (or within similar systems elsewhere: the same locations relatively)."

It took me quite some years to conclude that this resonance effect through time was not just in one particular place (with respect to everything within a similar system), but if there were no external perturbing forces such as gravitation for instance, from nearby planetary masses or even other suns and stars, on a much larger scale, which of course there are, then if two complex structures were to become so identical to relative quantum levels, either at the same time or at different times, then they would start to resonate and their internal motions tend to duplicate each other.

Considerations of this sort caused me to wonder about the effect of gravity which acts on everything especially on the cosmic scale, and having read as much as I could understand on the subject, I learned that nobody had a convincing theory about how or why it operated, and that although the three other forces of the strong nuclear, weak nuclear and electromagnetic had all been shown by the expert physicists to be all reconcilable with each other, mathematically at least, the force gravity was still very much at a loose end. Again, my curiosity was aroused since everything was affected by this oh so prevalent source and I thought it bizarre so little was known about its function. It was well known that it acted according the inverse square law and that it was accounted for further by Einstein's General theory, but I also read that it could not yet be rationalised with quantum theory despite attempts to do so.

I first had my curiosity piqued when I was maybe ten and my mother had taken my younger brother and I to the Science museum one half term, and there was the inevitable long queue for the ladies to deposit their coats in the cloak room. I was left standing to watch the huge Foucault's pendulum that in those days was suspended to swing majestically back and forth in the atrium adjacent to main lobby entrance to the museum: such a shame it has gone. Because I had nothing better to do I read the explanation engraved on the floor for the way which the pendulum swung in accordance with the stars and not the spinning Earth so that its angle of traverse swung deviated at quite an angle to its original zero line set down the middle when started, presumably at 9 a.m. as the museum opened. It took me some time to appreciate what was going on, but when I did, I could hardly believe it. The result was that the stars controlled the way in which it swung and not the spinning Earth on which we were controlled and existed under the influence of its force of gravity. Astonishing, and something I have never forgotten, and am still waiting for a satisfactory answer, to the extent that I have had to attempt my own. This will be featured later in chapter 12, but I mention it now since I see from my notes in late 1978, I had been considering the notion and definition and consequences of being in relatively the same place. From this I deduced that gravitation on a large scale seem to indicate that the same place is difficult to achieve on a large scale if it is assumed that the force exercised by the stars and other celestial bodies (dark matter?) is a crucial factor.

Having mulled over this surprising result, over many years, I was delighted to come across it when I first started to read Ernst Mach's book, 'The Science of Mechanics' (1883) and what is now known as Mach's principle which it seems he never encapsulated in a short definition. Perhaps the most concise description I once read was along these lines "When the subway jerks, it is fixed stars that throw you down." In other words, inertia and gravitation are dependent on the effect of every other mass in the universe. The question here seems never to have been finally agreed by anybody, but until somebody proves otherwise, my inclination is to agree with Ernst Mach who incidentally was regarded as a major influence upon Einstein's later work. However, my reading of Mach's books and also some others by Schrodinger started me to wonder about the influence of the total mass of the universe on every smaller mass within, and if so, did this gravitational effect act at light speed or was it instantaneous? Then again perhaps such large-scale considerations were in some way involved or tied up with the so consequential and absolute governing effect of light speed? Such questions started me to consider along these lines which led to some useful conclusions towards the end of 1979, as I have already described. The final results of such musings on the link between inertia and gravitation were finally concluded three decades later in my paper dated 2010 *(Appendix 10)*.

Meanwhile, to summarise again this time duplication effect in practical terms, if there is an alternating current which acts to push billions of identical electrons up and down a conductor, say a metal wire or aerial, the work done in constantly changing their direction back and forth will cause waves of EM action to be radiated in a sphere in all directions to all parts of space at light speed. If such a wave comes across another length of conductor at a distance, indeed any distance, but say a kilometre away, then the electrons in that conductor will duplicate the actions of the transmitting aerial. The current will not be so strong but the actions of its electrons will be exactly the same to resonate with the frequency of the original current. This how any information is transmitted from one place to another by radio or other sorts of waves, and it is also how sight and vision operate in principle. As already mentioned, DT holds the position that such EM actions are not transmitted by photons but rather as shivers or small distortions in the fabric of space time to draw out and duplicate the action and velocity of the singular rim. The latter is expanding out as a sphere at a velocity which serves to define the velocity of light or all EM radiation within the universe.

To test this hypothesis further I started to think about the various other ways of transmitting light. I wondered how this modus operandi applied to neon light emitted from a discharge tube which does not involved the passage of electrons down a conductor but yet resulted in the same effect. To briefly summarise the characteristics of an atom, of say neon, the main constituent parts are the positively charge nucleus of protons together with a few neutrons which are surrounded by negatively charged electrons. Although the latter have a tendency to fly off in all directions, they do for the most part remain at a predictable distance in orbit around the nucleus, producing a sort of three-dimensional cloud, or shell of electrons. Each of these shells has a particular quantum number and is differentiated into separate energy levels. The number of these shells and the numbers of electrons within them determine the form of the atom and from this there follow all the physical and chemical properties of the various elements.

After some thought it occurred to me that here was an electrical current being passed into the neon filled tube to cause it to emit a characteristic red light. What happens very roughly is that when the input of an external electron is inserted into the neon gas, it will transfer energy to the atom's outer electron causing it temporarily to jump up to a higher energy level. The latter is unstable and will revert back to a lower energy state to force a constituent electron, already in an orbit known as a shell, strongly held around the nucleus of positive neon protons, to emit a photon of radiation energy. Some of this radiation energy can be seen as a different colour of visible light, but there is no smooth oscillation to be duplicated externally, so what is happening with the neon discharge tube? The answer is that an electron jumps from one shell orbit into the next. Then I realised that in fact duplication theory could accommodate these bursts exceptionally well. When an electron jumps from one shell to another, it makes what is called a quantum jump, an expression which has come familiar in the vernacular. The electron apparently does not just jump from one orbit into the next. No, it disappears from the first and simultaneously reappears in the next orbit, in which case it is a singular event. It was this point that caught my attention: I had learned that wherever I recognised a new singularity, there would be curious side effects in the vicinity. In this case it is the emission of a quantum or photon of energy.

So, if there are billions of identical atoms with further billions of electrons jumping at regular intervals from one orbit to another, the same orbits in each case, then here was duplication on a very large scale of vast numbers of amazingly similar events. They would be much more identical than the flow of electrons in an alternating electric current, so that it might be reasoned that the duplication effect would be stronger. This is exactly so because the energy of the light radiation caused by the quantum jumps is far greater at the far higher frequency of visible light than that of radio waves caused by the alternating current. To give some idea of the difference, the wavelength of the latter can be thousands of metres, whereas the wavelength of visible light is between 4 and 7 thousandths of a metre.

A photon emitted with the specific energy caused by an electron jumping from one shell or energy level down to a lower level in an atom of, say, neon will have a specific frequency or colour. This is the familiar red illumination of the neon light emitted from a glass tube filled with neon gas across which an electric charge is placed. This photon travels outwards and when its strikes another neon atom in the external world, it will cause another electron to jump out to a higher energy level, so that the action is duplicated or registered by an observer as red light of that specific frequency. What bothered me among other things was the way in which that photon radiated out. Did it travel out in one straight line? The accepted answer seemed to be no, it travelled out on a wave front at light velocity, with an equal probability to be in any place on that wave front. This is the famous complementarity of light: it acts as a particle or burst of energy, created by this instantaneous quantum leap, but it spreads out as a wave and can materialise in any location on that wave front at any time, or so it seems. What makes it materialise again is when anywhere on that expanding wave front comes across another neon atom with an electron in the appropriate lower energy state, so that the photon is absorbed and the atom is put into the higher state.

If the edge of the expanding photon probability wave does not meet with anything, then that photon goes on expanding out into space at light speed, presumably until it does meet something. It seems that that particular photon cannot give up part of its energy: it has to give it all up in the form of making an electron perform that particular quantum jump of that particular energy level, which can presumably only be done within a neon atom. From this then, the photon will pass on through the universe undisturbed until it hits a neon atom. My first reaction was that this might be never since it is a very large universe not very full of neon atoms. It occurred to me that the photon could be regarded as a shiver of energy in space, expanding outwards from its source at light speed.

In terms of duplication theory, I could better visualise this process as a potential for duplication of the quantum jump, ballooning outwards on the surface of an ever-increasing sphere. I found it misleading to regard it as a particle that could materialise anywhere on this sphere the instant it met another sympathetic electron. Much better to think of the periphery of this ballooning sphere as a distortion in the fabric of space time, a sort of shiver, with the potential or capability to excite another similar electron, the moment the sphere expands into one. I saw it as a tiny wave of distortion expanding outwards like a balloon. I felt that duplication theory justified very clearly why the quantum jumps of the electrons between orbits around atoms produced radiation waves, also known as photons, of much higher energy than radio waves. I considered this was an entirely rational explanation and easier to understand than just being told that electrons making quantum jumps between shells produce more energetic photons than were produced by the mere oscillation of electrons.

The application of DT to explain EM radiation and the transmission of action through space is less compelling for me than is the basis of explanation for resonance through time of similar structures. There is no accepted mechanism yet for the latter although there clearly needs to be one if only to explain perfect recall and eidetic memory. There is already a formidable amount of scientific research carried out in support of the current understanding of EM radiation being transferred through space at light speed, although this subject is still fraught with disagreement at some levels., especially now that research on quantum effects has progressed over the last couple of decades to show that photons can be transferred, or more accurately correlated, over huge distances instantaneously. In short, our exiting understanding of EM radiation is by no means settled or agreed, especially at fundamental levels. It has been apparent to me that until we have an explanation for the mechanism behind gravitation, our grasp of the operation of the other forces will be incomplete. Possibly I should have left the subject well alone since it is still divisive between the experts as to whether it is a local force energized by exchange of physical contact, or non-local, which indicates force at a distance.

Meanwhile the next chapter describes a little more of how I was coping or not in the atavistic world of commercial property and life in the office, which might act as light relief for the reader. I have to say I wonder whether such a self-indulgent approach to the development of an attempt to understand the mind is a mistake, being possibly seen as an attempt to trivialise such a serious subject. But then so little palpable progress seems to have been made in this last century on this particular subject, despite the huge technical advances that have been achieved, that I am often given to wondering what would a Leibniz, or a Newton clone have made today had they been born again, given all the information that is now available?

Ethics, Estate Agents and Limited Progress: 1986

During the 1980s I worked in the office in Reading with my old-fashioned partners, the majority of whom were solid members of local rotary clubs, and who were used to dealing with local retailers and business owners. It transpired they knew very little about large development schemes that were beginning to flourish at that time in the Reading area which had become known as the Golden Triangle with the apex at Heathrow airport expanding out westwards. Directors of large American IT companies would fly in for a meeting and then fly out and it was far easier and quicker for them to attend a meeting West of Heathrow rather than fight the traffic into the center of London, where the rents on office space were eye wateringly high in comparison to those in the Reading area, which was also very well served by the 125 express train service from the West End of London. My first really unpleasant experience of the spirit of ruthless competition when big money was involved in development sites occurred in the middle 1980s and an explanation of how in property, when the going gets tough, the tough get going, although unscrupulous might be the better word.

A small local developer had bragged to me "Nick boy, I am now on to a really big scheme in Reading, just you wait to see." He did not identify the site of course, as I was not to be involved by him. I was interested but could not think what it might have been, unless possibly it was the old Courage brewery site which occupied at least eight acres, on the Southern edge of the town center. The old brewery was being moved to a new site on the M4 a few miles south of the town center. I thought it might be, but it was far too big a deal for this local developer to take on. I therefore thought I ought to put the possibility of a purchase to a developer of my choice, having first enquired of the large firm of London agents who advised the brewery as to whether it might be available.

The way that small commercial agents can make substantial profit from their local knowledge it to identify a possible site to a substantial developer by demanding an introduction fee based usually on 1% of the purchase price of the site and the promise of any ensuing work in letting or selling the completed development scheme a few years later. I had come across an amusing executive, Barry, of a very successful London based Development Company who had been established about ten years and which was known to bid very aggressively for a property if they decided to go for one. So, having done some business with them already I mentioned the possibility to him on the basis of the usual one percent introduction fee and any follow up work, the latter being usually joint with vendor's London agent. He said of course, and when I contacted the latter, they were cagy about whether it might be available but when I mentioned the name of my acquiring developer client, they agreed to a meeting to see if the matter might be taken further. It was set up but it was August and that fortnight I was in Cornwall for the annual fortnight's summer holiday so I did not attend trusting Barry to let me know if there might have been any possibility of a purchase. When I returned, he said the meeting had led to nothing, so that was that.

About a year later I was listening to BBC radio four whilst shaving one morning, and heard an announcement that the large Courage Brewery site in Reading had been purchased by a developer for £8 million, or perhaps a little more from memory. In 1985 that was a large sum of money and one percent was £80,000, but the follow up letting and/or sale work would bring in a number of hundreds of thousands. Naturally the first thing to do way to phone the recalcitrant Barry and ask what on earth was going on. He laughed and said not to worry, I would get paid a fee, but in the process of the acquisition negotiations, he had used another London based agent, who shall remain nameless, who was also a director of the purchasing company and therefore a colleague of Barry. I knew this nameless vaguely through friends in common, and an old friend of mine with whom he had shared a flat some years earlier. I was obviously very concerned at Barry's obvious duplicity but he was charming enough to allay my fears somewhat and after all, there was future letting and or sale work of the completed scheme in the future which would make the acquisition fee appear almost derisory.

Then sometime later a meeting was arranged in their West End offices with Barry, and a senior director of the Development Company, and nameless, the other agent. The latter never turned up, which I suppose should not have come as a surprise, and when the acquisition fee was discussed, the senior director at once announced that he was not in the habit of paying two agents for introductions, and after some further indignant expostulation, managed to offer my firm the modest share of £15,000 as opposed to the full £80,000 to which I was entitled in the circumstances. I was so shocked that rather than express forceful indignation, I just responded that I would have to consult with my partners before I could agree anything.

On return to Reading report to my partners, I suggested that we should stick at a proper one percent or £80,000 of the purchase price, and if they refused, then we should sue. There was fortunately some correspondence in the file between me and Barry to show the introduction had certainly come from me. My four partners did not seem to understand how introductions to development sites worked, since it was not the sort of thing they had ever done, and they just blinked at me incredulously when I mentioned the figures involved. I suggested we must accept no less than the full one percent and if they refused, set the lawyers on the opposition. They looked appalled and said we could not possibly get involved in litigation with a substantial London based PLC developer, and said I must settle at what I had been offered and be grateful. Lacking support within the partnership in the end I gave up trying to persuade them: they were totally unused to business on this scale and out their depth.

Having been a partner for less than half a dozen years, and not entirely sure of my ground, after much havering I had no option but to accept a much lower fee at the figure stipulated by their company director, bearing in mind that Barry said I would definitely be getting the follow up letting and/or sale work as their local agent which not be the case if I was awkward on the acquisition fee. I have no definite knowledge but I have always assumed that the nameless agent involved got the lion's share of the fee and most probably split it with Barry, which sleight of hand I have seen more than once or twice over the years since then, between developer's employees and their agents. Sometime later, maybe a year or two, I asked Barry what they would have done if we had instead sued them for the full amount. He laughed in his easy engaging manner, and said they would have paid without question since they were preparing to float the company on the stock exchange and any hint of litigation would critically affect the sale. Such was his charm and ability to see the value in a good site that I continued to send him possible development sites but with the terms made absolutely clear. When his company bought a more modest site in Marlow for a 20,000 sq. ft. office development, and once again he refused to pay the acquisition fee, I persuaded my partners to allow me not to instruct the usual Reading based partnership solicitor but instead to let me use my friend Julian, with whom I had studied law at university, to start proceedings for recovery. Jules initially made little progress and so he advised he send in some sort of application to the Courts for action preferably just before Christmas which would have to be answered very rapidly. Since no doubt the top executives would be going away skiing or to the Bahamas for a week or two, they would have to settle the matter before they went on holiday. This is indeed what happened, and I was paid very rapidly after a quick phone call from one of the two principal shareholders and directors of the company.

Returning back to what happened to the development of the huge 8 acre Reading town centre site sometime later, the planning consent originally applied for was mostly all offices but took so long to be processed that it came out to be only 170,000 sq. ft of offices on less than half the site. In the end planning was eventually granted for a large section of the site to be a huge covered retail centre, delighting in the name of the Oracle, (estimated cost in 1990 at £200 million for about 600,000 sq. ft. of shops, or about 13 acres of built space) and later on a mass of housing as residential became increasingly profitable. Needless to say, my firm never did get retained to become involved with the later lettings: the site as I recall, being sold on to a huge specialist retail developer and investor, Hammerson, in 1997, quite some years later. By this time, I had lost contact with the disarming Barry whom I later was told had been taken away by cancer. I have to say that this reduced my feeling of mortification and acrimony I experienced at his hands down to a more human level, and the presentment that perhaps after all, there was occasionally some justice in existence, or maybe just a supernatural sense of irony. It was the first time that I felt no regret in hearing of the early demise of someone I knew quite well.

This was also mediated a little further when the Oracle shopping centre was being extended down a side road, Minster Street, leading to directly to the main shopping drag of the town in the late 1990s, by which time I had left my partnership and had started up on my own. I was asked if I would act for a small local retailer who had a lease expiring in a few years' time but which the property was being acquired by Reading BC acting for Hammersons as part to the huge and extended shopping centre, still being built. He did not want to sell but had been losing money due to the blight caused by the construction works over a number of years of adjacent to his shop and now they were going to acquire his lease by a compulsory order. He was offered £10,000 compensation for him to get out before lease expiry by a large London firm of specialist surveyors, Drivers Jonas, but he could not afford the fees quoted by another London specialist firm, hence my involvement.

The client eventually managed to find the one firm of solicitors in Reading who specialised in legal aid cases and then promptly retained the barrister who wrote the most authoritative text book on Compulsory purchase law. In response to our estimated valuation of about £300,000 loss of earnings, the other side refused to budge from their offer of £10,000 compensation, and after some months of negotiation, they applied for the matter to be settled by the Lands tribunal, the highest court for property disputes. For a number of months, I prepared a proof of evidence under the expert tutelage of counsel, Barry Denyer Green, and two days before the hearing the other side offered £160,000 to settle and to pay all our sides costs which were maybe another £80,000. I felt honour was satisfied and that this was a fine example of taciturn men in suits, dull but efficient, acting for huge multinational companies grinding down small business men without any compunction. However, I anticipate that by then the original developer purchaser of the site was little, if at all, involved.

Before all this came to pass, I had fallen out in 1993 with my Rotarian partners, with whom I never really fitted in or had much in common. After an arbitration which turned nasty over the value of my 20% of the freehold of the property they occupied, they had to pay me substantially more than they estimated, and delayed in doing so after the arbiter had made his award. The then senior partner was a specialist in rating and the valuation of pubs, and was out of his depth when it came to office development sites which this was and which was sold as such a few years later at what seemed to me for too low a figure to a developer I knew well, and who turned it into a wine bar.

I took a small office in a series of dilapidated buildings along Queens Road, one of the main routes away from Reading town center. I had also managed to buy a small share of the Queens Road freehold with a local developer client, using the money which I had managed to extract from my former partners, The surrounding circumstances of this process were quite epic for me, far too complex to be described here in a book about the workings of the mind, although I suppose they might later form a diverting narrative, given time and the inclination to elaborate. After a few further years working in Reading the Queens Road site was sold for development and I made a comfortable profit. By 1993 having started up on my own as Severage Greaves, I moved from Reading in 1996 to share an office with a residential agent in Wallingford, a delightful Thames side town. I had a few loyal clients who wished to stay with me, and which provided me with an income albeit much less to start with than when in partnership. I was going to call my practice Champerty, Severage and Greaves which combination amused me since I saw it as the estates equivalent of Private Eye's eponymous firm of solicitors Messrs. Sue, Grabbit and Run. When deciding what to call my new practice, I recalled from my days as a law student there were still on the statute books the intriguing twin felonies of Champerty and Embracery: too wonderfully resonant of mediaeval law to forget. The former is when which an individual with no previous interest in a law suit, finances it with a view to sharing the future proceeds. However, I lost my nerve and settled for just Severage Greaves, but also with the rationale that a client's substance having been severed by professional fees, as is too often the case, would inevitably grieve.

I could not resist it, having once seen a brass plaque in London announcing Swindells and Gentry, and then I recall that I had another old friend Peter Sly who used to drink at the Flower Pot hotel at Remenham and he had a small estate agency for a while with a partner whose name was Sharp, and they did not hesitate to trade under the slogan Sharp & Sly, but I am not sure how long that lasted. All the same I did later start a little property company, Champerty & Severage, through which I later owned a small commercial property. To the discredit of the legal profession, not one solicitor with whom I had dealings over the next couple of decades, and there were many of them, had ever heard about champerty, although one or two recognised that Severage was almost an anagram of Greaves. One old friend, former neighbour and client delighted in addressing his letters to Sewerage Greaves: very satisfying. Perhaps this was one of the more useful, and certainly the most memorable result from four years of studying law in that ancient Irish university.

That is enough digression from the main purpose of this narrative on the mysteries of the mind, but it might shed some light upon an increasing lack of enthusiasm in my chosen career, and general disenchantment with the calibre of people taking important decisions in big business which affected public life. It now seems to me that as time passed, I would fall back with increasing nervous energy back on my spare time interest which never diminished.

It is now at least 35 years since Rupert Sheldrake published his first book which doubled my faltering belief in my own work, and which allowed me to continue to worry away at my obsession with the mechanism of mind and memory. One of the reasons so amazingly little is still known about the operation of the latter, despite the huge steps forward since the 1930s and the development of quantum theory, is that physics is labouring under a belief structure which is probably flawed by one or two fundamental issues. As already mentioned, one candidate that comes immediately to mind is the nature of gravitation and how and why it works. Nobody seems able to explain so we have to accept that it just does. Another major fundamental question springing to mind is light speed. Why is it measured to be at one apparently invariable constant velocity, and why does it happen to be at that one particular figure of about 186,000 miles per second? Again, there is no answer other than it just does. This blind acceptance without query or even much interest seems to me something of an obvious blind spot ignored at our peril, and suggests that it is a subject aching to be investigated. In fact it was not until 2010 that I finally drafted a paper which gave an answer of sorts to both this problem and also possibly to Gravitation and inertia by consideration of Mach's principle (see *appendix 10* for more detail). This was prompted by the intimations I had more or less dreamed up in the office in 1979 as mentioned earlier in the script. The latter was not because I was specifically attempting to solve such a major cosmological problem 40 years ago but rather that it was just an interesting implication of the light speed problem that occurred to me in passing. In the later 2010 paper I was instead trying to reinforce the second part of DT to show one effect was the direct corollary of the other transfer through time effect, when it occurred to me that my singular rim answer to the light speed problem might also be directly connected to inertia and gravitation.

Of all my ten papers I have put on out on the Research Gate and Academia.edu websites to date, the one that resolves this light speed question together with a simple illustrative explanation for the effects of special relativity, seems to be taken least seriously of all my content. Presumably this is because there is already what is a quasi adequate explanation for the electromagnetic radiation effect, despite the fact that some of the greatest physicists of the twentieth century were never happy with it. Sometimes I wonder whether my explanation is just so simple that interested specialists would have come up with the same proposal years ago if there was anything in it.

Well they have not as far as I know, but I am also aware that the research on the shape of the universe as it currently stands does not favour the spherical expanding ball version (closed finite and bounded) even though it is one of the accepted alternative possibilities. Having said that, at the time of drafting this paper, November 2019, I have just read of reports from Prof. Melchiorri of Sapienza university, Rome, backed up by astrophysicists at Manchester university, have indicated that the results from the final Planck satellite release might indicate the possibility of a round rather than a flat universe. We obviously have to wait to see. But then there are so many other answers proposed, all of which are either mindboggling such as infinite multi branching universes, or else so mathematically complex that they cannot be visualised in terms of our familiar three dimensions. I have always been worried by answers that are incredibly complex, and although sometimes complexity can lead the way, my gut feeling is that if so, such resolutions are only difficult because a large part of the evidence of surrounding facts is absent. Once all the relevant surrounding facts to any mystery are known then the answer will be simple and suddenly become obvious to any ordinary thinking individual curious enough to require an answer. In particular I am thinking this is the case with gravitation about which we know so little other than one mass attracts another and the way in which it does so varies with distance and mass.

Again, we do not know why, but just that it does, which is remarkably similar to the position of our lack of understanding on the absolute and perennial quality of light speed. Neither do we know much about inertia, or the quality of mass to resist being accelerated: it happens and we can calculate its effect but do we know why mass has such a resistance? No, not as far as I am aware, but surprise surprise, I have this possible answer to the connection between gravitation, inertia and Mach's principle which is an extension of the rationale set out above. At first, I did not take my speculations that seriously but with passing time, and with the recent announcements of revised calculations resulting from observations from the Planck satellite on the shape of the universe possibly being spherical (mentioned later in the text), there might prove to be increasing support for such a scenario.

Recapitulation from 1979 and Its Relevance to Intuition

So there I was out of London from mid 1979 with my family living in a semidetached farm labourer's cottage, with a pleasant view of distant fields and trees, in a hamlet called Upper Culham at the top of Remenham Hill outside Henley in the early 1980s. By this time there were also two small sons at the local primary school in the village adjacent at Crazies Hill, and we had pleasant neighbours, indeed very amusing and diverting neighbours, and this was all quite good. My wife Angela had installed her large loom in the sitting room, the ceiling of which had to be pierced through to accommodate its dobby mechanism sitting on top of the shafts, and she was working freelance and part time selling designs to mills and fashion houses for furnishing and fashion textiles. The local paper interviewed her with a photo of her machinery with the very appropriate headline 'Looms large in the Lounge', and she, I and Gussie, the oldest son, would attend trade fairs from time to time in Belgium, France or Germany where she would have a stall and buyers would examine and finger the designs and occasionally buy a few. She learned never to let a prospective customer holding a design out of her sight for a moment in case they quickly took a photo of it before return indicating it was not what they wanted. Once or twice I would take a day or so away from the office to assist and hold the baby if necessary and acts as Gopher with a few other husbands in attendance to provide sandwiches, tea, coffee and moral support in the event of no sales. Male textile designers at such fairs were very much in the minority.

But she was beginning to miss the company of working with friends and colleagues with similar back grounds and she was given blocks of teaching at the London College of Fashion for a few days a week, which made a stimulating change from school runs and minding the children 24 hours per day. The commuting was hard work of course but being back in the company of other weavers and students she found very worthwhile. So, life was not too bad with some help from au pairs and visiting grandmothers.

In my spare time when not getting involved with the mysteries of horticulture and a veg patch, I was working on a revised and more detailed version of a roughly drafted paper of about 65 pages completed in June 1979 which had been sent to Koestler and a few other prominent academics in the field. I then added an appendix in December that year to explain the isotropy of light and the supposition that its velocity was controlled by the expansion rate of the universe, and when I sent this proudly off to one very eminent physicist, a Nobel Laureate, he replied to point out that:

"The process of duplication clearly is one which does occur in nature, but generally by processes which are understood in other ways than your energy-of-interaction method, for which there is no real evidence. But it seems to me that you are basically describing a number of processes in terms of the concept of duplication rather than constructing a theory of them. For example, in the case you quote of electromagnetic waves, your approach would fail to give the quantitative predictions of inverse square law and angular distribution of the radiation emitted from a dipole that Herz derived from Maxwell's equations, which seem to be entirely adequate in themselves, and do not talk of duplication. To take another instance, your discussion of intuition very nearly assumes the result you wish to prove in order to derive it, and you would have to go more deeply into the mechanism involved for it to appear a useful theory. I must also point out, as you are probably aware, that a lot of the detailed physics is incorrect. But don't let me discourage you completely, as intuition itself can be very powerful, and it is quite possible that there are important things to be found out in the area into which you are looking."

Well, as a result, I immediately added another appendix in response to this criticism. Of course, he is right that I give no quantitative predictions of the inverse square law, and indeed I was describing a number of processes in terms of the concept of duplication but how else to attempt an explanation of any phenomena? I cannot see any other way of constructing a theory other than assuming a result intuitively and then seeing if it seems to work or not. As I described in chapter 4, the answer can come out pat, fully fledged, seemingly out of nowhere and then the reasons for the answer might be checked retrospectively, albeit logically, to back up the intuitive conclusion. That is the whole thing about intuition. That is how it works: one large leap to the right conclusion, and developing the logical deductive reasoning thereafter in justification, which later are little more than a construction of much smaller connected intuitive leaps.

But of course maths and precise physics were never my strong points, and I was then unable then to argue his criticisms here, but there is also the fact that despite Maxwell's equations being adequate in themselves without any talk of duplication, the explanation of how radiation energy is transmitted across space is known to be flawed as explained above. Still I was encouraged by his answer but took the matter no further, other than to write an appendix which I added later in January 1980 to satisfy myself as far as I could. On the subject of intuition, it seems a good moment to describe the connection that DT has with this subject, which I have thus far avoided in order not to appear to overdo things as a universal vade mecum for everything. However there was such a connection which occurred to me initially in late 1978 but which I developed into a more explicit form by late 1979, and in order to explain this I shall now quote extracts from a book which I started in 1985 a few months after I completed the more formal paper earlier in 1979 of about 150 pages.

This was a much longer version of this part autobiographical account I am drafting now, but by mid 1991 when six years later I had eventually reached page 180 of closely typed A4, much of it done on holidays, I realised that I was going to really struggle to get it published. It was too long and did not have enough back up evidence for a readership to take it seriously, especially so given the struggles I had experienced by then to get people well qualified in the subject of the mind and physics to read just short paper extracts of parts of my work. Since I reckoned that one of the strongest arguments supporting DT was that its principle seemed to provide answers across the board to so many otherwise diverse questions, too many really so that it would be expecting too much of the academics, never mind the everyday reader, to take it seriously. Why should they be inclined to give any credibility to someone outside academia making a claim that here was an alternative approach that resolved so many different problems, especially when some of them already had apparently adequate existing explanations? Furthermore by 1991 I had not made much progress even though Rupert Sheldrake was appearing in conferences all over the place and there were many interviews on his books recorded on YouTube, and although he had a strong following, he seemed to have a hard time gaining credibility with a large sector of the establishment.

His second book 'The Presence of the Past' came out in 1988, followed by the Rebirth of Nature in 1991. The former with its very convincing and well-argued pages on how light speed was possibly variable was a major eye opener for me since it reinforced my own ideas on the singular rim of the universe expanding out at light speed.

I gave up the book started in 1985, the working title of which was 'The mind at Random,' some years later in 1991 and instead started out on yet another approach to the apparently insuperable problem of getting my views on the operation of the mind out on print. I will mention what happened to this third attempt later on, but having read some of the 1991 uncompleted version again recently I shall now lift some passages from it in order to show how DT can offer an explanation for the mechanism behind intuition and also its application to the problem of consciousness.

A specific thought structure placed into a mind otherwise in trance is a distinct pattern of synapse firings set into the midst of otherwise formless random motion of the conscious part of the brain. As explained above in chapter 4 sections E & F, I saw here was a possible means of explanation of perfect recall across time, with the later same mind having initially been instigated momentarily into a mind in a state of random trance, given the appropriate source of prompt via a single engram or physically stored memory source. Once a specific thought is placed into the earlier mind it can appear and will be duplicated in a later trance state mind. The more perfect the degree of randomicity in both minds, the more chance there will be of a perceptible transmission being made between the two. Since this might also apply to two different but very similar minds (Identical twins for example), then here are grounds for a most convenient explanation for telepathy, either across time or simultaneously. However, I shall leave that possible avenue well alone, especially so since I saw that that here was also a possible explanation the les controversial subject of intuition. What was important here was that the later mind in deep trance state seemed to have an ability to copy, or make a duplicate of any other thought structure capable of being encompassed by another mind. That was the spin off result from this particular singularity state, an amazing capacity for duplication.

All I had read about the intuitive way in which scientific discoveries were made as explained in the section F confirmed I was coursing in the right direction. Further, my existing knowledge -not extensive, but sufficient- of how mystic religious beliefs bring intuitive enlightenment to their followers, confirmed the same thing. I was delighted, and I pursued headlong the various implications that occurred immediately to me. Thus far you, the reader might still be asking, so very well, where is intuition in all this in specific terms? There might be some potential here for a possible general explanation for the mechanism of intuitive enlightenment, but nothing very specific. But in order to give a more specific explanation, the concept of understanding or comprehension needs to be examined a little further, which I had also been considering at that time, in spare moments. The understanding of a concept must be based on an ability suddenly to recall from memory a sequence of earlier thoughts or holocepts which earlier were taken in over a longer period of time, probably in a number of lesser learning steps. This presents formidable difficulties.

Consider what happens in my mind when I say I understand something, say the operation of the ordinary petrol engine. At once I know I have in my mind the ability to recall if necessary, all the various movements of the reciprocating pistons in their cylinders, the valves opening and closing, the electrical circuits operating to produce a spark at the right moment. That is understanding. I understand the engine in principle, although a mechanical engineer's understanding will be much greater since his memory can also recall all the detailed working of the alternators and sophisticated timing devices and modern electrical circuitry that mine cannot. But although his understanding is more extensive than mine, he can recall it just as instantaneously as I can, or so it appears.

A maiden aunt's understanding of the petrol engine is different. It is noisy and vibrates when the ignition key is turned on in the dashboard: a large metal lump under the bonnet, covered in grease, dirt, tubes and wires, and it somehow contrives to rotate a shaft thing which is connected to the turning of the wheels. This is a lesser understanding with little detail. Viewed in these sorts of terms, I regard understanding as an ability to recall and recreate thought structures or holocepts of the engine in the mind. Auntie's limited understanding presents a fuzzy image of the engine. Contriawise, the engineer's holocepts are quite comprehensive and detailed, so that there is the instant ability to recreate (or duplicate) in the mind, an image of the full working parts of the engine.

I therefore see increasing degrees of understanding as the ability to recreate (or duplicate) in the mind in greater and more accurate detail the structure of the object under consideration. This means in the form of pictorial 3D images projected from the brain in holographic form. Using that handy device of extrapolation to the ultimate (or singular) circumstances, then perfect understanding of a concept, or more easily, a single object or specific structure, comes when a perfect duplicate of the object under consideration can be formed in holocept form in the mind.

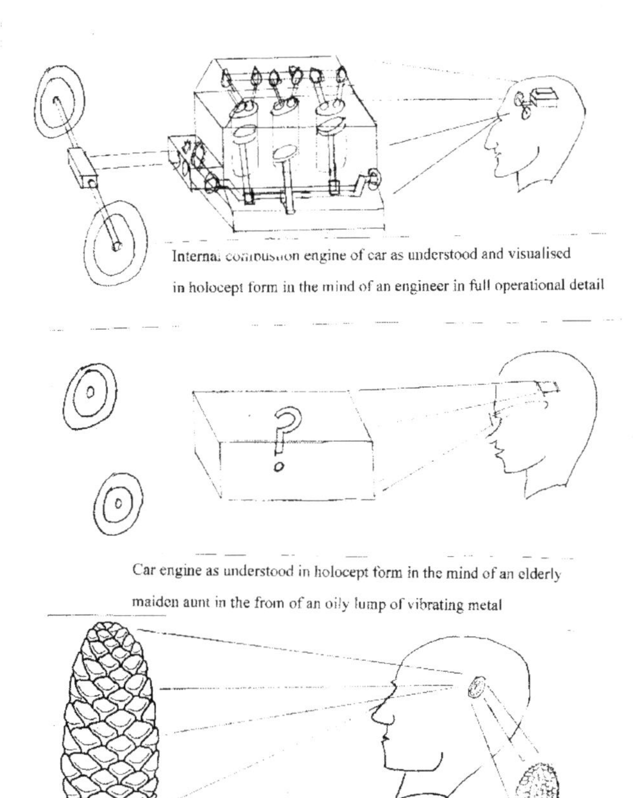

Internal combustion engine of car as understood and visualised in holocept form in the mind of an engineer in full operational detail

Car engine as understood in holocept form in the mind of an elderly maiden aunt in the from of an oily lump of vibrating metal

Pine cone as viewed by omniscient Eastern mystic or sadhu, well trained in voiding the mind into a state of near perfect randomness so that a perfect mental duplicate holocept is created, of not only its external visual image, but also, its internal structure and the way in which it grows and develops. A Western naturalist trained in biochemistry will also be aware of such structural detail governed by the mathematical Fibonacci series, and other theories but there is much else yet to be to be grasped before full understanding achieved.

Plainly this is going to be difficult for large structures, but there seems to me to be no real reason why it should not be physically possible that the structure of say, a small twig or pine cone should not be recreated in the mind in holocept form, correct in every detail down to molecular if not atomic detail. But I have already shown that if the mind can be stilled to a state of near perfect randomicity, then it has the potential to duplicate perfectly the structure of any object that might somehow be instigated in sketchy form within that trance state.

Thus, an accomplished eastern mystic might have been considering this pine cone set before him, concentrating on it for hours, until he has taken in as much information about it as his conscious mind allows: the touch, the feel, the smell, the shape. Then, he stills his mind to random motion through contemplation as far as he can, whilst still retaining slightly above all the other totally subdued conscious senses, a vestige of the image or holocept of that pine cone, or any such complex object. There should come a stage when the increasing randomness of his mind will reach a point near enough to singularity state so that it will start to duplicate in holocept form the nearest convenient object. Provided that a great degree of randomness is achieved, then the retained vestigial structure of the pinecone in the mind will suddenly start to act as a seed pearl. Once the duplication process is initiated, then a chain reaction could result, like the precipitation of crystals in a supersaturated solution, and a perfect copy will be produced instantaneously. The reason for this is as described earlier, is due to the minimum energy principle. The holocept will therefore have the potential to duplicate the structure of the actual cone, inside and out, down to maybe large molecular level, or whatever degree of detail the complexity of the neuron circuits will allow.

Thus, a sudden intuitive total understanding of the cone might be achieved, at a stroke. It exists in holocept form in his mind down to impossibly minuscule levels of detail. He therefore not only knows all about it, but he can effectively say he has become that pine cone; it exists in his mind as a near perfect duplicate. That I take to be true intuitive understanding, and the mechanism through which it is achieved. Such an explanation for the intuition depends in turn on the almost embarrassingly simple definition of understanding to be the production of a holographic image by interaction the brain cells. (Just to clarify one possible point of difficulty, the holocept or holographic image is created by the firings of the synapses within the brain, but the image created by the interference patterns projected beyond physical dimensions of the body.) The more detailed and precise the image, the greater the degree of understanding, although it is not limited to a mere a visual image, since it also comprises the interior workings of the structure as well. It is a three-dimensional duplicate image, inside and out. Image is too weak a description: the holocept is another entity in itself. This talk of images immediately raises the question of how this image is viewed, which is of course one of the big-time philosophical quandaries, and I will come to this within the next few pages.

But, in the meantime, I had developed my hypothesis of intuition to the point of a rather general, but plausible explanation for intuitive understanding of small structures via trance or contemplation, and I needed to bolster this up to an explanation for ordinary intuition in everyday use. One further point came to me which reinforced my ideas thus far, was as follows. Duplication theory indicates that as one structure starts to duplicate another to near singular tolerances, there is an increasing potential for the mass of the particles involved to start converting to radiation energy. But it then occurred to me that it is an energy release of sorts that is experienced when intuitive truths are realised. Not more than a few molecules would need to be converted to produce an energy release significant enough to be detected by the nervous system of the body. When understanding breaks through, when the truth makes itself manifest in that sudden shaft of light, this is usually accompanied by a wonderful sense of elation and well-being. Could not this sense of exhilaration be caused by a small creation of energy from just this duplicative process? Even if this sounded at first romantically farfetched, the more I considered it the more I liked it.

Furthermore, consistent with this line of reasoning, the concept of the truth could also be defined very neatly. The truth in these terms is an accurate holoceptual image in the mind of how things actually were in nature, in the external world. The closer to the truth of any subject under consideration, the more accurate would be the holoceptual image of that subject, in the mind of the individual concerned. Perfect truth would create an energy of its own in the mind beholding it. Perhaps this also gave a rationale to the concept of beauty, the inexplicable thrill that the fortunate can experience when observing an object or concept of beauty, especially for the first time. Perhaps this was what the poets and the mystics had been droning on about for centuries. At last I could make some logical sense out of the quotation from Keats that had been drummed in to me, with others, for exams in English literature at school:

"Beauty is truth, truth beauty: that is all ye know on earth, and all ye need to know."

Indeed, according to this rationale, anything can be beautiful once it is properly understood. All that is needed is perfect understanding. Paul Dirac, one of the most eminent of British Physicists said:

"It is more important to have beauty in one's equations, than to have them fit the experiment."

Frankly it was considerations of this sort more than all the rest that encouraged me to think there must have been something in my speculations. I found them very exciting. My next step was to try to reconcile the mystics' intuitive method of gaining knowledge in single large leaps into the void, with the apparently contradictory Western method of logical deduction and analysis, step by laborious step. I have considered the scientist and the mystic in a little detail, but not yet given much space to the arts, the proponents of which seem to act in a way which has more in common with the mystic than the scientist. One of the tasks of the artist is to communicate to others his own particular view of a fundamental truth of nature in as compact a medium as possible: a single picture, a few lines of verse. Perhaps it is the fortunate choice and order of a few words of poetry that can set off in the reader's mind a heap of similar associations, so that the emotions experienced by the poet himself can to some degree be shared with his public. The same with a painting: a few inspired lines of brushwork might be able to so much catch the essential spirit of a scene that the viewer feels himself to be transported there, or at least to some degree shares the same insights that the artists felt when painting the scene. It does not take much stretch of imagination to see that there is a form of resonance at work here. The calling of the artist is to see the external world in a new light, and then somehow to share that vision with his fellow men, transmitting it in whatever way is most suited to his particular talents.

In terms of duplication theory, he strives to evoke in the minds of his public viewers duplicate holocepts or thought structures he has experienced. He does this by catching the essence of a scene in his chosen medium of expression, and hopes that these carefully chosen words, chords of music, structures of paint, or whatever, will act as engrams in the minds of others to instigate the vestige holocepts of similar scenes which, because they are true to nature, will then unfold in accurate detail so that they can experience his own observations and the emotional response they caused in him, strong enough to wish to transmit it to others. It is this fact that the artist's original observation must be true to nature, so that only a suggestion of it in someone else's mind provoked by observation of the artist's work, is then enough according to the minimum energy principle for the full holocept or observation to be fleshed out by the resonance/duplication process. Presumably it helps if the initial impact of the artist's work is staggering enough to strike the observer's mind into a moment's stillness, so that the resonance process can then more efficiently take place. I have often read how it is the first ever sight of a particular painting by a sensitive observer that makes the biggest impact, and causes the strongest emotional response. This would tally with the first shock of the observation stifling the observer's mind into a moment's trance state, so that it is then at its most suggestible potential.

On the other hand, the scientific way of sharing new knowledge or information comprehended about nature and the true state of the external world appears to be completely at odds with the intuitive methods of the artists and mystics. The scientist decides to examine one tiny section of nature, say to ascertain the molecular structure of a particular substance, and he carries out exhaustive tests and experiments in the laboratory, until a pattern of order emerges that will allow him to deduce that the structure must be thus. A development of many small laborious steps will eventually allow him to make his small breakthrough, so that for the first time, the required molecular structure is ascertained, and a little more knowledge is added to mankind's store. Whether or not it will be of any use is another question, but at least knowledge and understanding has been increased.

To most scientists a few decades ago the mystic method of stifling the mind to acquire wisdom was anathema. It seemed to be a contradiction in terms that an Eastern ascetic could sit still in a cave for years doing nothing and yet becoming wiser, especially to the Western scientist who sweated hours, days, months and years to acquire one small piece of new information, so small in itself that it could hardly be called more wisdom. The disparity between the two approaches seemed impossibly at odds. It would also maybe seem unfair to the scientist that the mystic did not have to do anything except just sit there, and concentrate on doing nothing. It is not until one has tried to do nothing for hours on end, and tried to empty the mind, that one realises the impossibility of the task. Of course, unless it could first be explained to the Western scientist why in logical terms such a practice might lead to the acquisition of knowledge, then he is not going to believe there is any point to it. He will therefore never go through the years of training and contemplation that must be undertaken before the mind can be cleared at will. However, I am now suggesting that duplication theory indicates that fundamentally both methods of acquiring knowledge are the same. It is just that the eastern mystic or artist makes one or two huge intuitive leaps to gain instant massive insights on the nature of the external world, whilst the scientists make collections of very small such leaps.

The scientist, say a chemist seeking the molecular structure of a chemical compound (perhaps a new superconductor), probably has a sketchy idea of the class of answer he is seeking. Perhaps his problem is that he knows the four elements of which this new material is comprised, but he does not know their respective quantities, their structure, and the way in which they are all joined together. He then carries out all manner of experiments and tests to observe how the compound behaves in varying different circumstances. In selecting these tests, he will follow hunches that the compound "might just have this structure in which case it should respond in such and such a way to this test: let's try that therefore."

In other words, although he is apparently logically carrying out a number of tests from which in the end it will be said that he is capable of deducing the correct solution, in fact the way in which he decides on those tests, the critical part of the whole process, is purely based on little intuitive hunches. It is the choice of test where he can make inspired guesses, and then when enough tests have been carried out, a pattern of behaviour emerges for the material from which it might be relative child's play to extract the required answer. In short, the rational deductive processes of modern science are nothing more than a series of connected small intuitive leaps forward, gifted guesswork if you like. The artist and the mystic use single large intuitive jumps to increase their knowledge by improving their perception of the external world, and although such methods might appear to have nothing to do with scientific method, the basic mechanism involved is the same.

Thus, I was able, using this fairly general explanation for the mechanism of intuition, to reconcile the two opposite poles of East and West and their apparently contradictory teachings of the way to gain wisdom. I was delighted with this really very simple explanation, and today, some decades later, it is perhaps the one application of duplication theory with I am most pleased.

In these speculations first made in the early 1980s I was still very aware of a number of weak points in the argument. The first, was the mechanism for the production of the holographic image or holocept, which is viewed by the mind as thought. Well, in the last three or four decades a number of psychologists, neuroscientists and physicists have written persuasive papers showing how the process within the brain are connected with electromagnetic field theories which I find supportive especially the holonomic theory of Bohm and Pribram. The latter are remarkably similar in essence to DT.

The other weak link was the question of how this holocept or image was perceived in the mind. What was it that actually observed this image? This is perhaps one of the most baffling problems of philosophy: the problem of self-consciousness or self-awareness. What is it and how does it work? What is the self, the 'me' in the mind, and how do I come to be aware of myself? There is also the same problem on a different scale in science in that it is now thought that the observer of an experiment might have some effect on the quantum scale, in which case, this involvement should be written into any mathematics describing such an experiment. Perhaps the most convenient way to summarise the problem is to give a quotation form Professor Arthur Eddington's most excellent book written in 1929, "The nature of the Physical World". In this passage, Eddington is discussing 'Actuality' and the problem of what he calls 'the identity of Mr. X'. He starts by discussing the nature of gravitation and showing that any complete explanation must be cyclical.

"The definitions of physics proceed according to the method immortalised in 'The House that Jack built': this is the potential, that was derived from the interval, that was measured by the scale, that was made from the matter, that embodied the stress, that.....But instead of finishing with Jack, whom of course every youngster must know without the need for introduction, we make a circuit back to the beginning of the rhyme: that worried the cat, that killed the rat, that ate the malt, that lay in the house, that..... Now we can go round and round forever.

But perhaps you have already cut short my explanation of gravitation. When we reached matter you had had enough of it. 'Please do not explain any more. I happen to know what matter is.' Very well; matter is something that Mr. X knows. Next question, What is Mr. X? Well, it happens that physics is not at all anxious to pursue the question, What is Mr. X? It is not disposed to admit that its elaborate structure of a physical universe is 'The House that Mr. X built'. It looks upon Mr. X -and more particularly the part of Mr. X that knows - as a rather more troublesome tenant who at a late stage of the world's history has come to inhabit a structure which inorganic Nature has by slow evolutionary progress contrived to build........

From a broader point of view than that of elaborating the physical scheme of law we cannot treat the connection with mind as merely as incident in a self-existent organic world. In saying the differentiation of the actual from the non actual is only expressible by reference to mind, I do not mean to imply that a universe without conscious mind would have no more status than Utopia. But its property of actuality would be indefinable since the one approach to a definition is cut off. The actuality of Nature is like the beauty of Nature. We can scarcely describe the beauty of a landscape when there is no conscious being to witness it; but it is through consciousness that we can attribute a meaning to it. And so it is with the actuality of the world. If actuality means 'known to the mind' then it is purely a subjective character of the world; to make it objective we must substitute 'knowable to mind'. The less stress we lay on the accident of parts of the world being known at the present era to particular minds, the more stress we must lay on the potentiality of being known to mind as a fundamental objective property of matter, giving it the status of actuality whether individual consciousness is taking note of it or not.......... A little reflection will show that the point of contact of mind with the physical universe is not very definite. Mr. X knows a table; but the point of contact with his mind is not in the material of the table. Light waves are propagated from the table to the eye; chemical changes occur in the retina; propagation of some kind occurs in the optic nerve; atomic changes follow in the brain. Just where the final leap into consciousness occurs is not clear. We do not know the last stage of the message in the physical world before it became a sensation in consciousness....... Mr. X is one of the recalcitrants. When sound waves impinge on his ear he moves, not in accordance with a mathematical equation involving the physical measure of a number of waves, but in accordance with the meaning that those sound waves are used to convey. To know what there is about Mr. which makes him behave in this strange way, we must look not to a physical system of inference, but to that insight beneath the symbols which in our own minds we possess. It is by this insight that we can finally reach an answer to our question, what is Mr. X?"

I had often pondered the problem of self-awareness, not quite in the terms above, but rather by setting myself the simple question, who am I, and what is this thing which I refer to as myself? How do I think, how do I remember things, and how do I understand things? It all seemed quite insoluble to me at first. Ever since I first started to remember my dreams, I realised that there was more to reality than just the world of consciousness, and I had over the years come to consider that the world of the mind might be the only reality, and that perhaps it was the external universe that was the dream. By my early thirties, I was beginning to accept that it was probably just part of the human condition that we should never know the answers to these questions. And then came

DT with its surprisingly simple answers to parts of these questions, one of which was for self-consciousness as follows.

The answer to Eddington's question was that there is no Mr. X. There was no need for him, or for some metaphysical scanning device to observe the holocepts. I had already speculated that the sense of wellbeing that comes from intuitive breakthrough was merely a few molecules or atoms of a structure in the mind converting to radiation energy when that holocept duplicated some structure, object or concept in nature to near singular standards of perfection. There was no observer of the holocept, no Mr. X, but just the ability of the whole nervous system of the mind and body to respond to the external world by producing increasingly accurate images of parts of it.

When this occurs the resulting glow of wellbeing that inevitably follows any accomplishment or increased understanding can be explained as a resonance with nature which creates this small amount of duplication energy, or possibly just the increasing potential to do so, which can actually be detected by the brain, and then maybe the whole metabolism generally. Certainly, my own experience of sudden enlightenment or even just doing anything constructive, is that I immediately feel better humoured, and rejuvenated. I am sure this effect is not merely subjective and that everybody experiences it all the time to a greater or lesser degree. Indeed, I have often wondered about this feeling in the past, and asked myself why this should be so, so palpable can such an effect be.

Just in case I have not managed to describe DT in an adequately concise or particularly memorable manner so that its key principles and rationale will inevitably not yet be as clear as they are in my mind as the author, I have attached as appendix 9 a recapitulation of DT on one page and the way it has explanations for a surprising number of phenomena as explained above in chapters 3 and 4. This is as brief as I can make it and still hope that it is intelligible, and I repeat it here purely as an aide memoire for those who might still be having trouble getting a hold on the salient points. This might be useful on consideration of the issues raised in the next chapter.

Voiding the Mind and Consciousness

Following on from the last chapter on intuition, increased understanding is derived from the ability of the mind to create progressively accurate holocepts of the structure of concepts or objects in the external world. Although when left in the random trance state, the mind will automatically tend to produce increasingly accurate mental duplicates of nature, this rarely occurs since the conscious mind is usually trying to ensure that its supporting body stands the best chance of prolonging its own survival. Dreaming about in trance is more likely to minimise the chances of survival in this rough world where the fit and physically strong tend to survive longest.

As a result, the normal conscious state is the antithesis of trance, with the mind constantly at work anticipating what to do next to avoid trouble rather than taking in truths of nature. After all, there does not seem much point in being able to comprehend these eternal truths if one is not going to be around long enough to appreciate them, having been felled by the nearest predatory beast or one's fellow man. Perhaps that is why in the material Western world we seem to have entirely lost the knack of stifling the mind. Now that we have conquered through technology most of the day to day problems of survival, and now that we have the security, affluence and time to consider the question of accumulating wisdom for its own sake, we are in a good position to start again to explore the benefits of contemplation. The brute beast has to concentrate nearly all its faculties in just staying alive, whereas more intelligent life forms, having perfected survival techniques, can afford to start to wonder about the reason for the ability to survive in the first place. According to DT the best way to produce results here is to behave in a contradictory way by emptying the mind rather than by keeping it constantly active, which was-the most effective method of ensuring survival at a physical level.

To go back again to Mr. X, the observer of thoughts in the mind, he is a myth since there is no need for him. The mind and the whole metabolism of an individual responds through resonance to nature and therefore the structure of the external world by reproducing parts of it in holoceptual form as thought. The more detailed and accurate the holocept, the greater that individual's understanding of the external physical world, and the more he is able to feel at one with the universe. Combined with this will be an increased feeling of wellbeing, and not only is the otherwise insoluble problem of how thoughts are observed neatly removed, but if this were justifiable, then a mechanism to explain self-consciousness and self-awareness very easily seems to suggest itself and maybe a few hard problems melted away to nothing.

Reverting back to my description of intuition’s operation, consider the mind contemplating some intellectual problem. A great deal of generally relevant factual information surrounding the problem will have been observed and recorded, but in total disarray so that the task is to fit all the disparate pieces together into a cohesive pattern, rather like doing a jig saw puzzle in three dimensions. When complete, this would then provide an explanation in the form of an accurate reflection of nature in the mind, in other words complete understanding. So, when it seems that there is no more generally relevant information to be taken in, then the mind is stilled and set into random motion. If there is a serious, almost obsessive drive to solve the problem, then perhaps with the mind operating ninety percent randomly, a vestige of consciousness could be retained, enough to keep all this relevant information near the surface. If then this small part of the mind operating at a conscious level, runs through a number of possible combinations of the assorted facts in attempts to produce a solution, the rest of the mind operating randomly should tend to resonate with greater perceptibility to actual structures in nature, whenever these arbitrary attempted combinations come a little closer to the truth.

If the rest of the mind were random enough with all other structured thought excluded, then according to DT the answer, the correct holocept, should pop up at once when given just the slightest instigation by the presence of the few relevant facts or thought structures comprising the problem. Remember, this is because any holoceptual structure imposed on otherwise random motion, according to the minimum energy principle, will tend to resonate with the object most similar to that structure in the external world of nature, and thus duplicating its structure more exactly. I am convinced that one purpose of the intelligent animal organism, the whole metabolism and not just the brain, is to recognise and detect this resonance, which represents a lower energy level and therefore more stability, which should be more acceptable to nature. This would also represent a tendency towards a more ordered state of affairs, by arranging previously jumbled bits of information into a coherent thought structure which accurately reflects nature in the mind: in other words, entropy is reversed as more order is bought into the world through understanding. But of course, this is just the embodiment of the process of life: cells duplicate themselves again and again to produce organic development and increasing degrees of order, which is the essence of DT. It is also all to do with biochemistry, about which I know little and which is under the expert auspices and jurisdiction of biochemist Rupert Sheldrake, and leave that all to him for explanation.

The physical body and brain of an intelligent organism exists to detect duplication and indeed to exert itself on the external world to bring about an increase in degrees of order. This activity is in itself the operation of self-consciousness, and it would seem this is a fine example of a teleological argument. Mr. X is not a viewing mechanism of any sort. He is the result of the resonance of duplicate structures: a process to detect the true structure of the nature: more simply, the 'truth'. As I have already mentioned, when an answer to a problem is sought and then found, its resolution produces not only intellectual pleasure, but also a physical sense of wellbeing, depending on the extent and the complexity of the problem. All human beings strive to increase their pleasure or enjoyment in life, so that it could be argued that if the resolution of truth represents the highest form of pleasure, then the purpose of human intelligence is to detect more and more truth in the universe. In this respect the 'truth' means the accurate portrayal in holocept form in the mind, of structures in the external universe.

Accurate memories can be regarded as truthful holocepts, perfectly duplicating nature, and it is only because our conscious memories are so inefficient that the world is currently governed by records on paper or magnetic discs. These represent more accurate and permanent recall of facts or structures in the past than can be recorded mentally (Western man having lost the trick of contemplation and perfect recall), and so today the whole of the civilised world is ruled by documentation: the only convenient form of recording exactly what happened or what was said at an earlier time. Individuals who are proficient in the written word and its manipulation become secure, wealthy and powerful rather than those who have a genuine facility to recall the truth. However, the structure invoked in the mind by the written word is not very complex, and the truth or accurate representation of certain facts that occurred, or might occur, is very limited. In other words we have to make do with the written word, as an inefficient medium of description and recall, because it is the most common place means of record we know how to use at the moment, other than perhaps the relatively recent arrival of audio visual electronic recordings, not mention the further resulting influence of algorithms.

All the same, it is fascinating to note that it is this ability to recall exactly some past occasion or structure, however imperfectly, through the documentation that controls the world and the rules of civilised human behaviour. It is not the paper or the written words themselves that are important -they are just the means- it is the fact that documents can duplicate or accurately recall something from an earlier time which makes the ability to write and read the single most important instrument of control for the last three or four thousand years. In short it is the ability to reproduce exactly something that occurred previously that is crucial. If we each could be trained to have this ability in our minds without recourse to the mechanical recording devices, then our behaviour should take a major step forward. This ability to recreate previous occurrences and structures is so crucial to our lives, so intimately bound up with our psyches that we cannot see it for what it is: the lynch pin of our existence.

The 'self' or ego of an individual, or however personality is described, can be seen to be dominated and formed by the vividness of past memories and the impression they made upon the individual at the time they were first observed. This is because intelligence operates through recalling past observations which might be relevant to current external circumstances, and how they might best be adapted to enhance that individual's chance of survival. This description of the operation of intelligence is of course at a level much lower than its ultimate purpose, described above as the imposition of order onto the external universe. However, before any such intelligence can impose such order, it must first be able to physically survive above the brute beast level of having no time for leisure pursuits above the basics of eating, finding adequate shelter, sleeping, and instinctive procreation. Therefore, these basic ingredients for survival must first be met, before consciousness can be developed.

The self can be regarded as a jumbled assortment of memories and inherited memories (genetic behaviour patterns). If the memories are repeated enough, they become lodged as engram patterns creating conditioned reflexes, then to become permanently engrained into the gene pattern in the chromosomes of the body's cells. The memories in this collection comprising the self will be the more vivid and the more deeply engrained, the closer they are to reality. In other words, the more accurate such holocepts are to nature, and the closer to the truth, the greater the resonance and the stability and the value of these memories. However, these accurate memories of great comprehension will be mixed in the mind among memories of less consequence from different times and places in a random morass. The higher the function of intelligence beyond that of ensuring mere survival, the more it will attempt to arrange and combine these holocepts into more ordered and meaningful patterns, so that wider and more accurate representation of nature can be formed in the mind.

Memories might stick in the mind for no apparent reason and which by themselves appear to have no great significance. Later, further observations might be made, which when considered with the earlier memories, combine to form a significant holocept reflecting accurately a larger slice of nature. This constant sorting out of recalled holocepts into new combinations, which are realised to be significant when they duplicate nature, is a process which results directly from the phenomenon of the resonance of similar structures. The mind detects this resonance in the same way, say, as a meter measures increased electrical potential and interprets it as a feeling of both intellectual and physical wellbeing throughout the whole body. This ability to detect resonance or full understanding of parts of the external world seems to be a fundamental component of how the existence of sentient beings can be improved. As such it might be argued to be an integral part of how consciousness works, and the urge to sift through myriads of combinations and permutations of holocepts can be seen as curiosity, the great driving force behind intellectual progress.

All these reflections appeared to flow so easily from the subject of intuition's operation that it seemed to me that there had to be a strong connection here with problem of the composition and operation of consciousness. The more I thought about it, the more I saw that holocepts of the external world, both observed and recalled, would comprise increasingly accurate duplicate images/holocepts of its true nature which would incrementally deepen the observed understanding of it and existence. I was inevitably worried about whether an increased potential for mass to be converted to radiation energy was capable of being detected if such a physical conversion did not actually take place occur, lest the whole premise falls to the floor, but at least it gave some sort of partial insight to the great problem of consciousness, or so it seemed to me twenty years ago, and still does.

I was aware from the history of science that in the past the most apparently insoluble problems were sometimes resolved at a stroke once a certain fundamental principle was realised, to produce an amazingly simple answer. Often, so obvious was the answer to the problem that succeeding generations would wonder not at the ingenuity of the solution, but rather at the fact that preceding generations could have been so blind. For instance, the orbits of the planets (the Greek word planet means wanderer) troubled astronomers for centuries. They just could not work them out, and produced all sorts of amazingly complex geometric devices to rationalise their apparently erratic behaviour. However, the answer was obvious in principle once the theory of Copernicus became accepted that the planets revolved round the sun rather than the Earth being the centre of the universe. The answer then became more mathematically precise once Kepler realised that the planet's orbits were not circular but ellipsoidal. Then after all, if my version of that part of quantum entanglement involved with mind and memory, turns out to acceptable or not far off the mark in due course (modesty prevents further comment), then one might expect some of the great problems of qualia and whatever else that philosophers have argued about amongst themselves for millennia, might fall to the floor.

Another derivation of my hypothesis of understanding and intuition that immediately occurred to me at the time was that if you extrapolate it to infinity (always a useful gambit), then the following results. An individual mind should be capable of understanding (duplicating in holocept form) any single structure or concept in the universe, although it obviously has restricted capacity to replicate vast amounts of interior detail of large objects, due to the physical limits of the size of the brain producing those holocepts.

However, if a number of minds could join together to act as one through some form of telepathic connection, then there might be the capability to produce a joint and extended holocept. But DT is nothing if not a possible explanation for telepathic communication in the resonance of similar thought structures, both past and future, in otherwise random blank minds in the trance state. I have not gone into the explanations which the theory might provide for paranormal effects such as this, not wishing to aggravate credibility any further, but the possible explanation for telepathy through resonance should stick out a mile. But first of all, the problem of recall of events from the past has to be dealt with and one would have thought this might not be impossible. If it turns out to be nothing like my version of DT then somebody else should be able to come up with something before another decade passes. That is my presentiment, and that is when things will start to change, and I hope I live to see that day for the following reasons.

When once the mechanism behind memory and thought is mastered, it should be possible via reverse engineering to be able to have two separate minds networked together in the way that computers can be combined today. The result of many minds being combined together into one vast system of intelligence should be not too farfetched a concept. This should then be capable of producing a far more detailed replica image of the universe, or large parts of it. If all the separate life forms in the universe were able to communicate telepathically together, once they have all developed far enough to understand the operation of the mind, then it might not be too much to suppose that they were together capable of producing a perfect enough replica universe in holocept form, that the two would interact to convert totally to radiation energy, the whole boiling lot reduced back to the lowest energy state.

It was at this time that I first started to think along these general cosmological lines, and developed them a little later, as I shall show. However, they followed on so immediately from the explanation I came up with for intuition and an outline version of consciousness, that I thought I would mention it in passing at this stage, so exciting did I find these sorts of implications at the time.

Little Progress Until Support from Quantum Entanglement

In 1984 we moved from the cottage at the top of Remenham Hill to a bigger house on the edge of Watlington, which is either a small attractive town or a large village (nobody is ever quite sure which) on the edge of the Chiltern hills in South Oxfordshire. It had then about 20 shops, a Coop (wonderfully open every day eight till late), a surgery, a primary and secondary school which made for an easier life in such a community rather than in a hamlet of half a dozen houses. Before the war it apparently had about 20 pubs reduced to six by 1984, and now down to three, although the fine old Memorial club where the beer was never expensive, is now a continental diner.

We still live there today and the children, three boys by this time, all went to the local primary school, and then on to a private day school at Abingdon, which I could just about afford as a commercial surveyor working in partnership in Reading. After a couple of years, the town was threatened with an extra 400 hundred houses in order to fund the construction of a ring road around its edge, and I joined the parish council to help thwart excess development. Life was generally busy enough as the house we had bought required a great deal of work to get it redecorated, sort of insulated and relatively watertight, not to mention the gardening and cultivating the veg path, at which I was not that proficient but enjoyed. There was not that much time for further work on my spare time obsession with understanding the mind and the point of existence.

As mentioned earlier I did manage to produce 193 pages of a narrative account from 1985 to 1991 of my labours in this respect titled 'The Mind at Random' which I never completed. I reckoned that it would be impossible to ever get into print having made a few approaches to a few publishers and literary agents. It was too technically detailed for the general public without a relevant background in academia and a complete lack of credibility for an academic readership, lacking peer reviewed material, never mind its radical and alternative approach. Then in 1993, I fell out with my partners and started work on my own as Severage Greaves, which was a worry enough to distract me from matters of the mind for some time, but by 1995 I had decided to try another approach to publication.

Some years later I was chatting to Rupert at about the time of the millennium, complaining to him that with my lack of any relevant academic background, it was almost impossible to get anybody who was well qualified in physics, psychology or biochemistry to take my duplication theory at all seriously. I was well aware how hard it was for him to get the more conservatively minded academics to take on his morphic resonance proposals, so how much more of an uphill battle was it for me as a provincial estate agent to get such paragons even to look at my work. I commented facetiously something along the lines that I might do better to gain some attention if instead I wrote a black comic novel along the lines of the estate agent who thought he was Einstein as a vehicle to contain my ideas. I was a little taken aback when he enthusiastically agreed that might be the best way for me to go forward.

However not that much later in early 2002, having no better alternatives, I thought it would at least be worth having a bash at drafting something along those lines. I would describe a narrative of the early days of my life in W11, just off the Portobello Road from 1970 before Notting Hill started to get trendy and affluent. It was to be written in the third person singular under the pseudonym of Julian Weatherby together with his friends and flat mates of those bachelor days, (mine and theirs thinly disguised) in a relatively light hearted vein, to include much more narrative account of life in London in those irresponsible times.

I enjoyed drafting some of the more diverting episodes of my life in London, which I thought might appeal to the average reader who might not be too struck by the detailed explanations of physics even if I managed to make them less complex and lengthy. There was ample material with pub life in the evenings in that part of London, with the early days of the Notting hill carnival in August, which paled in excitement compared to the political infighting of the communal garden committee of the crescent of which I became a member. So wonderfully rancorous were the disputes within the committee, the result of one minor misunderstanding was having battery acid poured over the bonnet of my old Renault six.

The owner of the first floor flat Nick who was training to become a barrister, suggested that we should attend the AGM of the committee in an upstairs room above a pub, and it transpired there were three or four other attendees besides us, together with the current committee. The chairperson evinced great disgust at the lack of support and asked if any of the audience would like to volunteer to join the committee, since the existing committee were minded to resign en bloc due to the lack of support. So Nick looked at me and said he would propose me if I would propose him, which went through effortlessly nem con, and then the old committee rushed to join again.

I recall the chairman of the paid gardener for the gardens was the husband of the lady chairman of the committee. He only had one arm and could only bend over with great difficulty, and so it transpired there was a fair amount to sort out. I recall later on going through the minutes of former committee meetings: a source of bitter narrative and amazing conflicts, quite hilarious, to the extent I thought it would make excellent copy for a BBC 4 radio miniseries. Four or five years later I was gob smacked to see large vans with TV cameras in the adjacent part of the crescent. They were filming a new series to be called 'The Cres' based on the adjacent community gardens, their up and coming occupiers and their committee in the adjacent and rather smarter section of Elgin Crescent than ours. I considered the plot of the few I watched rather weak in comparison to the minutes of our more scruffy slice of garden life.

Back to the new proposed book: the initial working title for this effort was 'Schrodinger, Zen, and the Art of Estate Agency' but I was stuck at page 17 until late 2002, after which I set more time specifically aside to progress the book further. So much did I enjoy describing carefree life in London and the antics of old friends and accomplices not that thinly disguised, that I had written more than 16,000 words before I actually got as far as Julian taking time off to work in the BM. By the end of 2004 I had written about 142 pages, and it was once again getting far too technically inclined for easy reading. Besides the narrative had reached only as far as Julian working in the reading room in late 1978, so I decided to can this second exercise. Once again it was just too long and involved, although possibly the informal presentation of life in W11 in the early 1970s might have made for easy reading.

Over the years from the middle eighties after the move to Watlington I corresponded with a fair number of experts, some of whom were interested, some of whom were not and failed to reply, and a small number of whom considered that such approaches were not much more than impudent. John, one of the notable Beloff family, and who had set up the Koestler chair of parapsychology at Edinburgh university, was a regular correspondent over 20 years, very charming and helpful, and on checking my files recently, I note that he sent some of my papers to physicist Peter Higgs who was not yet well known as he was to become in 2012, but nothing came of that particular foray on my behalf. Not much of note then happened until I managed rather late in the day in 2007 to put up my own website which is still more or less in its original format with little amended since that time (www.mindandmemory.net) This meant if I found someone who seemed to want to know a fair amount about DT or whose work seemed to me to be fairly similar, then I would just refer them to my website. This made the process of communicating with possible like-minded individuals much simpler. The website gives a detailed description of Duplication theory together with a curtailed narrative account of the way in which I built up my conclusions from the late 1970s, and it now requires much updating and some deletion of earlier sections which are clumsily worded, and at the time of writing I have not yet managed to do this.

However, I now rely much more on the two academic websites mentioned above to propagate the central theme of DT via about 10 papers and the various improvements therein that have occurred to me since 2007. Since there is more comeback and response from the Research Gate and academia.edu websites, I now tend to rely on these for explanations of parts of the detail of DT rather than flood an interested party with the whole shooting match of all its various applications. There is an almost embarrassing number of the latter, which worries me that it might appear so wide ranging as a universal panacea and answer for far too many unknowns that nobody could take it seriously, given its lack of provenance and peer review. Of course, such an extent of resolutions should in theory be a source of encouragement, but it could also be seen as just ridiculously over ambitious and a pipe dream.

My discovery of these two academic websites in 2016, where almost anybody can place their papers without the delay and necessity of peer reviews and publishing costs, changed my approach to getting papers out in the ether. Over these last few years since 2016 it has changed the way in which I can easily find on the internet others whose work appears to have something in common with mine, and then contact them if the similarities of rationale seem compelling enough, and which occurs occasionally.

Otherwise these were busy years domestically from the mid 1990s with the two younger sons completing their studies at university, the youngest at Durham studying theology, and the middle son having completed his medical studies at Oxford to become a doctor in 2005, and then on to Harvard and Imperial to specialise in public health, which arcane subject seems to me as an outsider to have more to do with statistics than anyone other discipline. My oldest son left for Australia in 1997 not having bothered with A levels to learn how to live an independent life and a fair amount about building sites, a very useful qualification, together with an award for second best didgeridoo player in Sydney. He would have come third but his didge teacher, in a state of too much drink having taken, never quite made it to take part in the competition.

During the nineties and the first decade of the new millennium I did not do very much in the way of new written theoretical work, none at all really although I wrote to a fair cross section of people interested in the same questions that I was pursuing. There did seem to be increasing numbers of the latter as time passed, but I found they would tend only to express some interest in my material if there were some strong similarities in approach, and there were not that many of the latter. Number one son Gussie, having originally settled back in UK in 2003 after eight years in Australia, well qualified to teach the didgeridoo, and also well able to supervise and work on the conversion of an old stable block at the bottom of my garden, to be later sold. He then set up as a builder in London and when buying furniture for his room in a shared flat in Clapton, North London, he had bought a side board from a second hand shop, which he had noticed was built by his grandfather's firm, Greaves & Thomas long since defunct, for a few quid. He did it up a bit and then discovered it was then worth about ten times what he paid for it, that sort of modernistic design from the nineteen fifties being very fashionable. He had obviously inherited his mother's designer genes because my sentiment about that sort of furniture was that I would have to be paid to have it in my house. So anyway, he started in business with a website, buying from E bay, and other sources, until by 2016 he had taken a lease on a shop in Hackney Wick.

In 2010 I completed a paper on the Absorber theory mentioned above, to show how this also could account for the way in which gravitation and Mach's principle could be reconciled, and I have attached as *appendix 10* rather than go through the initial part of it again that already described above in chapter 8. This paper contains three possible alternative answers to the mechanism behind gravitation, one of the last great unknowns. Because the third alternative might seem totally counter intuitive in that it defines gravitation as a repulsive force or tendency, with the mass of stars, black holes and galaxies within acting in a blanketing capacity from the huge mass of the expanding out spherical singular rim of the universe, and will doubtless appear counter intuitive but it is the one which gives me the most satisfaction, not least since it gives a very simple answer to dark energy, and also possibly one for dark matter, albeit less well founded. I was enormously pleased with this paper at the time of writing however unlikely it was to be taken seriously having to do with cosmology, not my subject, and seemingly unconnected with DT. However, there was a strong correlation with that part of DT that explains Electromagnetic radiation as already detailed.

Furthermore, I found irresistible the fact that the fact it dealt seemingly with Mach's Principle, gravitation and inertia, the existing explanations for which I have found to be almost nonexistent, never mind inadequate. Even better, I made my conclusions unprompted by any particular desire at the time to specifically resolve these problems, dating right back to day dreams in the office in 1979. They just suggested themselves almost effortlessly as an implication of DT: nothing if not a consistent set of belief structures.

There was one instance during this time that was encouraging. My friend Stephen, my friend and great enthusiast for Duplication theory, Stephen, was a member of an academic group called ANPA, Alternative Natural Philosophy Association which meets once a year to discuss presentation given by members, and he gave talks on duplication theory on three separate occasions. Stephen is very confident and fluent on the rostrum, which I never have been, with his own slant on DT. I never attended, but he always reported back. On one occasion an eminent topologist commented that there was a very interesting and important paper published in 1982, the 'No-cloning theorem' which seemed to be quite similar in some ways to one of the basic tenets of DT that it is impossible for one structure to be exactly identical to another. I checked this out on Wikipedia later and read: "In physics, the **no-cloning theorem** states that it is impossible to create an identical copy of an arbitrary unknown quantum state. This no-go theorem of quantum mechanics was articulated by James Park in proving the impossibility of a simple perfect non-disturbing measurement scheme in 1970 and rediscovered by Wootters, Zurek and Dieks in 1982. It has profound implications in quantum computing and related fields. The state of one system can be entangled with the state of another system."

I found this tremendously encouraging. Over the years when I have tried to explain DT to physicists, a number of them might mention politely enough that it was incorrect to speak of actual structures of particles in space since quantum physics ought more accurately be considered in wave form, rather than as collections of connected points in an outdated classical from of physics. I could see this was certainly possibly a serious problem. But sometime later I was told about the Fourier transform by another friend I encountered on the internet in 2016, Shelli Joye, who had some very similar views to mine on the way that the mind operates.

Shelli is a qualified electrical engineer and explained to me how in 1822 Joseph Fourier had discovered a mathematical equation which showed that information from the frequency domain could be transformed into the time domain, and this would apply to the formation of holographic images from physical actions within the brain. Her papers posited that the connections between the neurons via synapses and also dendritic connections in the brain would be complex and ordered enough to create holograms of memories in the form of structures created by past experiences and thought patterns. These would then be projected from the brain as holographic images which I described as holocepts.

Thus, it might not be so much the actual structures of electro chemical currents flowing within the brain that were being duplicated close to singularity state, but rather it was the created holographic images, the holocepts, that could not ever be identical to those from the past, and which would therefore resonate. Since this ability to duplicate earlier similar structures is a quantum effect then the no-cloning theorem will apply. These holocepts might never be able to be identical they could certainly be very close to that singularity state. To learn about the Fourier transform and the No-cloning theorem almost forty years after I had first deduced this fundamental element of DT by observation, this was very reinforcing and gratifying. Furthermore, I read from the so useful Wikipedia (yet again),

"**Quantum cloning** is a process that takes an arbitrary, unknown quantum state and makes an exact copy without altering the original state in any way. Quantum cloning is forbidden by the laws of quantum mechanics as shown by the no cloning theorem, which states that here is no operation for cloning any arbitrary state perfectly..........Though perfect quantum cloning is not possible, it is possible to perform imperfect cloning, where the copies have a non-unit (i.e. non-perfect) fidelity. The possibility of approximate quantum computing was first addressed by Buzek and Hillery, and theoretical bounds were derived on the fidelity of cloned quantum states. One of the applications of quantum cloning is to analyse the security of quantum key distribution protocols. Teleportation, nuclear magnetic resonance, quantum amplification, and superior phase conjugation are examples of some methods utilized to realize a quantum cloning machine. Ion trapping techniques have been applied to cloning quantum states of ions."

In any event the next major step forward started to impinge upon me much later in about mid 2016. A few years earlier I had read about experiments carried out by Professor Anton Zeilinger, a quantum physicist of Vienna University, and who in 2004 teleported a photon (light particle) from one side of the Danube River 600 metres to the to the other side. But the photon didn't cross the ground, nor did it fly through the air. It moved from one place to another without travelling through any of the in-between places, and it was done instantly and not being limited by light speed. This quantum teleportation, as it has come to be known, is made possible by a process called "entanglement" on which subject Einstein speculated, having observed that pairs of particles sometimes act as if they are connected. If you poke one, the other jumps instantly.

Amazingly, this is true no matter how far apart the particles are (Einstein talked of entanglement as "spooky action at a distance"). Scientists first suggested that entanglement could be used to teleport particles in 1993, but it was Zeilinger who put the theory into practice in Europe. Then in 2012 he carried out a similar experiment over 143 kilometres between two Canary Islands using two optical links, one with quantum entanglement links and the other ordinary classical light beams, with the former demonstrating instantaneous connection.

I had read earlier that this might be theoretically possible as a result of a paper the physicist John Stewart Bell had written in 1964, which became known as Bell's inequality theorem. This was based on a discussion on a paper written by Einstein and two colleagues in 1934 and known as the EPR paradox (Einstein, Podolsky & Rosen), and showed that two separate but formerly entangled photons with spin can demonstrate non locality according to quantum theory. This means that two separate events can be shown to happen at the same time at any distance apart, unaffected by the usual limiting effect of light speed: in other words, instantly. According to the original established rules of classical physics this was not possible, since nothing could travel faster than light speed, and so Einstein and colleagues concluded that there must be a fault or what was called 'a hidden variable' in the quantum theory rationale. However, thirty years later Bell's theorem proved that in quantum terms this instant connection was indeed possible mathematically. This became known as a non local effect.

Although via Bell's theorem instant connection regardless of light speed was known to perhaps be possible, it was not until much later when practical experiments were carried out that it started to be taken very seriously. As a result, the extent of the subject and nature of physics had to start to be seriously reconsidered, and which process is today at the forefront of scientific research. For instance, eminent particle physicist Henry Stapp of Lawrence Berkeley National Laboratory was been quoted as saying: "Bell's theorem is the most profound discovery of Science."

I first started to read a book on the subject by Anton Zeilinger, 'The Dance of the Photons' in 2015 and I foundered after the first 100 or so pages, not being able to grasp the detail. The blurb on the dust cover stated that "In the Dance of the photons, Zeilinger, winner of the prestigious Wolf Foundation Prize in physics, tells the story of his life's work in a lively, folksy anecdotes, and an engaging sense of humour, rather than abstruse mathematics, to convey the profound significance of findings in his field." This indeed he does but I could not hold the detail in my head and follow the line of argument. I then left the book abroad somewhere but a year later realised I had to understand more about the subject and bought another copy to have a more serious attempt at its mastery.

I had read more in general terms about the consequence of entanglement and how it was essential to the construction of quantum computers on which huge amounts of funding are being poured. The hope is to build an effective working device far more powerful than standard digital computers can currently manage, although this has not yet happened as far as I know.

From my reading more on entanglement I also had an intimation that the way in which the holocepts formed by interference patterns projected from within the brain seemed to have a supporting justification in terms of instantaneous quantum effects. In fact, it was more than just a subjective intimation since a number of physicists and other experts were of the same inclination, although initially there was the problem that quantum entanglement acted simultaneously and apparently not over time.

I still cannot get a comprehensive grasp of entanglement's mechanisms to enable me to explain Bell's theorem to anybody else but I what I can appreciate is that the way the experiments are carried out are surprisingly similar to that part of DT which relies on the mind's neurons firing as close to randomly as possible before a structure can raised in holocept form through resonance with another similar structure. What I learned from Zeilinger's book was that randomness is a fundamental feature of the quantum world, and that for instance the transmitting source of photons has to be able to fire its photons in a way as close as possible to perfect random motion, and the way in which two such entangled photons are then detected and measured also has to be carried out in a completely random manner. When I read this and took in some more detail about such experiments carried out in the last 30 years, which I still found hard to grasp, it became clear to me that there was a very close link here with the fact that many aspects of DT also revolve around the crucial quality and effects of random motion.

This was exciting, and to attempt show why, I will try to explain a little more detail about quantum entanglement. There is a problem here since it is such an complex subject that it seems only physicists with competent mathematical ability are able to fully understand the detail of the mechanisms involved, but enough successful experimental work with mainly photons (quanta or particles of light energy) has been carried out in the last decade to be sure that this entanglement and that this quality of quantum non locality really does exist. This means that the action of one photon when it is measured and which was entangled with the other but is now at a distance, has an effect on the latter, however far apart they might be at precisely the same instant. The nature of this second photon is at once known. In other words, information between the two is transferred at once and unlimited by light speed, which forty years ago was regarded as impossible, other than the very few physicists who understood Bell's calculations, always assuming they took them seriously.

So, despite my lack of mathematical ability I shall now try to convey my understanding of the way in which quantum entanglement operates and which will change everything about the way we live in due course, once the experts have been able to understand and hopefully simplify its description. I have little doubt they will be able to do this, after more research has been carried out to then render the whole business more or less obvious, and easy to understand for anyone interested as is usually the way with scientific progress. How long this will take is another matter.

A photon is an elementary particle and effectively a quantum of electromagnetic radiation such as light or any other electromagnetic field, and which carries force across space at light speed. It has zero mass and is in the class of particles which are knows as bosons. In terms of quantum mechanics electromagnetic (EM) waves can also be viewed as streams of particles or photons. When viewed in this way, the polarisation of an EM wave is determined by a quantum mechanical property of photons called their spin, which can be either one way or the other: horizontal or vertical for instance. The wave form of a photon is transverse, and it oscillates perpendicular to the direction of motion and it can be polarised by passing the photon through a filter. The usual way to produce entangled photons is usually to fire a laser beam through a certain type of crystal which will cause a very few of them to be split into pairs of entangled photons which are emitted in different directions.

This means that the energies of the two new photons must add up to the energy of the original photon and likewise its momentum. But the energy and momentum of each photon is unspecified. If one photon is measured, it instantly assumes some energy and momentum and the other photon then has to have the corresponding energy and momentum to fulfil the energy conservation laws. Each photon from the crystal will be polarised either in one direction vertically (V) or horizontally (H). It is not completely decided which of the two situations is actually the case, until both are measured, and until that happens, they are indistinguishable, effectively the same entity. If we measure one of those particles, the entanglement disappears, the joint wave function collapses and if the measured particle becomes a vertical spin, then the other at once becomes a vertical spin, and vice versa.

It is worth repeating this astonishing process again. When the photon emerges as two separate entangled photons in separate beams, it is in a superposition of two polarisations H and V. But when we then put one detector into the path of each emerging beams, the photon will be registered in one of them. That photon will therefore also have a definitive polarisation, vertical V or horizontal H, depending on which beam it is found in. But crucially if one detector registers the photon, the other one will not register. The experiment confirms that only one of the two detectors registers a photon but never both. So, the question is then how does the second detector know that it should not detect the photon? It is because until the photon is registered there is an equal probability for both detectors to detect the photon. In the language of the quantum, the photon was in 'superposition' of both possibilities, and this superposition collapses the moment when the photon is detected by either one of the detectors. It is only at that moment that the photon decides which path it is to take: before that it was an absolutely random possibility. But instantaneously and faster than the speed of light, the other detector knows it cannot register the photon. An experiment to demonstrate this was first carried out by John Clauser in 1974 in America and then in France by Alain Aspect in 1986, and in 2018 Chinese physicists carried out the same sort of experiment between a satellite and an observatory on earth 150 miles below to prove the same instantaneous effect.

I have to say I find the full detail of polarisation of these photons and the actual way in which these very tricky experiments are carried out with very sophisticated electronic equipment hard to grasp, but what is clear is that although the mathematics of Bell's theorem is beyond most people. What I can see is that this proven fact of instantaneous connection between locations thousands, millions and possibly light years apart, will force us to radically reinterpret the way in which we understand time and communication.

Currently our measurement of the passage of time can only be done by referring to the effect that light speed has on the way that simultaneity is described. If an event takes place on the sun, say a major explosion such as a huge sunspot, then we cannot know about this until eight minutes later since that is how long the light from the event takes to reach Earth. But in the quantum world it would be possible for this to be registered at once. In short, our whole experience of time is changed.

Everything is instantly interconnected, so it seems to me that the whole concept of the passage of time is directly linked to this limiting factor of the speed of light and the rate at which the latter might be variable. As a result, I anticipate that our understanding of the passage of time and how it affects our experience of existence will change radically when we become far better acquainted with the quantum world than we are now. It seems there is a basis for anticipating that everything in existence is interconnected not only through time but distance as well. See *Appendix 11,* a short paper on 'The Nature of Time' for a little more clarification here, completed in March 2018: simple enough, if a little controversial.

It was not long after I learned about the no-cloning theorem and realised that it could be conveniently applied to the production of singularity state holocepts (holograms produced and projected from the brain (chapter 4), as a simultaneous effect as well as one transferred across time as memory. The part of the brain that controls vision is the occipital lobe, a large area at the lower back of the brain which is one of the four main the processing centres containing most of the anatomical region of the visual cortex. Visual nerves run right from the eyes to the primary visual cortex which then passes information, and a great deal is known about where such information is passed to in other parts of the occipital lobe, but nobody has any indication of how this is converted into images which every sighted person experiences. I have to say I know little about the detail of this very complex subject on which much research has been carried out, but I have never heard of any even part convincing explanation of how vision is experienced. Neither am I going to suggest one in any detail at all now but just suggest a modus operandi in principle. This is offered by the combination of the holocept and the connection of DT with Quantum entanglement that I described briefly above.

It occurred to me that if one of the functions of the visual cortex was to run as a random motion generator so that its neurons and/or other components started to fire randomly when the eyes were opened, the following was a possible result. Highly structured visual information would pour in from the field of vision of the external world via images recorded on the eye's retinas. As explained in Chapter 4, if there was initially nothing but random chaos in the brain, the moment some order and structure was introduced externally, the brain's randomly firing neurons would start to duplicate such introduced information from outside bought in via the eyes, ex hypothesi. The images or holocepts produced would be duplicates of objects in the external world observed in the direct line of sight of the eyes. These would be created instantly and projected out as holocepts and registered by the brain as vision. These holographic images created would be compared automatically with holocepts from the past store of engrams to see if they were similar in any way and then decisions made as to what action might need to be taken to avoid strife and conflict.

In short vision and sight was another instant entanglement effect to which brain would take microseconds to be able to respond no doubt. This was yet another conclusion that I had not been looking for, but as occasionally seems to be the way, possible solutions precipitate out into useful conclusions when they are least expected. Strong conscious intention to reach a specific goal can sometimes be an impairment or so it seems to me, ex hypothesi. I do not have the wherewithal to take this hypothesis any further although I am delighted by its apparent simplicity and conformity with the general thrust of DT, even though it is of course only a top down premise and cannot be validated until much further bottom up research work has been done. But perhaps it is not a bad pointer of the way to go in the circumstances, which might be worth checking out to see whether signs of the ability for the occipital lobe to function very randomly are present in the brain. I imagine that this should not be impossible.

One further point has occurred to me that I should attempt another paper on the crucial quality of vision and sight, and its connection with the subject of mathematical ability, so much part of physics. Without the ability to produce images in the mind (holocepts) the mathematical equations and calculations would not have existed in the first place. Their existence is secondary to the ability to form images in the mind which can then be translated into the very precise and demanding language of maths. But it is a language and there are some crucial issues to consider here but which I touch on now.

The first which occurs to me is that for instance, Einstein's general theory used very complex maths to give a proof for his brilliant theory of general relativity which equated mass with energy and gravitation. It describes gravity as a geometric property of space and time, and rationalises all that with the special theory of relativity rather than the older classical theory of Newton. But there is a problem in that it has not been not been reconciled with the laws of quantum physics to sort out a system of quantum gravity, and in my non mathematical view, this indicates to me that there is something substantial missing from our understanding of the way in which gravitation and inertia work, and more likely this is due to lack of adequate information by accurate observation.

Effectively this means we require more information from the astronomers as to what their instruments can tell us of what goes on in the universe. The fundamental process involved is observation which is purely visual via instruments and then the mathematicians can apply that information to see if it can be codified into their own wonderful and highly esoteric language. But maths is a secondary, albeit very useful function derived from the pictorial holocepts projected from the mind duplicating the external structures of reality. If this argument is seen as a partial excuse and apology for my unfortunate lack of ability in maths, so crucial in physics, then I have to agree but I am convinced that without the initial ability of visual images, the human race would never have developed to extent it has today.

An example of this is my own attempt at understanding gravitation and inertia (see *appendix 10)* by making an assumption of the very fundamental question of the shape of the universe to be bounded and finite, expanding outwards. The cosmologists have been arguing amongst themselves at almost internecine levels about this question. I assume that this is because they are well aware that until they come up with some sort of reasonable answer to this and the existence of dark matter, our knowledge of cosmology is pretty much hamstrung: if we are aware of the makeup of only 5% of the contents of the universe, it is not too surprising that the experts should be aware of the irony of themselves all fumbling in the dark. This has to be directly connected with the lack of understanding of the nature of gravitation, and how and why it operates

Before I move on to the last chapter with a few predictions of how events might pan out in the future assuming there is substance in the operation of DT, there is one other experimental result which appears to me crucial and which needs a brief mention as follows. An increasing amount of experimental research work has been done over the last couple of decades showing how instant communication over distance can be carried out via quantum entanglement, but my original interest was memory and to show how information could be transferred from one moment in time in the past to another in the present. The contents of chapter 3 showed how there could be a resonance effect through time between structures of holographic images because they were identical to near singular levels of accuracy, and effectively the same object. But the rub was that because it is impossible to have two identical objects in the universe at the same time, or at any other time due to the Uncertainty principle, such a precise duplication can never be achieved. However, there could be a sort of resonance effect between the two if a very close approach was made to such perfection, and what is more I deduced it could be across both time and space.

In summary another succinct way of describing this is to say that if it is impossible to have two identical objects then the closer they become to that state, the more one or the other will tend to have to disappear or cease to exist, and presumably because the one earlier in time cannot now change its structure then the one in the present instead has to take some sort of action. In memory's case that is to move on to follow or duplicate the internal movements of the structures of the earlier object, the elements of which will be in motion on a minuscule or vibratory level. This results in the tendency of a sequence of earlier experienced events to be followed as flow of Memory. Then I attempted to show at the beginning of this chapter 12, how when one of an entangled pair of photons is measured (detected), the other one simultaneously disappears: it is effectively the same entity but does not becomes so until it is detected at which moment the other one suddenly cannot exist, according to the no-cloning theorem. This same rationale also applies to powers of visualisation if Heisenberg's uncertainty principle is first taken on and properly understood in the way that DT explains memory's operation. This really does not need complex maths ability, to be able to grasp, but just a different approach.

But thus far I have only mentioned experimental results which prove simultaneous quantum connection across space but nothing yet about across time in the form of experimental back up for my original thesis for memory's power of recollection. Fortunately, I am aware that there has been one experiment carried out by Anton Zeilinger to this end, the details of which I have not seen together with a more recent one to successfully show this effect. Surprisingly little interest has been shown in them, despite it seems to me a very important result, but then it is very early days yet. It is important for DT because it provides a proof in principle to reinforce my rationale for memory.

In 2013 Eli Megadish and a team of physicists in the Hebrew University of Jerusalem reported that they had successfully entangled photons that had never coexisted. This means that a quantum link between particles in different times is possible, more formally described as temporal non locality. So this is the start to providing a basis of possibility of transferring information across time as DT invokes, and provides reinforcement for my original premises first conceived in 1978 that it is possible to transfer/correlate information over time, past to present, although then I had never heard of quantum entanglement, never mind what little was appreciated about it then by those who knew something about quantum theory.

One further revelation for me occurred recently in May 2019 when a retired Doctor friend Peter to whom I was trying to describe the essentials of Duplication theory, commented that it sounded something like the free energy principle of Karl Friston. I knew nothing of his work but on checking, discovered he was qualified in psychiatry and now a professor of neuroscience University College London specialising in brain mapping. He is also an extremely competent mathematician and his Free Energy Principle shows how biological systems maintain their order by restricting themselves to a limited number of states. This is done by referring such systems to be enclosed by a 'Markov Blanket' and the result shows that the brain operates as an 'inference engine'. Effectively this means it becomes self organising, which is exactly what DT delivers in its explanation of memory and thought. In the past when I have explained DT to many physicists and/or scientists in general, I am often asked if there was a mathematical proof for this self organisation effect. A year ago, I was unaware that one existed and this usually ended the dialogue. Now there is such a proof, although inevitably it will take time before it is tested adequately to become acceptable as any such major radical proposed breakthrough will.

Finally, my friend Stephen sent me extracts from a journal, Quanta, reporting that a paper was published in Nature Astronomy on 4th November 2019. The authors argue that the universe may curve around and close on itself like a sphere, rather than lying flat like a sheet of paper as the standard theory of cosmology predicts. The authors have reanalysed data from the Planck space telescope's observation of the cosmic microwave background (CMB) to claim it favours a closed with a 99% certainty. This has been proposed by Alessandro Melchiorri of Sapienza University of Rome and Eleonora di Valentino of University of Manchester, supported by Joseph Silk FRS of Oxford. The team of experts behind the Planck telescope reached different conclusions in 2018, and maintain that this most recent interpretation of the evidence indicating a closed universe is a statistical fluke.

We have to wait to see how this pans out but the rationale on which DT is based supports a closed universe. This is demonstrated by my paper attached as *appendix 10* "Inertia, Gravitation and the Absorber Theory" (2010)

And If So, What Next?

This last chapter is to show how DT has implications for the operation of artificial intelligence (AI), and then to summarise a few other possible effects, implications and applications that arise therefrom. Since this is all highly subjective and conjectural, there will be much use of the first person singular in the descriptions of how I see what might happen in the not too distant future.

I have given explanations of how it should be possible in principle to transfer information both simultaneously across any amount of space and also how it might be transferred across any amount of time, both via procedures involving quantum entanglement. For time transfer, all that is needed are two similar systems both capable of firing perfectly randomly so that if into the later system a structure can be inserted similar enough to quantum levels with an earlier particular structure, then the latter will start to resonate and duplicate the sequence of movements of the original structure. In very simple terms, this is because the two structures are the same object and, until the later surrounding circumstances are disturbed, can only act as one.

Anticipating that once the theorists have a better understanding of both these entanglement procedures, and the practical technocrats start to implement quantum computers or whatever devices they might develop to implement applications of the theory, then by reverse engineering they should be able to manufacture an approach to a simplified replica of certain parts of the human brain: AI in short. This will be unlike any so-called AI device that might have been produced or envisaged today, since it will have some degree of intuitive ability that current computers are without. They will be very different and capable of producing degrees of order and pattern from swathes of randomness that will have to be incorporated into the process which ordinary digital computers cannot get near today.

If I make a not impossible assumption that it should be possible to network a number of such artificial intelligences together, then the combined amount of information and intuitive reasoning in such networked device ability will increase. However, once the mechanism of mind and memory is ascertained then there would really be no need to manufacture AI machines/computers to emulate human intelligence, especially since initially their component parts would presumably be much larger than the tiny filaments of nerve endings that are the composite parts of the brain.

Furthermore, it should be possible for individuals to be able to network their minds together, either by standard electronic wiring but also later by the entanglement procedures that should have been mastered by then. This would be brought about by setting up a group of similarly inclined empathetic minds together by initially setting them into some form of self-induced trance state that would ensure random firing of the neurons, into which a specific thought structure from one individual could then be invoked and transmitted instantly to all involved. I also assume that those involved could be far apart although coordination of the timing would presumably be easier initially if they were close at hand.

It would be a form of telepathy, which subject is often regarded as anathema by many scientists, and understandably so, at least according to their own parameters of belief, which dictate that if a specific result from an experiment cannot be reliably repeated, then it cannot be regarded as genuine example of reality. In short telepathy cannot exist for those of conservative mindsets. It is a sound point of view in many ways but memory certainly does exist, and once we have understood its mechanism and understood how images from the past can be recreated, it does not seem that unreasonable to me that a simultaneous effect (telepathy) or time reverse (precognition) should be not be possible. This is especially so given that we know so little about the nature of time, and since we now know that instant communication via entanglement can and does occur, and can also do so over time (the Megidish experiment), this now indicates that the whole question of the passage of time has to be reviewed. I shall make an attempt on this latter problem further on in this last chapter, but reverting to the networking of minds together, the rationale of DT suggests it should be possible for a group of individuals to empty their minds and then be put into some form of telepathic communication, although presumably one individual would have to be the instigator of mental proposals which would be transmitted to and shared with the others.

So if holographic images are projected and viewed by this one individual's mind, I have assumed that a sequence of thoughts (holocepts) can be transferred to the mind of another by some form of instant entanglement procedure, once the latter has been mastered in a great deal more detail than the very modest amount that has been achieved to date. This smacks more of ESP than science, a subject much excoriated by many, due to the current embarrassing lack of understanding of the mind's mechanism. Once the latter has been mastered, then on the assumption it is on a basis of entanglement as suggested by DT, the next step would be to understand how such holographic images of one mind might be transferred across both time and space to others. That such a deeper understanding of the quantum world would help develop these psychic abilities should at least be considered as not absolutely impossible by the more traditionalist and conservative rationalists of science.

As such communication techniques improve, I make the assumption that it should be possible for individuals within such a group to converse mentally and share experience and thought structures resulting in a sort of group mind. Rupert Sheldrake goes into this subject in the way that groups of insects and animals, bees, termites, swarms of birds, shoals of fish all indubitably demonstrate a group mind and inclinations separate from individual behaviour patterns via his morphic resonance. One result of this might be the development of a sort of super mind as a combination of many individual minds gained from the multifarious experience of all involved. In discussion with friends and colleagues in the past on this point, there has been some opposition to the prospect of loss of individuality in the process of joining in with the crowd and in any event, if such a scenario was possible, there would be the risk that one determined and negatively intended member of the group could disrupt and maybe take over the whole concern.

Well yes, I see the possible danger but posit that this would be offset by the fact that in order to join the group in the first place, an individual has to clear his mind, ex hypothesi, completely of any thought structures at all, malign or beneficial, to achieve near perfect randomicity of the cognitive mental centre. This would be a sine qua non for any unsuitable person to be able to become involved. I imagine that to qualify as a member of such a group there would have to have been a training period acquire the ability to void the mind, no doubt akin to meditation or other similar depersonalisation exercises. As anybody who has attempted such contemplation exercises will know this has never been an easy task: almost impossible indeed to levels of perfection. So, if these exercises had not been incorporated then such a disruptive individual would not be capable of becoming part of a group mind in the first place. Maybe if he/she did, then the breadth of knowledge to which they had gained sudden access would sort out any such venal inclinations of self-promulgation. I suppose what I am saying is that in order to become part of the group, only applicants who had advanced themselves enough above personal ambition and self-advancement would be capable of becoming an active part of such a group. There would be an automatic inbuilt exclusion mechanism. I have attempted to explain the consequential qualities of randomness in the quantum world, and here is yet another example of how fundamental that subject is.

I consider it a reasonable possibility that research on the mind might have developed to a stage within the next two or three decades, given the astonishing rate of technical progress over the last half century, and that we might have reached a state where such communications were possible with or without telepathic communication. That is always assuming our political leaders and autocrats have not managed pollute the atmosphere with radioactive dust clouds created by a nuclear war between two irresponsible warring minor states. I fear this is by no means impossible judging by the current unpredictable and erratic behaviour of our political leaders. I am also inclined to think that we have reached such a tipping point on the ability of the human race to either destroy itself or qualify to advance to a different level of existence. It could just as easily go one way as the other: a sort of test as whether we qualify to move up another level or fall back to square one to start the whole shooting match all over again.

Having made many wide ranging top down conjectures on how the mind operates, it would then be pusillanimous not to attempt a prediction of the results of such a scenario, and since my view of the future based on the potential of future research on the quantum world is teleologically optimistic, I now do not hesitate to do so. Duplication Theory explains that there is this self-organising tendency which is there to counter the other fundamental tendency with which we are all too familiar, that of entropy, the principle that all systems run down into increasing chaos. As Schrodinger observed in his perceptive 1945 short book 'What is Life' that in order to explain life there must be a principle of 'Order from order' to counter that of the other great principle behind quantum theory, which explained so much but which could be very simple described as a principle of 'Order from disorder'.

There are these two opposing tendencies, one dispersing and running down into the unpalatable heat death of the universe, but this is countered by this organising tendency for complex structures to duplicate themselves, which at its most basic level is that of simple cells starting to duplicate themselves into more complex and repetitive structures, manifesting themselves as life. The further implication of the ability to produce increasingly complex structures is that as life evolves, it also develops consciousness and the ability to understand nature and the external world in the form of duplicate holographic mental images of the latter. Thus, increasing intelligence is a result of this self-organising tendency and I see its purpose is to counter the effect of entropy and stave off this bleak prospect of the pointless heat death of the universe.

I anticipate such mind sharing techniques could be developed with practice so that eventually increasing numbers of sensitive and intelligent individuals would be able to develop this mutual empathy to such an extent that they effectively could be in some form of mutual or telepathic contact with each other. What is more they could do this if they so desired with large sections of society similarly trained and endowed, so that their brains and minds were effectively networked together like groups of networked computers. I imagine that there would have to be some sort of routine or exercise to go through, perhaps similar to entering into a self-induced trance before one joined into such a group mind. But think of all the advantages of having this enlarged memory and information at hand.

Eventually I doubt whether anyone of any intelligence and judgment at all would want to be left out of such an experience, so that there would be this huge joined up intellectual system, effectively a super mind. Thus armed, humankind will be capable of making large technical advances at a rate well above that experienced over the last 50 years or so which have been impressive enough after all. If my extrapolations are not completely awry, then within another 50 years or so, and maybe even after only another couple of decades, with the benefit of this new intelligence, we should be capable of making contact with other intelligent races, and be able to network with them if we so desire. Just imagine the amount of information that would be available then. This raises the question that if there are such other intelligent races then some of them will inevitably be well advanced beyond our current stage, so why have they not contacted us already?

Duplication Theory is a result of this self-ordering tendency acting as a counter tendency to entropy and increasing chaos. The latter causes the universe to be constantly expanding and running down, whereas life is increasing order and understanding of the universe, and just as fundamental as entropy. Duplication and the self-ordering process cannot be stopped, although in some very hostile environments it will develop very slowly and in forms which will be very alien to us, perhaps not using the familiar elements on which our organic chemistry is based: carbon, oxygen, hydrogen, and phosphorous. I reckon there will be different intelligence systems on different scales of dimensions as well, but let that alone for now.

As for the reason we have not heard from any of these more advanced races yet, they will be aware if too much information is given to a system in advance of its own natural rate of organic and uniform development, then that will not turn out well. If one part of a system starts to develop at a much faster rate than the rest, then this will have a sort of cancerous effect and destroy the equilibrium and hierarchy of the rest of the system resulting in serious disruption. I have assumed it would be a mistake to attempt to artificially accelerate the rate of development of any organism beyond that set by the rate of expansion of the universe since I anticipate the two are interlinked.

These other more advanced civilisations will wait until we, or any other candidates who have reached the stage of joined up thought, are ready to join up into a large super intelligence. On this basis there is not a problem in finding life elsewhere in the universe: it is everywhere and will be hard to avoid in one form or another. This is based on the assumption that the self-ordering tendency exists to counter and eventually balance the effect of expansion and entropy. I also suppose it could be argued that in the early life of an expanding universe, not long perhaps after the big bang, entropy will be the overriding tendency at first.

So that deals with extraterrestrial life and those who anticipate that we shall have difficulty finding it elsewhere in the universe. If I extrapolate the position from when the human race gets its act together and links all its separate minds together, I conclude the following.

When human mental abilities have been developed by the group mind, the result would be that they would in time be capable of reaching out through space to contact other similarly developed minds. They would then be able to network with them and further develop their intellectual ability. If this could be done in an ordered and not too hasty manner the result would be the eventual existence of a vast system of combined intelligence and understanding. The next step in such a scenario that occurred to me was that such an entity would have an almost godlike capacity, especially as by the time this degree of connectedness had been achieved there could perhaps be a diminishing need for some form of corporeal identity. If so, I conjecture that there would be little need for such an advanced entity to be supported by a material physical system. If that could be done away with, then the result is effectively an all-seeing, all-understanding and even all-forgiving God, very much in line with the belief of a large number of religions, especially Christianity and Buddhism.

I also consider it likely, having taken a leaf out of Rupert Sheldrake's book on this subject that the rules of nature are probably not static but are evolving. If so, then why would not such an omnipotent intelligence hesitate to accelerate, moderate or alter such rules of nature that we take as given constants currently. Until recently there were a number of established constants of which light was perhaps the greatest, and most familiar, but there was also the important Cosmological constant, as well as a few others. But then in 1998 the astronomers discovered from observation of supernovae, the universe was apparently not only expanding which they had known since Hubble's observation in 1931, but the rate of expansion was increasing as well. In short, they had got it wrong implying it was a positive non zero value for which Saul Perlmutter's team were awarded the Noble prize in 2011. There are a number of other standard figures taken as constants but there is one less now and decades of mathematical discussion and predictions on the shape and characteristics about the nature of the universe changed overnight. I have to say this is one of my concerns about the nature of modern science: too much time and energy spent of algebraic theorising and figure work involving thousands of hours' production of learned papers and disputation by the academics involved, that suddenly becomes irrelevant once a particular new observation is made.

Within the expanding universe, life is duplicating itself constantly increasing its understanding of its own existence until it attains a state of being able to do what it wants with the universe of which it is a part, and not only a part, but possibly becoming the controlling interest. It occurs to me that such an omniscient life form, understanding how much suffering of its forebears' miserable earlier experiences had all been a necessary part of such evolution, it might well want to make amends for that. If I was part of such a system, then I would want all its component former life forms and sentient beings that had ever existed in the past to be able to see and properly understand how that, and they, had all been part of the way nature progressed. After all, the very existence of life is down to the fact that structures duplicate themselves and become more complex and more ordered as time passes. So how are we able to manage to justify existence as fair and equitable when there has been so much pain and suffering in the past?

At the moment as far as we know there is a problem in that astronomical observations have shown that the universe is expanding at an accelerating rate, and that this is driven by dark energy which they calculate makes up about 68.3% of the mass in the universe in terms of energy equivalence. In order to avoid the heat death of the universe where everything disappears out of sight, or possibly the Big Rip, where electrical and nuclear forces tear atoms apart, this giant combo intelligence would have to slow down such uncontrolled expansion. One answer is to make the assumption that when fully developed the super mind would be capable of doing this by psychokinesis.

This conjecture, for that is obviously what it is, that psychokinesis could be invoked, just like that, sounds far too convenient, even assuming that such ability existed. However, I shall proceed with the conjecture, why not? All the giant intellect has to do is to wait until it has developed enough to be capable of creating a hologram of the universe, which ex hypothesi it should will be capable of doing which is so accurate that it would be impossible to discern which is the real article and which the holographic image. Having reached that near singular state, the intellect consciously starts to slow down the expansion of the universe in its mental holoceptual form and the real thing should follow suit.

This may sound very farfetched but it corresponds in some way to a recent theory by Dutch physicist Erik Verlinde, whose thesis seems to indicate that gravitation is explained as an entropic force in which space is emergent through a holographic scenario. If the super intelligence requires to move the external object in accordance with its wishes, all it has to do is adjust the structure of the holocept and reality will follow. This would be so, ex hypothesi, simply because with such an accurate all-encompassing hologram neither is more real than the other. But if the mental image is then changed by intent and/or a palpable act of will, reality will follow to maintain the lowest energy state or maximum stability as described as one of the basic maxims of Duplication Theory.

Well, this is only a conjecture but it is at least consistent with the modus ponens constructed by DT, and it would represent a specific and explicable explanation of the destiny of us all as part of that great entity. Better still, it would effectively be a combination of all existing intelligent life, with all of its previous existences, and could be seen as a sort of judgment day once this stage is reached. Every individual and every moment of their separate existences will be available and exposed to all the rest. Nothing would be hidden, which is one of the conclusions of DT, in that everything experienced can be recalled, and not just by the individual who was originally involved. All those needlessly cruel and violent actions ever taken by any individuals would be understood in the light of their backgrounds, and the gene pool passed on to them by previous generations, which I suppose would be some sort of justification for so much individual stupidity and needless cruelty. Nevertheless, I imagine it would be suitably embarrassing for the individual former minds forming part of that huge intelligence to have their actions available for display in every single little graphic detail.

So then what? I reckon that this huge disembodied intelligence would not want the universe to go on expanding to the heat death that would otherwise occur if nothing else was done about it. A very unsatisfactory state of affairs and worse, it would not observe the requirements of everything being symmetrical that the scientists seem to consider an absolute must, and which seems intuitively sensible enough to me. In which case this intelligence would want to slow down the outward expansion, and then reverse it until the big crunch was achieved, and in doing so, time would need to be reversed (see *appendix 11* for an abbreviated paper on the nature of time). So once this super mind was comprehensive enough to be able to duplicate the universe with its own holocept, perfect in every detail, as I have said, it could then slow down the expansion of this holoceptual duplicate and the real one would duplicate its action to do the same.

One absorbing result of this scenario would be that each individual part of the super mind would be able to experience his or her own life in reverse, and observe, played out in front of them albeit backwards, all the crass mistakes and nonsense for which they were responsible. These embarrassments would not matter to the all-seeing and understanding super mind as a whole, but even so, each former individual as part would have this galling experience set before them. I see that as a sort of purgatory where the foolishness of their early existence is beholden to all with the accompanying subjective ability to see just how trivial their behaviour was. Not exactly a harsh physical penance, but one which would presumably be acutely embarrassing to the individual concerned with the knowledge that such information was accessible to every other entity that has ever existed. That might be some form of a downside to having been Hitler, Stalin or Genghis Khan, especially as such people seem to suffer worst from pride and ambition than any other failing.

This suggests that such an embarrassment is a universal solution or sort of compensation for an individual's appalling performance in life, which might not seem an adequate recompense for those that suffered. However, I am trying to describe the feelings of this omniscient intelligence system which is supremely understanding and empathetic. From personal experience I have to say that for me, apart from physical incompetence and actual pain, the worst form of mental suffering is the recollection of past events when I did something unforgiveable and so embarrassing, that I would rather forget, but cannot. How much worse would such a sentiment be for a part of a now hypersensitive being, had he been Stalin when alive? I think even his victims in their now supremely understanding capacity would feel horrified and sorry for the past stupidity and ignorance of such primitive human individuals, now comprising part of that combined intelligence and whose past performance is held up for all to perceive.

Well that at least is my attempt at solving the problem of pain and suffering, crime and punishment in this world. It may be delusionary but at least it is an answer of sorts to a problem on which I have never heard or read much of a satisfactory answer from anybody yet, other than the standard version of the righteous but oppressed shall sit on God's right hand on judgment day and variations on that theme. Good enough for some if they are prepared to rely on faith in their beliefs to carry them through, but if one can have a bit of a rationale to qualify the apparent unfairness of existence in order to dilute the need for blind faith to explain everything, then that has to be a good thing. It might seem a paltry reason for the reason for the universe to come into being, so it can then snuff itself out in order to maintain a nice symmetrical shape, but that is all I currently can suggest having considered over a number of decades the implications of the way in which mind and memory operate, assuming DT has a basis of probability.

Until somebody else comes up with any modus operandi for memory which explains and makes consistent such a large number of other phenomena which previously had been thought to be completely unconnected, it is at least a reasoned proposal. It is based on a background of by no means illogical observations derived from principles of physics, somewhat amended in parts, allied to some very striking recent experiments carried out on entanglement which are starting to turn current beliefs upside down.

I suppose I will continue to think along these lines, especially now I have this hypothesis of resonance, unless as I have said already, someone comes up with a simpler and better general alternative. The whole system seems pretty much all of a piece with so many phenomena brought together which have formerly not been capable of any reasonable clarity, at least not to my mind. Having little ability in mathematics, instead I have to be able to create mental images of how things might work. If some algebraic proof on which a theory is based is so complex, say string theory, that only a handful of top mathematicians and physicists have a grasp of it, then that is a warning sign for me. Whereas I would not presume to say it is wrong, I would say that it is probably incomplete and that some piece of the jigsaw is missing, or that some basic assumption on which the theory is based will be flawed, or both. For instance, my interpretation of the photon is very different to the established belief, much simpler, as is my explanation of gravitation and inertia.

As far as I know there is no accepted explanation for why mass resists acceleration. It is just what is observed to happen: no reason given at all, but presented as an observed fait accompli. Duplication Theory gives it a rationale in that structures resonate with themselves through time, and the more complex their composition, the stronger the resonance effect. This will result in a tendency to resist any external force that might act on such an object or structure. This is compounded by my postulate of the pressure exerted by the motion of the outward rim of the universe acting on any piece of matter within to resist any tendency to change its velocity or motion in a straight line (*appendix 10*).

I suppose it could be argued that DT's statement that similar structures tend to duplicate themselves through all time in one location is just as much a given fait accompli as saying mass has inertia and resists being moved, so why is it an improvement? It is because my answer seems deeper, given that it is a direct corollary and therefore tied in with the mechanism behind EM radiation, as well as being just the result of the simple observation that mass resists force. We know and see that similar actions tend to duplicate themselves through all space at one time in EM radiation.

This observation is so far reaching with applications to such a wide range of previously considered unconnected phenomena that it has to be more fundamental. I have always understood that it is the purpose of science to link together all phenomena under one basic explanation. There is this need to establish a TOE, or Theory of Everything, and under one heading or basic principle if at all possible. DT has not done that but it seems to me to have made a step in the right direction in that connects a few phenomena that were formerly thought very disparate. It also disposes of some current givens, which otherwise have to be accepted without adequate explanation for why they exist.

As for what happens after time reverses and all sentient beings as part of the super mind live through their former experience of existence with the benefit of full understanding of how and why it came to pass, I have no inkling. Start the whole shooting match over again in another universe which bounces out of the big crunch is the only rather insipid answer that occurs to me and that some form of existence and motion is better than nothing at all, which is not unlike some of the ancient Hindu teachings in the Vedanta.

Appendices

Appendix 1:
On the Significance of Singularity States

I use the word singularity state to describe a state or system the conclusion of which may be closely approached but can never be achieved and I use it in a number of different pursuits: gravitational singularities, mathematical and geometrical singularities, isolated and moveable singularities.

Some of the more obvious examples are light speed, absolute zero of temperature, the notion of infinity, black holes, the minimum intervals of Planck length and time. My first fundamental observation is that whenever a singularity state is ascertained or discovered, and increasingly close approaches are made towards that state, it becomes apparent that the laws of nature as they were formerly understood have to start to be radically amended, which observation I now expand and qualify below. The most obvious example and archetype of a singularity state is light speed. It is impossible for anything to do with mass to attain its velocity, but we have known since the early 20th century that although it cannot be achieved, when close approaches are made to that velocity, those very strange effects start to happen. Time slows down and mass starts to increase exponentially. This is familiar today to most but it was entirely unanticipated in 1900, and would not have been believed were it not for those early mathematical proofs and later experiments.

Another obvious singularity state is the absolute zero of temperature. This cannot be achieved but as it is approached, superconductivity and super fluidity effects start to become apparent, not anticipated before such close approaches were first made possible. The curious qualities of Bose-Einstein condensates which have been produced relatively recently at temperature very close to absolute zero are another example of weird effects resulting from such close approaches. A black hole would seem to be in a different category of singularity since it can certainly be approached, but it is not possible to discern what happens in its interior and it has to be assumed that the laws of nature as we are familiar with them will be very different within.

Then there are the more theoretical singularity states such as infinity and the definitions being derived from the latter such as parallel lines meeting at infinity, the fifth axiom of Euclid on which the fundamental laws of geometry were first based. Once the concept of infinity was first analysed constructively by Zeno and Anaximander to start to develop mathematics and that ability to the point where Leibniz speculated about infinite numbers and produced his infinitesimal calculus as a result. Once Planck, rather to his surprise, discovered that it was impossible for dimensions of time and space to exist below a certain dimensions, the whole concept of physical science started to change radically and is still causing concern due to the consequent lack of full understanding of Quantum theory: another example of the discovery of a singularity state changing the laws of nature as they were then understood. I suppose it might be considered just coincidence that whenever a new singularity state is ascertained, and close approaches made thereto, that sometimes anomalous effects become apparent, requiring established known laws of nature to be amended. This has to be wrong, and a reasonable conclusion is that whenever we register a new such approachable yet unattainable singularity state, then we should expect to meet with surprising side effects as a matter of course.

One of the most challenging conundrums in physics at the moment is why the rate of rotation of the stars in elliptical galaxies is not in accord with the laws of motion as we currently understand them. The possible presence of dark matter indeed has been put forwarded as one of the possible answers, but again it seems possible that some sort of singularity state is at play here which once registered might open up a new vista of a crucial part of scientific understanding. This mystery must obviously be resolved if advances are to be made in the understanding of the universe, and this required advance has been signaled by yet another singularity state. The most striking examples of these that occur to me are: superposition in quantum theory, renormalisation in quantum electrodynamics, the existence of dark matter, and why gravitation still eludes reconciliation with the other three fundamental forces, and quantum mechanics. These are all well-known problems yet to be resolved to everybody's satisfaction.

This indicates to me that wherever there is some doubt and obfuscation about circumstances which are not yet clearly explicable, then there will probably be an as yet unidentified singularity state lurking about. This might not always be so, but as far as I am concerned, that is the case in the operation of memory, and from that, much of the mind's operation in general terms. Research being done by a few physicists and neuroscientists on the latter seems to indicate that they are getting close to recognising the possible role of quantum entanglement in the mind. One crucial element of the theory and experimental work in quantum entanglement is the importance of randomicity (a word I prefer to the clumsier randomness), which I reckon is a new and crucial singularity state although I dare say others have reached that conclusion via a different route.

My postulate is that since it is obviously possible to have varying degrees of randomicity, it is then impossible for a system to attain perfect randomicity. But when close approaches are made to that singularity state, for that is what it is, unfamiliar effects should begin to be experienced which currently cannot easily be accounted for. The case of memory the unexpected spin off effect is that complex structures, similar to near quantum level, have an increasing ability to resonate (duplicate themselves and their ensuing actions) across both time and space) provided the initial surrounding circumstances were capable of near perfect randomness. What has caught my attention within the last couple of years is that recent experiments carried out on quantum entanglement are reliant on the systems involved being able to run absolutely randomly.

The way in which this entanglement can be rationalised mathematically is by reference to Bell's inequality theorem, the maths of which is well beyond my grasp, but which theorem has come to be recognised as a major paradigm of 20th century physics. It seems that for photons which have been entangled and are later any distance apart, certain of their characteristics of these two separate photons such as their spin or polarisation, once one is ascertained, then the state of the other is instantly also determined and known. It thus appears that one particle of an entangled pair "knows" what measurement has been performed on the other, and with what outcome, even though there is no known means for such information to be communicated between the particles. In short there is instant communication between the two separate entities not limited by any notion of the limiting speed of light. Such an astonishing result has smacks of having the potential to introduce a new a paradigm or at least of changing the way physicists approach their subject: a veritable cat amongst the pigeons.

Further to experiments carried out initially in laboratories by Alain Aspect of France in 1982 and others later, Anton Zeilinger demonstrated in 2012 instant communication between observatories more than 140 kilometres apart between the Canary Islands. This has now been updated by experiments in China in 2017 carrying out the same sort of experiments between satellites and observatories on the Earth. The crucial part in this for me is that Zeilinger's book 'The dance of the Photons' explains how this teleporting process is totally reliant on the systems at either end of the transmission process being able to act as randomly as possible. At the risk of repetition, the following attempts a brief description of the significance of Bell's theorems and the experimental results based thereon. It is possible for two objects such as photons or matter particles to enter into an exotic condition called entanglement, in which their states become so utterly interdependent that if a measurement to determine the property of one, the corresponding property of the other is instantaneously known, even if the two objects are separated by huge distances. This result was anticipated by physicist John Bell in his 1964 inequality theorem, and has been proved experimentally correct over the last two decades. It is quite clear the theory and the experimental results require that the source of the generated entangled particles must be random and also that the measurement device or detector at the receiving end must also act completely randomly. These experiments have to be carried out with quantum random number generators: the results are not satisfactory if the equipment involved cannot operate in a purely random manner.

In 1978 I attempted an explanation for the operation of memory in that it might be possible to transfer information across time if two structures were similar to almost quantum levels, although I had not heard of quantum entanglement as presumably not many had 40 years ago. It was only in 2016 that I started to try to understand the mechanism behind quantum entanglement, after which I was struck by the similarity of the principle involved to that on which duplication theory was based. One of the crucial assumptions of my theory is that perfect randomicity is an unattainable singularity state but that when close approaches are made thereto, the laws of nature with which we are currently familiar need to be amended in order to be better understood.

By late 1979 I had set out in a brief draft paper the principles of this theory (more correctly hypothesis) in an attempt to demonstrate that a structure at one moment in time will start to resonate and interact with a later structure if it were similar to a point of near singularity on the further assumption that the surroundings of the two structures were similar, or as relatively similar as possible in an expanding universe. If this was the case then it provided an explanation in principle how information in the form of a structure of firing neurons, a particular thought or perhaps a recorded visual image, might be transferred from an earlier to a later time in the brain. In short it would be possible to explain perfect recall by a system of resonance. The conclusions of duplication theory transpired to be remarkably similar to those of biochemist Rupert Sheldrake's hypothesis or morphic resonance to explain formative causation in the way cells develop, as set out in his first book published in 1981, which I read in 1984, albeit from a very different approach.

The thought process to arrive at an explanation for the mechanism behind memory was briefly as follows. I had observed on a number of occasions that in a state of hypnotic trance, individuals were capable of not only perfect recall but also of being regressed to some earlier period in their existence to appear to be reliving it moment by moment. Whatever was going on in such hypnotic trances, it was clear that there was a very different mindset involved than was in normal consciousness, and one in which the subject could demonstrate capabilities out of the ordinary. Having read a fair amount about the subject, I made the assumption that when in the trance state, until the subject had been requested to carry out some specific instruction, that part of the brain that controlled consciousness would be totally relaxed, effectively blank and not registering actions of the external world observed through the senses.

Since the firing of brain's synapses between neurons never cease their action, then in trance state they would have to continue their motion passing electrochemical impulses between the neurons, and this action would therefore have to be random, without form or order. I was then able to apply this assumption to general observations on the nature of singularity states, which I had already subjectively defined as a condition where close approaches in nature might be made but never achieved. As already set out above, I had concluded that whenever a new singularity state was ascertained, bizarre side effects might be expected.

When considering that in trance the neurons of the brain controlling consciousness were firing in random motion, it suddenly occurred to me that here was possibly another singularity state. There have to be increasing degrees of near perfect randomicity, so that if two similar brains, one in the future, the other in the past, were both exhibiting states of near perfect randomicity, they would be effectively identical, or as identical as it was possible to be at different times. If they were strikingly near perfect duplicates of each other then it might not be unreasonable on the premise conjectured above to suppose that there might be observed some unexpected side effects, probably not yet acknowledged to exist by established scientific beliefs.

There is an explanation in more detail on my website using the Heisenberg's uncertainty principle (and also Pauli's exclusion principle) to justify why it is impossible to have two absolutely identical structures existing at the same time or indeed at any other time: another singularity state in short. But as close approaches are made to perfect duplication they start to interact at different times as if they were the same identity. I also realised that the firing the neurons and synapses would cause billions of electrochemical currents to flow between them within the brain and this would have to create complex interference patterns. If it was assumed that these patterns were highly ordered, then it was not impossible that their structure could effectively be the cause of holographic images projected out beyond the brain. This possibility was first suggested to me by the work of neuroscientist Karl Pribram who worked closely with eminent physicist David Bohm on consciousness. This would present a simple model for the operation of mechanism of memory and thought, and I was also to devise a simple possible answer for the way such images were experienced, but again any interested party will have to read the paper or the website for that.

When I first came up with such a scenario in the late 1970s, I had not heard about quantum entanglement and arrived at this general conclusion via a somewhat different route as a resonance basis. Quantum entanglement as first anticipated by John Bell's inequality theorem has now been demonstrated by Anton Zeilinger and others to transfer information (or rather correlated information) instantaneously over many kilometres, and I now understand a little more clearly that this process is totally reliant on the systems at either end being able to act as randomly as possible. My hypothesis for the working of memory is based on a surprisingly similar premise which I would like to think was not coincidental. Since there is not yet any rationale of how memory operates, none at all of any demonstrable viability, as far as I am aware, I find this encouraging.

Nick Greaves
ResearchGate
November 2017, abbreviated March 2019

Appendix 2 – Letter from Arthur Koestler (1978)

8 MONTPELIER SQUARE,
LONDON, SW7 IJU
01-589 6700.

June 15th, 1978

Dear Mr. Greaves,

I find your speculative essay most attractive and since you ask my opinion, I should certainly advise carrying on with it. The idea that bits of mass should have a sort of romantic longing to occupy one and the same place appeals to me very much, but I can't grasp intuitively the suggestion that the next best thing for a frustrated bit of mass is to duplicate itself. However, I may have misunderstood.

I am afraid I cannot go into more detail because I have such a vast input of books, offprints and manuscripts sent to me that to enter into correspondence would leave no time for any other output.

With kind regards, and best wishes for your continued work,

Yours sincerely,

A. Koestler

Arthur Koestler

Appendix 3 – Letter from Arthur Koestler (1979)

8 MONTPELIER SQUARE,
LONDON, SW7 1JU
01-589 6700.

February 20th, 1979

Dear Mr. Greaves,

Thank you for your letter of January 31st and the essay.

I found it immensely stimulating and particularly liked your resonance hypothesis. But I am of course no physicist and not qualified to judge. I have a hunch though that David Bohm may react positively, if you send him a copy.

With best wishes,

A. Koestler

Arthur Koestler

Appendix 4 – Letter from Karl Pribram (1979)

STANFORD UNIVERSITY
STANFORD, CALIFORNIA 94305

DEPARTMENTS OF PSYCHOLOGY AND OF
PSYCHIATRY AND BEHAVIORAL SCIENCES

NEUROPSYCHOLOGY LABORATORIES
JORDAN HALL

July 23, 1979

Nicholas Greaves
175 Sussex Gardens
London, W.2
England

Dear Dr. Greaves:

Thank you very much for yours of June 21st. I spent considerable time going over your manuscript and have the following comments to make. First and foremost, you have thought deeply and surprisingly well regarding the problems that you raise. I, too, am not qualified to handle the physics that you cover, and knowing David Bohm, I doubt that he is answering any mail, but I may be in error here. Perhaps you can find some other physicist friend who will take a look at the manuscript.

My own uninformed opinion is that the manuscript, as now written, is somewhat rambling and that you could say things more succinctly if you choose to revise. Just as an example, you point out that as objects begin to reach the speed of light that strange things begin to happen, and in one place even point out what these strange things are. This is of course nothing more than the Doppler Effect which we know so well in the realm of sound and we also know that we now can penetrate the sound barrier. The big question is what lies on the other side of the light barrier if anything. This is just an example.

With regard to the basic duplication theory, I think what you are saying is so, but that a more sophisticated form of it might be in Leibnitz's monadology or Gabor's holograms. Duplication is there, but in a highly nested form. That is, the whole is contained in every part. This does not as yet answer the question of how we transform from the ordinary domain to the holographic domain, and this is where Prigogine may come in.

Finally, I did find some of the things you said about brain function just a bit on the wooly side, but certainly in the right direction. Might I suggest that you take a look at Languages of the Brain which is now out in paperback and available from Brooks/Cole. I am enclosing an order blank for Languages and reprints of more recent articles so that you can see how my own thinking has been developing.

Appendix 4 (continued)

Dr. Greaves
July 23, 1979
page two

I do think you have written a most interesting piece and found your writing style to be superb. There are many quotations that you have gathered together that would be most useful to me in my teaching. In short, you have done an excellent piece of scholarship, and with some revision and bringing up-to-date it might well be worth publishing.

Sincerely,

Karl H. Pribram

KHP:lmcl
enclosures

Appendix 5 – Correspondence with Rupert Sheldrake

Nick Greaves to Rupert Sheldrake dated: March 18, 1983

"I have at last got hold of a copy of your book, and almost finished it. It is of course excellent, and anyone with half a brain should be able to see that there has to be something in what you say. Personally, I say a great deal more than that, and my only criticism is that you do not go far enough developing your theme and the consequence of your speculation. Not only do I agree with what you say, but I have developed almost exactly the same theme only approached from a completely different angle, and I have attached a few extracts from a paper I wrote for my own amusement in 1978/9. I call it duplication theory, but I nearly called it resonance theory........

I was staggered when I read your book. My reaction was that here is Sheldrake saying that there must be this morphogenetic field which causes things to repeat themselves in certain circumstances, and which acts through time and at a distance, and here am I, not only suggesting the same thing, however clumsily, but furthermore, giving an explanation for such a field's operation in terms of principles of quantum theory. You simply must read what I have to say: I am sure that I am not far from a version of the truth, as no doubt you are, and I am equally sure that your ideas are complementary to mine. Mine are far more detailed, and far wider, but hopelessly expressed as far as the academic world is concerned.

You are the first biologist/biochemist I have approached, and I await any response with interest. Physicists I find are infuriatingly blinkered, to the extent that although I am confident enough about the validity in general terms of my work, I am certainly not at all confident about how long it will be before any serious acceptance might be gained. I have almost resigned myself to having to wait for someone else to come along to come up with the same ideas and to express them more convincingly than I can, in the correct academese. Still, Kepler managed without the jargon of the time. I hope this finds you: I understand you are in England currently. Yours sincerely, Nick Greaves"

Sheldrake replied very promptly by return dated: Nov 3, 1983

"Many thanks for your letter and your writings in duplication theory. In essence, it is indeed similar to the theory I am putting forward; and you explore many of the same areas. It seems we must have been writing at much the same time (1978-79, when I was drafting my book in India). So, ex hypothesi we may well have had some influence on each other....... I included a more extended discussion a more extended discussion on ritual, but removed this as unnecessary for presentation of the main ideas. I too am fascinated by inertia and suggest (on page 119, note 4) an idea similar to the one in the main text of your theory. This seems different from your later speculation along Machian lines, which I find less convincing.......... I have to say that interesting and suggestive though your essay is, I don t think you will have much chance of getting it published. I myself had the advantage of academic credentials, 3 1/2 years to devote myself to full time writing and rewriting, comments by over 100 scientists, philosophers, personal contacts with people in the publishing world etc. But in spite of all that my book was rejected by 12 publishers before I finally got it accepted by Blond and Briggs. Perhaps the best bet would be to work out some particular aspects in detail for publication as articles in open minded magazines."

Appendix 6 – Brief Summary of Morphic Resonance

Here is an extract of Sheldrake's introduction, which forms an excellent definition of the problem he tackles:

"At present, the orthodox approach to biology is given by the mechanistic theory of life: living organisms are regarded as physico-chemical machines, and all the phenomena of life are considered to be explicable in principle in terms of physics and chemistry. This mechanistic paradigm is by no means new; it has been dominant for over a century. The fact that this approach has resulted in spectacular successes such as the 'cracking of the genetic code' is a strong argument in its favour. Nevertheless, critics have put forward what appear to be good reasons for doubting that all phenomena of life, including human behaviour, can ever be explained entirely mechanistically. (Russell 1945; Elasser 1958; Polyani 1958; Beloff 1962; Koestler 1962; Lenartowicz 1975; Popper and Eccles 1977; Thorpe 1978) ....

The most important organismic theory put forward so far is that of morphogenetic fields (Weiss 1939). These fields are supposed to help account for, or describe, the coming-into-being of the characteristic forms of embryos and other developing systems. The concept of morphogenetic fields can be of practical scientific value only if it leads to testable predictions which differ from those of the conventional mechanistic theory. And such predictions cannot be made unless morphogenetic fields are considered to have measurable effects.

The hypothesis put forward in this book is based on the idea that morphogenetic fields do indeed have measurable physical effects. It proposes that specific morphogenetic fields are responsible for the characteristic form and organisation of systems at all levels of complexity, not only in the realm of biology, but also in the realms of chemistry and physics. These fields order the systems which, from an energetic point of view, appear to be indeterminate or probabilistic; they impose patterned restrictions on the energetically possible outcomes of physical processes. If morphogenetic fields are responsible for the organisation and form of material systems, they must have characteristic structures. So where do these field-structures come from? The answer is suggested that they are derived from the morphogenetic fields associated with previous systems: The morphogenetic fields of all past systems become present to any subsequent similar systems by a cumulative influence which acts across both space and time.

According to this hypothesis, systems are organised in the way they are because similar systems were organised that way in the past. For example. the molecule of a complex organic chemical crystallises in a characteristic pattern because the same substance crystallised that way before; a plant takes up the form characteristic of its species because past members of the species took up that form; and an animal acts instinctively in a particular manner because similar animals behaved like that previously. This hypothesis is concerned with the repetition of forms and patterns of organisation; the question of the origins of these forms and patterns lies outside its scope. This question can be answered in several different ways, but all of them seem to be equally compatible with the suggested means of repetition."

In his first chapter Sheldrake points out a number of unsolved problems in biology, where an organicist approach using these morphogenetic fields could provide satisfactory answers. These problems are morphogenesis, evolution, behaviour, the origin of life, psychology, and parapsychology

In Sheldrake's third chapter, the causes of form are discussed, and the concept of causative formation introduced:

"The hypothesis of formative causation proposed that morphogenetic fields play a causal role in the development and maintenance of the forms of system at all levels of complexity. In this context, the word 'form' is taken to include not only the shape of the outer surface or boundary of a system, but also its internal structure."

In the fifth chapter, 'The Influence of Past Form' he introduces the concept of morphic resonance, which more or less states the principle of my space duplication thus:

"A resonant effect of form upon form across time and space would resemble energetic resonance in its selectivity, but it could not be accounted for in its terms of any of the known types of resonance, nor would it involve the transmission of energy. In order to distinguish it from energetic resonance, this process will be called morphic resonance. Morphic resonance is analogous to energetic resonance in a further respect: it takes place between vibrating systems. Atoms, molecules, crystals, organelles, cell tissues, organs, and organisms are all made of parts in ceaseless oscillation and all have their own characteristic patterns of vibration and internal rhythm; the morphic units are dynamic, not static...... What is being suggested here is that by morphic resonance the form of a system, including its characteristic internal structure and vibrational frequencies, becomes present to a subsequent system with similar form; the spatio-temporal pattern of the former superimposes itself on the latter. Morphic resonance takes place though morphogenetic fields and indeed gives rise to their characteristic structures. Not only does a specific morphogenetic field influence the form of a system (as discussed in a previous chapter) but also the form of this system influences the morphogenetic field and through it becomes present to subsequent similar systems."

In summarising his hypothesis, Sheldrake goes on to point out that:

"All similar systems act upon a subsequent similar system by morphic resonance. This action is provisionally assumed not to be attenuated by time or space, and to continue indefinitely; however, the relative effect of a given system declines as the number of similar systems contributing to morphic resonance increases. The hypothesis of formative causation accounts for the repetition of forms but does not explain how the first example of any given forms originally came into being. This unique event can be ascribed to chance or a creativity inherent in matter, or to a transcendent creative agency. A decision between these alternatives can be made only on metaphysical grounds and lies outside the scope of this hypothesis........ The most frequent type of previous form makes the greatest contribution by morphic resonance, the least frequent, the least: morphogenetic fields are not precisely defined but are represented by probability structures which depend on the statistical distribution of previous similar forms. The probability distributions of electronic orbits described by solutions of the Schrodinger equation are examples of such probability structures, and are similar in kind to the probability structures of morphogenetic fields of morphic units at higher levels."

The above should serve to give some ideas of the similarities of our ideas and the completely different directions from which they were derived.

Appendix 7 – Correspondence with Art Chester (1984)

Correspondence with Art Chester, Laser Physicist from 12/01/84

Having read a paper by Art Chester late 1983 with a few copy extracts of a paper at that time, and after having read his paper on similarity, which had a number of points similar with Duplication theory, although his work was mainly maths based and fairly impenetrable to me in that respect. He replied on 12/01/84 at length over 8 closely typed pages a few extracts are copied below.

"It is difficult to know where to begin. I am not put off by your lack of physics training. Indeed, it seems to me that you have read very widely and have done an incredibly good job of synthesizing concepts from far and wide. The sheer scope of your considerations takes my breath away. At the same time, I recognise that my own approach to this many faceted thing we call Truth is rather different, and comes abot because of my training in theoretical physics. Modern physics does such a neat job of dealing with measurable phenomena (and of course defines itself in terms of measurable phenomena) that my knowledge of its successes prejudices me strongly to work on theories that don't disagree with modern physics.

I tend to think of 'reality' as being strongly subjective, and I would not argue for my more mathematical approach in favour of your more conceptual one. This subjectivity I mean in two senses: one philosophical, in the sense that truths can be perceived which lie totally outside the current scientific paradigm (in the sense of Kuhn's Structure of Scientific revolutions), and the other physical, in the sense that different observers occupy different parallel universe and may validly perceive the truth in different ways. ---- Although all objective measurements will find them in agreement......

However, I did not want to replace the known laws of physics which seem to work so well. What I wanted was a way in principle to permit ESP phenomena to exist, wedged if you like, in the cracks between our laws of physics, but not violating them. I can't tell you that I "believe" in telepathy and such, but it seems more plausible to me to accept its existence than to argue that years of dedicated investigation have been conducted by frauds and nitwits: it also seems a way to accommodate the coincidences we observe in everyday life which just might lie outside the boundaries of chance.

It took me 12 years of part time work at home to find way of expressing my simple principle mathematically without having its predictions clearly violate every day physical reality. To write down all the mathematics and explain it took 300 pages which probably no mathematician will trouble to read (because they do not have a compulsion to accommodate ESP) and non-mathematician will fully appreciate. The article you have read is the most detailed explanation that anyone is willing to publish, and at least describes the general principles. However, I, if your curiosity extends so far, I'll gladly send you a copy of the full write up. It does not have the scope of yours, but just as yours, the implications of the theory extend far beyond the realm of ESP which is used to formulate it. As you point out yourself, introducing any pattern-dependent principle which is independent of time and space radically changes our understanding of everything, -- it is necessary to think quite carefully to pick up most of the implications and check their consistency with what we know.........

Let me lay off from this discussion of my own work and give instead my impressions of the relationship between yours, mine, and Sheldrake's. In your work, it seems to me, that the real strength is in the breadth of concepts, the intuitive coupling of very diverse phenomena (biological, physical, astronomical, cosmic, atomic, mind, Newtonian, relativistic) and the recognition of possibly related patterns in widely separated places. Its weakness is its lack of mathematical formulation (which would permit quantitative predictions) and you interest in applying the theory in every possible place (even those where adequate explanations may already exist).

In Sheldrake's work, the strength is in its systematic coupling of a number of phenomena which seem to depend on replication of a pattern in space or time and in his forthright predictions of testable implications. His weakness lies in a treatment of mechanism that is infuriatingly vague to a physicist (it makes me suspect that he would predict things we just don't see). If I were knowledgeable in biology which I'm not, I suspect that I'd also be bothered by his total rejection of the adequacy of genetic-biogenetic-biochemical mechanisms in development. These mechanisms are probably more robust and capable of accounting for observations than he gives them credit for. In my own work, the strength is in its mathematical concreteness and its full consistency with conventional physical laws in the limit of simple patterns or isolated particle. Its weakness lies in the mathematical complexity (probably too complex to be correct, or at least needing another form of expression), its 'untestability' by conventional scientific means (despite its ability to make mathematical predictions) and its neglect of possible applications in biology and cosmology.......

Frankly I do not know how to find my way through this thicket of differences. If Sheldrake's theory is indeed undergoing experimental test, that is good. A clear positive proof would vindicate him and probably you as well and certainly stand science on its head. My own theory predicts that such tests will be as elusive and no-repeatable as the evidence in parapsychological studies---suggestive enough to probe the case for sympathetic observers, and inadequate to change the minds of sceptics. If that's the case, as I expect, there is no chance for a radical shift in the world's view of itself until much more work is done, or until an unexpected factor changes our paradigm completely."

Art's next six pages methodically go through my paper to make suggestions and corrections in an amazingly thorough and considerate manner. He very much liked my explanation memory and intuition, which was a source of pleasure to me, and the reason why I started work to find an answer to specifically this problem in 1978.

Appendix 8 – Letter from Henry Margenau (1979)

Yale University New Haven, Connecticut 06520

PHYSICS DEPARTMENT
217 Prospect Street

November 5, 1979

Mr. Nicholsa Greaves
5 Upper Culham
Near Wargrave-on-Thames
Berkshire, England

Dear Mr. Greaves:

Your manuscript is fascinating and enormous in scope. While I have not read it in its entirety, perhaps I have understood enough of it to make the following comments.

You are aware, I am sure, of its discursive character and of its lack of mathematical precision, which will make it difficult to have it published. Nevertheless, the range it covers recommends that it be presented to public view.

I will not criticise your fundamental postulates, for they are not stated in a sufficiently precise form. But your duplication theory has appeal, especially since it attempts to explain phenomena of consciousness. Let me, therefore, set down a few marginal comments for your consideration.

A physicist would not accept your description of the movement of electrons in a current carrying wire.

Free electrons do have a rest mass.

You often use the term "free energy" in a non-technical sense.

Electrons and photons (I call them onta) are neither particles nor waves. Enitities too small to be seen need not have visualizable properties.

What is meant by "degree of spin"?

Action at a distance does occur in modern physics: cf. the behavior of electrons in obedience to the exclusion principle.

Memory is a conscious process, information in the technical sense is not.

Fechner's statement of the causal principle is wrong. The relation between brain processes and consciousness is not illuminated by duplication theory.

Time forbids me to give detailed reasons for these remarks. However, you will find each one discussed in my published books.

Yours sincerely,

H. Margenau

Henry Margenau

HM/lf

Appendix 9 – Brief Summary of Duplication Theory

Brief summary and aide memoire of Duplication Theory and some of its Applications

The brain is composed of complex networks of interconnected neurons, dendrites, synapses, axons and it is not known how these operate to comprise thought, vision and cognition. DT assumes that electrochemical currents involved create interference patterns which form holographic images which are projected in 3 dimensions from the brain. Some of these are experienced as vision (sight) via the retinas, memory and thought in different degrees of detail and intelligibility, but being led by the visual sense.

Pattern and order are no more than repetition of similar intervals in space which can be perceived out of former randomness. Once a structure thus created becomes established, then form manifests itself where there was formerly nothing but disorder and chaos.

A singularity state is defined as a circumstance to which close approaches may be made but never be achieved. Examples of such states are light speed, infinity, and absolute zero of temperature, the Planck dimensions of minimum time and space which cannot be achieved. By observation it is clearly apparent that whenever a new singularity state is ascertained, the laws of nature and physics have to be amended to accommodate the new behaviour patterns that result.

Two structures can never be exactly identical due to the Uncertainty principle which shows that two particles with mass can never occupy exactly the same space at the same time, perfect penetrability, in line with Heisenberg's

Uncertainty principle. It is impossible for an observer to be certain of the precise location of any small particle in motion because it takes time for light to travel from a particle to an observer. A familiar and equivalent example of an approach to near perfect penetrability of two particles is the fusion of two hydrogen molecules to convert to one of helium to occupy, resulting in the conversion of a small amount of their combined original mass being converted into EM radiation.

The contention of DT is that an equivalent process results when close approaches are made to perfect duplication of similar structures at different times and/or at different locations. In other words, a resonance effect starts to manifest with the ability to duplicate or correlate such similar actions through both time and space. The conversion of the mass of a later structure identical to an earlier one never occurs since the particles of both systems are in constant motion and the minimum energy principle will instead bring about a continuing sequence of the earlier actions instead.

If two separate but very similar systems of particles are considered, each in similar states of random motion, then although they will never be identical, as each approached perfect randomness, they would start to make close approaches to perfect duplicates of each other. Such perfect duplication would be a singularity state which ex hypothesi would tend to bring about side effects not currently familiar or easily explicable. One result would be that if a specific ordered structure is suddenly inserted into one random system, then another system at a distance, similar to almost quantum levels would tend to duplicate or resonate with that other structure. This is because it is not possible to have two such identical structures, but which they will attempt to achieve do in order to satisfy the minimum energy principle.

It is posited that this is why the Eastern sages and mystics spent a major part of their lives attempting to empty their conscious minds of thought and intention in order to ensure the neurons, dendrites and other networks of the brain fire as closely as possible to perfect random motion. It is certainly evident from observation that a mind under hypnotic trance has capabilities very different from possessed in usual everyday waking state. Thus, it is possible that once a stream of recollection of past events is instigated via a molecular stimulus, described as engrams and with little doubt similar to DNA molecules capable of huge storage ability, acting as an initial prompt. This would provide long term memory flow with no need for physical storage other than the initial prompt, and then everyday working memory would be a series of curtailed such sequences to remind the proponent of what had occurred in the past similar circumstances and how they might best be dealt with in the near future, enhancing future survival.

As a result, it is postulated that intuition works best when the mind is firing randomly with little intent or purpose in mind. It is then more likely to be able more able to duplicate accurately circumstances as they occur in nature and the external world, that had been perhaps the subject of an earlier unsuccessful attempt to resolve a connected problem on which much time had been spent fruitlessly sorting out almost innumerable combinations and permutations of possible alternatives..

Appendix 10 -
Inertia, Gravitation, and the Absorber Theory

In 2010 I drafted three very speculative papers together as variations on a theme, abridged as follows:

Synopsis Paper One

This conjectures how it appears possible to reconcile gravitation and inertia with Mach's Principle. Some assumptions have to be made. The first is that the universe is closed and finite, expanding out equally in all directions as a sphere, and that the distribution of mass is not uniform therein but that there is a large preponderance moving near light velocity at the outer edge with much smaller quantities of matter closer to the centre point moving out far less rapidly as one might expect from visualising the motions of a big bang explosion. The effect of large amounts of mass near the outside edge moving out at near light velocity enhances the gravitational effect relativistically to strongly affect the motion of all matter further within. This is the universal effect demonstrated by Mach's Principle and Foucault's pendulum, and which also suggests a simple rationalisation of inertia.

The assumption here is that matter near the edge will be travelling at close to light velocity, so there would be far larger concentrations of matter distributed nearer the rim as far as an observer within, much closer to the big bang centre, due to the relativistic effects hugely increasing its mass.

The mass of the outer edge galaxies would be relativistically huge if they were travelling at near light velocity in relation to galaxies further in moving out at much lower velocities, regardless of whether the matter distribution was homogeneous or not. The attractive force of gravitation exercised by this vast mass moving out would be experienced by all lesser matter within. If there were to be some force tending to accelerate the motion of the latter away from their motion in a straight line, they would experience a pressure against this: inertia. Such a scenario appears at first sight to satisfy Mach's principle. Mach never defined in specific sentences his principle, although its most graphic verbal form attributed to him was "When the subway jerks, it's the fixed stars that throw you down." His principle can be defined in simple terms as follows: 'Every particle of matter in the universe, and its motion, has an effect on every other particle elsewhere in the universe.'

Thus, the very substantial quantities of matter near the periphery moving very rapidly outward and certainly well beyond the limits of visibility from Earth, would exercise a huge attractive effect on all matter further within the universe. If for instance the attractive effect of just one nearby section of the universe on, say the Earth, were considered, and if the inverse square law were invoked, this would be exactly countered by the much large section at the opposite end of the universe, albeit it so much further distant. In Diagram 1 the forces from opposing sides of the universe are shown to balance out on a stellar mass two thirds of the distance from the centre. In short there would be equilibrium of all such forces of attraction assuming the matter were moving at a constant velocity rather than accelerating.

Such a scenario would be the basis for a revised definition for Mach's Principle, and it would also deliver a basis for the concept of inertia to be redefined. The force of attraction of the vast masses near the periphery would be equal in all directions (inverse square law), and would act on all matter within the universe so that their initial motion expanding outwards would be unaffected whilst at constant velocity, but which would resist any acceleration so that the effect of inertia would be inextricably intertwined with the attractive force of gravitation. There would be no effect of inertia without the existence of the huge hidden mass of the universe expanding out near its periphery.

Figure 1

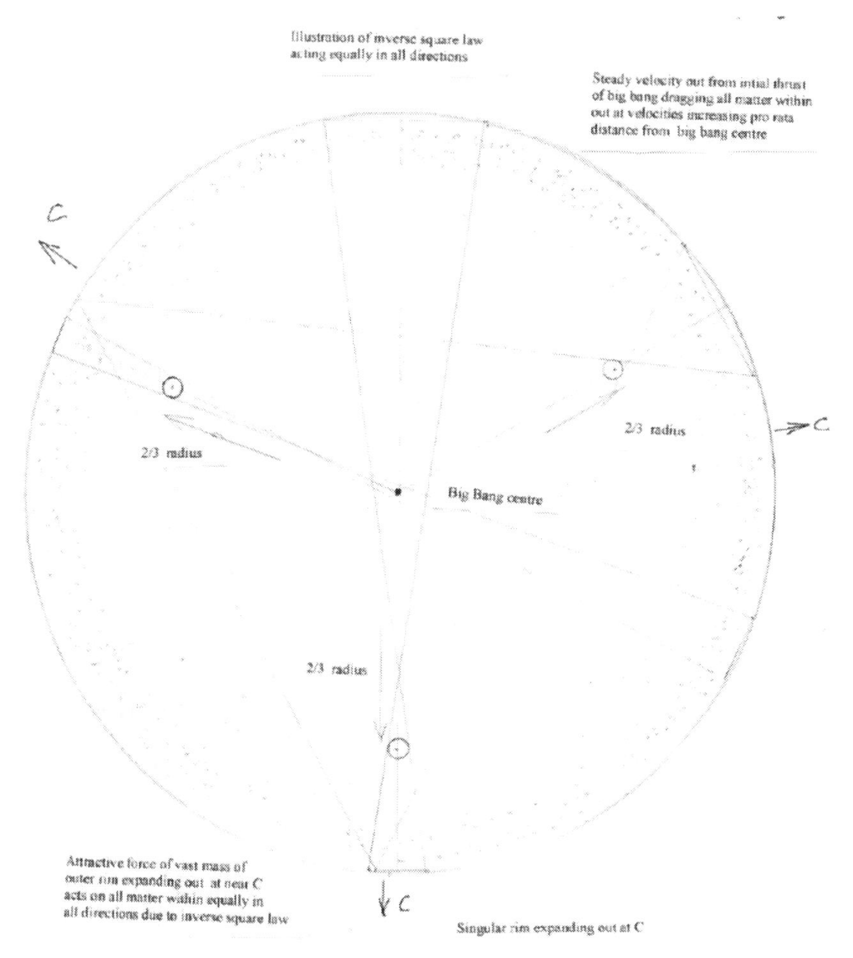

Since this conjecture relies on the fundamental assumption that the universe if closed and finite, I will conclude by a quote from Einstein in an address to the Berlin Academy of Sciences in 1921:

> I must not fail to mention that a theoretical argument can be adduced in favour of the hypothesis of a finite universe. The general theory of relativity teaches that the inertia of a given body is greater as there are more ponderable masses in proximity to it; thus, it seems very natural to reduce the total effect of inertia of a body to action and reaction between it and the other bodies in the universe... From the general theory of relativity, it can be deduced that this total reduction of inertia to reciprocal action between masses - as required by E. Mach, for example - is possible only if the universe is spatially finite. On many physicists and astronomers this argument makes no impression.

Synopsis Paper Two

A further assumption is made here that there is an edge to the bounded universe expanding out at light velocity from the original big bang burst of radiation energy, beyond which is singularity without dimensions of time or space: another continuum. A further assumption is made that the velocity of any source of EM radiation will be drawn out in all directions to exactly duplicate the outward action of this large singular rim. This renders the universe to appear isotropic and homogenous to an observer based within the universe on any planet system moving out, whereas viewed externally this would not be the case which reinforces the argument set out in part one, this being contrary to current evidence suggested by the cosmic microwave background. An implication of such a scenario is that were the rate of expansion of the universe to alter so would then light velocity. The Absorber Theory is then briefly explained which requires for its operation that the universe be enclosed in an opaque container, which would be a result of a finite and closed universe. Similarities of the Absorber Theory with the current subject proposals are discussed along with some crucial differences. The variation and possible reversal of the expansion of the universe with the implications for passage of time and the retention of symmetry are proposed.

The eminent Oxford mathematician Arthur Milne controversially argued that under Einstein's special relativity it was impossible for an expanding universe to have homogeneous matter distribution. He also proposed the universe does have an outside edge, and that the whole universe was created at a single point in flat space-time, and thereafter occupies the interior of a bubble that expands at the speed of light into previously empty space. This Milne model is also isotropic so that there was no difference between the fast-moving galaxies near the rim and galaxies at rest near the centre of the bubble, since any galaxy and its neighbourhood will subjectively appear to the occupants to be at the centre by the Lorentz transformation. This is remarkably similar to the assumptions made in the first section above. An implication is that if this outside edge is moving out at light speed its time will not have changed since the moment of big bang: no time will have passed. Together with the assumptions made in the first paper, if two further are made, then the behaviour of Electromagnetic radiation can be qualified in a manner in many respects similar to the results of the Absorber Theory by Wheeler and Feynman in 1945. The first assumption is that there is an outside edge to the finite universe formed of radiation that was first emitted at the initial moment of the big bang. Within this volume the universe has the continua of space and time with which we are familiar, but beyond there is nothing: no time, no space, and thus the biggest singularity conceivable. The big bang has created a universe of time and space the outer edge of which is Electromagnetic (EM) radiation, the singular rim expanding out at light velocity. The second assumption is that the EM radiation generated by every source or oscillation of charged particles within the universe is drawn out to exactly duplicate the action of this singular expanding rim. This is the corollary effect of Duplication theory to explain the way in which EM radiation is transmitted across space, and is also consistent with the isotropy of light well explained by the special theory of relativity. Diagram 2 below will assist clarify the position here and also gives a very simple explanation of the foreshortening and other effects of Einstein's special relativity.

Figure 2

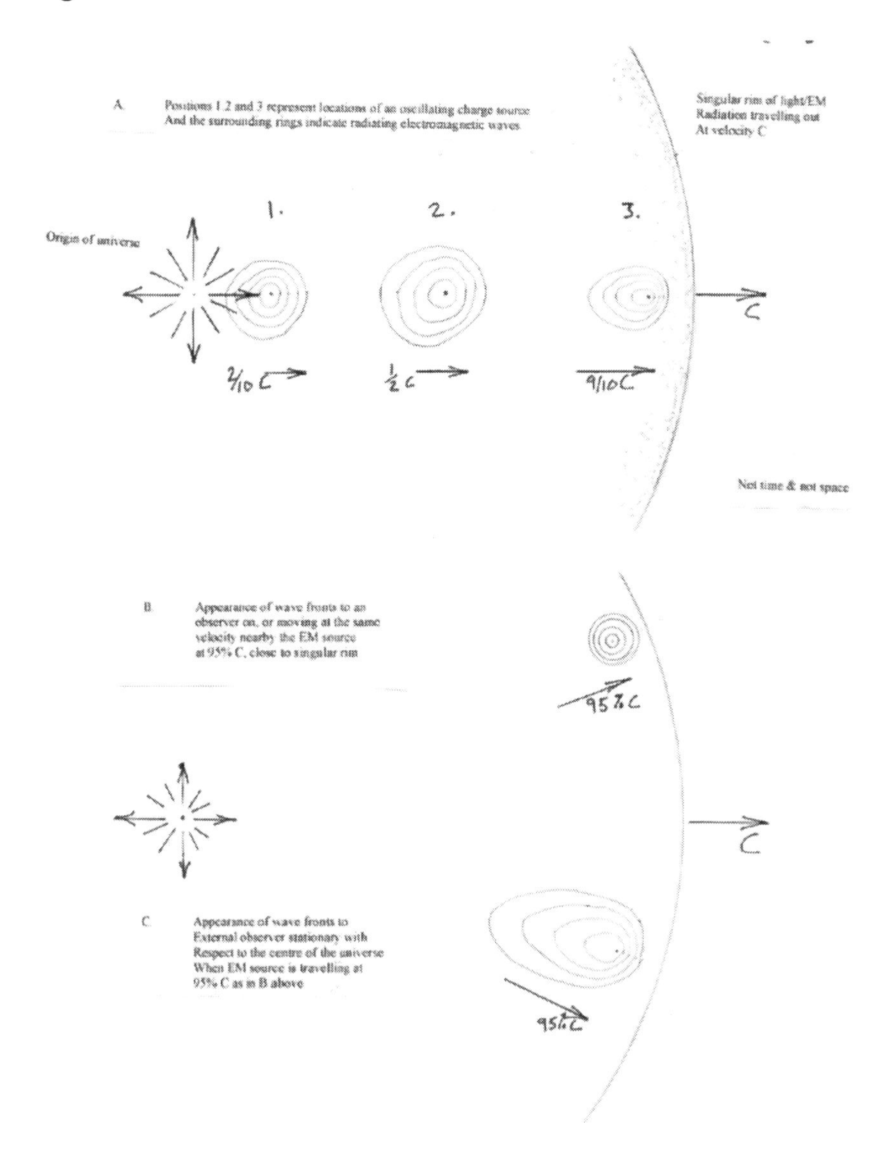

If the singular rim of radiation on the edge of the universe is travelling at light velocity then time will have stood still for this edge from the moment of the big bang. If it were to slow down, and with it, ex hypothesi, that of light velocity within, then the passage of time will presumably change and slow down pro rata within the universe. If the expansion were to reverse into contraction then by this supposition time the passage of time would also reverse, as would also all EM radiation to perfectly duplicate its earlier actions, thus restoring symmetry to the universe in accordance with Maxwell's basic equations, and it would also dispose of the problem of renormalisation that the physicist Dirac so disliked. However, as we currently observe and understand them, waves of radiation are only spreading out one way in time, and this lack of symmetry is the cause of mathematical difficulties which have yet to be resolved. This current lack of symmetrical behaviour in cosmology was one of the reasons why Feynman and Wheeler sought to produce their Absorber Theory in 1945 to reconcile this difficulty, as discussed later below.

I was struck that one of the conditions required for its operation was that the universe be enclosed in a perfectly absorbing opaque container. I saw at once that my notion of universe bounded by a rim of singularity fitted other considerations I had about cosmology. I found the theory to be best explained in a book 'Space and Time in the Modern Universe' by P.C.W.Davies, at Kings College London. Radio or EM waves travel forward only in time, whereas Maxwell's theory requires that EM waves should be symmetrical through time. However, this lack of symmetry causes formidable mathematical difficulties which have always plagued the descriptions of the interaction of charged particles with the EM field. Wheeler and Feynman sought to resolve these problems by analysing what would happen if an accelerating charged particle emitted radiation equally onto the past and future. Clearly this type of behaviour is in contradiction with experience, but they found the following remarkable result. Suppose a single, charged particle in empty space, when set into motion, radiates symmetrically one half advanced waves into the past, and one half retarded waves into the future (the latter being ordinary radio waves with which we are familiar). Then that same particle, when placed into an opaque box, will only fully radiate fully retarded waves into the future. Open the box and the advanced waves will reappear for reasons which are ably explained Davies's book.

A development of this argument showed that electromagnetic waves could be considered as perfectly symmetrical in time, and it also showed that, instead of the concept of the electromagnetic field, this would have to be replaced by the concept of direct action-at-a-distance between the charged particles. This latter would probably not be the instantaneous type, which characterises Newton's theory of gravitation, but a delayed action, propagated at light speed. This action would operate both forwards and backwards in time. An implication of this Absorber Theory can also be shown to be that the universe will collapse back to a point, reversing the big bang. Another is that the passage of time is directly related to the rate of expansion (or contraction) of the universe.

Duplication theory explains the way that EM radiation is transmitted and presents a different hypothesis to that put up by Wheeler & Feynman, but there are some striking similarities, and my version is much easier to visualise with the notion of advanced waves being hard to conceive. The closed universe as I have described it is effectively an opaque box as required by the Absorber Theory, all the more so if for whatever reason the universe started to contract rather than expand: all EM radiation within would also reversed and presumably run backwards through its original course of actions. Effectively time would be reversed except for that of the outside rim of the universe, which with its motion at the mediating speed of light, would never have progressed from the first moment of big bang. If the universe eventually contracted back to nothing then the action of EM radiation would have been perfectly symmetrical as required by electrodynamics and Maxwell. One final quotation on the subject of constants, variable or not, which is relevant to the above and is worth quoting from Paul Dirac is as follows:

"One field of work in which there has been too much speculation is cosmology. There are very few hard facts to go on, but theoretical workers have been busy constructing various models for the universe based on any assumptions that they fancy. These models are probably all wrong. It is usually assumed that the laws of nature have always been the same as they are now. There is no justification for this. The laws may be changing, and in particular quantities which are considered to be constants of nature may be varying with cosmological time. Such variations would completely upset the model makers."

3. An inversion of paper 1 to account for Dark Energy and the expansion of the universe

Synopsis Paper Three: *This section is similar to the first but that instead of gravitation being a force of attraction, it is reversed to one of repulsion. All the same assumptions in sections 1 & 2 have to be made together with some further conjectures. The first is that since two separate particles of mass cannot occupy the same space at the same time: matter repels matter. The fact that gravitation is experienced as an attractive force is rationalised as follows. The effect that the respective masses of two stellar objects (stars, galaxies or lesser masses) will have on each other locally will act to blanket off the repulsive effect of the outer edges of the universe in all directions other than that between the two masses. Some implications of this scenario are given for Dark matter and dark energy.*

This third paper is very speculative indeed. It is based on the fundamental assumption that like repels like, and in the same way that opposite electric charges repel, so units of mass repel each other, for the same reason at a fundamental level that two separate particles of mass at whatever microscopic scale cannot occupy the same space at the same time. Everybody is aware that gravitation is a force of attraction, but on the assumption that the universe is closed and finite, then due to a blanketing effect, gravitation could be operating repulsively on the macro astro-scale despite our contrary experience in the local small-scale dimensions of our observable universe. Such assumptions would appear to allow the quandary of Mach's principle to be rationalised with gravitation, and for inertia to be presented in an altered perspective, similarly to that demonstrated above in paper 1, and such a scenario would also give a rationale of sorts to entropy in general and for the outward expansion of the universe.

There has been some theorising that dark energy might need to be represented generally in the form of negative gravitation since the universe appears to be expanding faster than anticipated. Dutch physicist Erik Verlinde who came up with a proof in January 2010 indicating that gravitation is not a fundamental force but rather an emergent phenomenon that arises from the statistical behaviour of microscopic degrees of freedom encoded on a holographic screen. This encouraged me to reconsider some conjectures that occurred to me on the subject of Mach's Principle in the middle nineties, but dismissed as too fanciful at the time. Given this more recent information coming in from the observations of the astrophysicists, and having again been able rationalise a new framework to present a simple explanation of how Mach's principle and gravitation interact as above, the position on the relativistically vast mass close to the rim is as described in section 1 above still holds good, showing the universe with most of the matter near the outside edge expanding out at close to light velocity

If the universe is finite and bounded and most of its mass is close to the outside edge and traveling outwards at near light velocity as described above in paper 1, then this would have an interesting effect on slower moving galaxies well within the universe. As before the mass of the outer edge galaxies would be relativistically huge if they were traveling at near light velocity. If there was this repulsive effect between separate masses (galaxies, or clumps of galaxies), the repulsive force thus exercised on the interior galaxies would presumably be balanced out in accordance with the inverse square law, so their velocity would not be affected. However, if there were to be some force tending to accelerate them away from their motion in a straight line, they would experience a pressure against this: inertia. As before, Mach's Principle would be endorsed.

This conjecture is confounded by the fact that a dropped weight falls to Earth rather than shooting upwards. However, a simple possibility recently occurred to me which did not seem too unreasonable, and which can best be described as the possible existence of a blanketing effect. Such an effect certainly exists when a mass of conducting material is placed in the way of EM radiation. If my assumption were valid that gravitation was to act in much the same way as EM radiation, like repelling like, then there should indeed be such a blanketing effect. To rehearse my hypothesis, if gravitation were repulsive then the very substantial quantities of matter near the periphery moving very rapidly outward, and certainly well beyond the limits of visibility from Earth, would exercise a huge relativistic and repulsive effect on all matter further within the universe. If the repulsive effect of just one nearby section of the universe on, say the Earth, were considered, and the inverse square law invoked, this would be exactly countered by the much larger section at the opposite end of the universe. In **diagram 2B** the forces from opposing sides of the universe are shown to balance out on a stellar mass two thirds of the distance from the centre. This is very similar to diagram 2 above, except that the forces are outgoing instead of the reverse. In short there would be equilibrium of all such repulsive forces assuming the matter were moving at a constant velocity rather than accelerating so that there would be an inertial effect on this interior matter if it were to be made to accelerate.

However, if two stellar bodies or planets were to approach each other **(Diagram 3B)**, the proposed blanketing effect would start to push them together so that they would start to curve towards each other and when they reached distances close enough that they could not escape, they would fall into an elliptical orbit. It appears that here is some sort of alternative scenario for the explanation of gravitation as a repulsive force. In order to rationalise the extreme case of the attractive gravitational forces of neutron stars, it has to be assumed that the repulsive force created by the prolixity of stars and galaxies at the outer edges is vast and all pervasive which it will be if every object with rest mass is subject to inertia. It has to be assumed that the shielding effect is incremental, so that the repulsive force of the universe's outside edge is far greater than the repellent force that will also be exerted on a planet by for instance, a neutron star. This blanketing ability will increase in effect with the increasing mass of the two relevant masses concerned.

Such a scenario would be the basis for a revised definition for Mach's Principle. In summary it would do away with the notion of gravitation as a separate effect but instead allow the repulsive force driving the expansion of the universe to also define inertia. This force, being equal in all directions (inverse square law), would act on all matter within the universe so that their initial rate of expansion outwards would be unaffected whilst at constant velocity, but which would resist any acceleration. This is all as before in paper 1.

See Diagrams 2B and 3B below

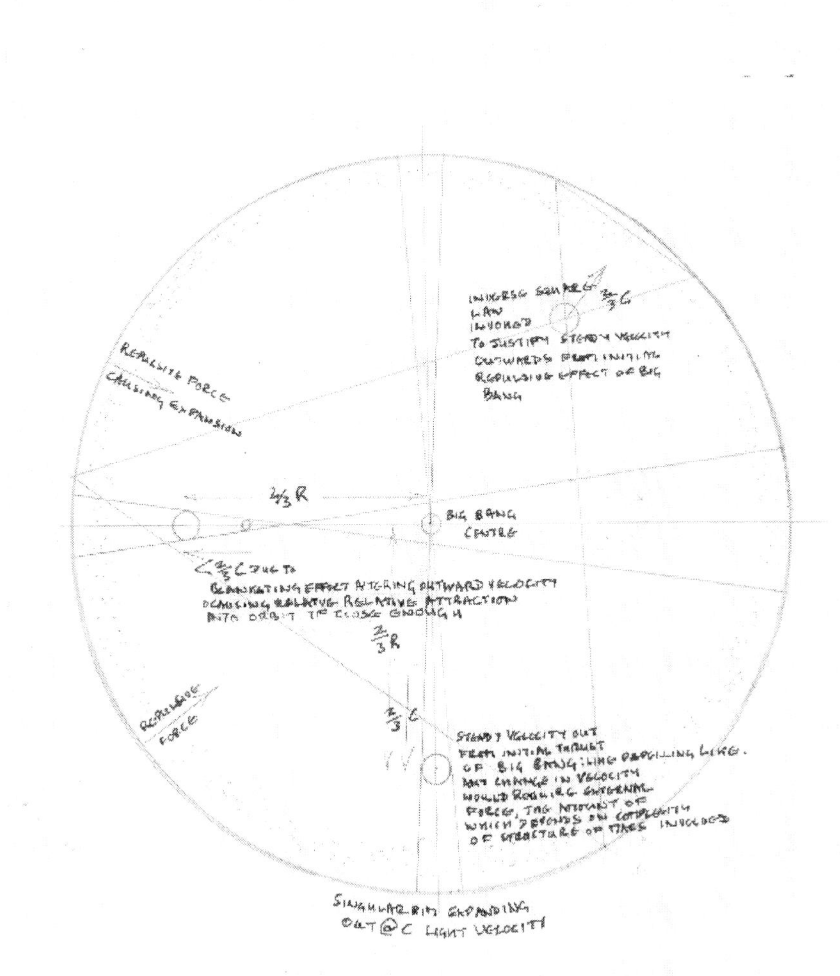
INVERSE SQUARE LAW INVOKED TO JUSTIFY STEADY VELOCITY OUTWARDS FROM INITIAL REPULSING EFFECT OF BIG BANG
2/3 C
REPULSIVE FORCE CAUSING EXPANSION
2/3 R
BIG BANG CENTRE
2/3 R
2/3 C
STEADY VELOCITY OUT FROM INITIAL THRUST OF BIG BANG
ANY CHANGE IN VELOCITY
FORCE
SINGULARITY EXPANDING OUT @ C LIGHT VELOCITY

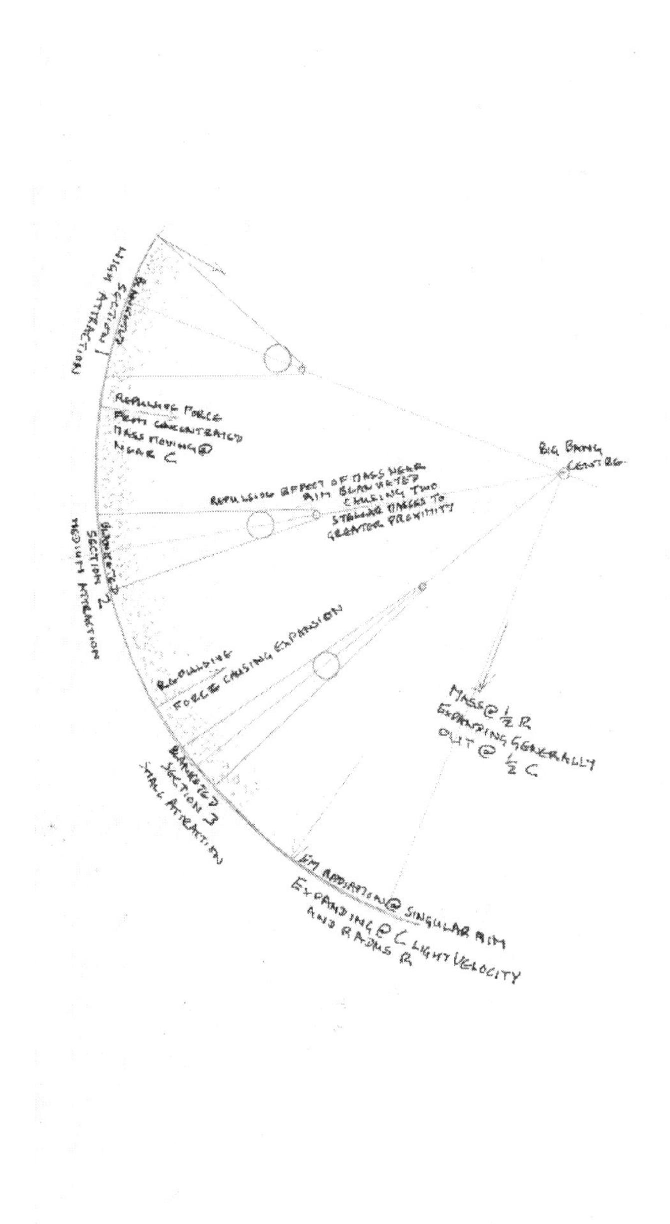

If gravitation were a repulsive force which could be blanketed by intervening mass then a basic rationale for dark energy and indeed the big bang at once suggests itself. A section on the problem of dark energy in Paul Davies book 'The Goldilocks Enigma' seems relevant.

"In the mid 1990s two groups of astronomers stunned the scientific community by announcing that the expansion rate of the universe is actually speeding up, as indicated by observations of supernovas in distant galaxies. That is, the universe is now expanding faster than before, and looks to run away with itself if the trend continues. The discovery rocked the foundations of cosmological theory, built as it was on the firm conviction that gravitation acts as a brake on the expansion, serving to slow it down from its explosive start at the big bang to the relatively modest rate observed today. Now the name of the game had changed. A mysterious antigravity force is opposing gravity and has succeeded in transforming deceleration into acceleration.......

It is too soon to predict that the force causing the universe to accelerate is one and the same as Einstein's original antigravity, although that is certainly the simplest explanation. As I have explained, antigravity can be considered as a consequence of the energy- and the concomitant negative pressure- of empty space itself. Alternatively, we can attribute the energy and negative pressure to an invisible field that permeates space. Either way, we don't see anything of it, so the generic term dark energy is used to denote all these possibilities. Astronomers are planning better measurements to find out more. Whatever it is, if you add up the dark energy responsible for making the universe accelerate, you find that it actually represents a total mass that is more than all matter-visible and dark- put together. It seems that dark energy constitutes most of the mass of the universe yet nobody knows what it is......"

In further support although the connection is not immediately obvious due to the technical nature of the paper, in December 2009 year a Dutch physicist, Erik Verlinde (see http://staff.science.uva.nl/~erikv/page20/page18/page18.html) came up with a theory which has caused some interest and comment from the physics fraternity. It is a theory that derives Newton's classical mechanics. This was followed by the publication of 'On the Origin of Gravity and the Laws of Newton' on 6 January 2010. The abstract reads as follows: "Starting from first principles and general assumptions Newton's law of gravitation is shown to arise naturally and unavoidably in a theory in which space is emergent through a holographic scenario. Gravity is explained as an entropic force caused by changes in the information associated with the positions of material bodies.

A relativistic generalization of the presented arguments directly leads to the Einstein equations. When space is emergent even Newton's law of inertia needs to be explained. The equivalence principle leads us to conclude that it is actually this law of inertia whose origin is entropic."

My proposal of repulsive gravitation agrees with Verlinde's statement that Gravity is not a fundamental force but an emergent phenomenon. There is also a correspondence in his involvement of the holographic principle with my other work which is not covered at all in these three papers having little apparent relevance to cosmology but the implications of which led me to the conclusions above.

References

Davies, P: The Goldilocks Enigma, Allen Lane 2006
Verlinde, E On the Origin of Gravity and the Laws of Newton, Institute for Theoretical Physics, University Amsterdam, Jan 2010

Nick Greaves, Watlington 17/11/10

More recent after thought:

When recently considering the search for dark matter and the nature of WIMPS or MACHOs, I came to a solution of sorts in line with the above proposals as follows. I was aware that one of the reasons for the estimate of dark matter and energy taking up 95% of the universe's mass was also based on the original observations of Astronomer Vera Ruben from 1980 when she published a paper indicating that the stars on the outer reaches of the galaxy were observed to be travelling at much the same velocities as those further in which conflicted with the inverse square law. It was reasoned that the reason for this must that there was a large halo of dark matter stretching out to these outer reaches. No other evidence of this has yet been found, although there have been many experiments searching for rare massive particles and also theories that the laws of Newton do not prevail at such distances.

It occurred to me recently that in a spiral galaxy, such as our own, a star in the midst thereof would be blanketed from the repulsive (or attractive) effect of the outer rim of the universe by all the surrounding stars in that one plane of the spiral on the assumptions made in this paper. When such galaxies are viewed from a distance it is quite possible to see how relatively crowded the stars are placed around the centre of the galaxy. In that plane the usual accepted rules of gravitation and motion might not apply in the midst of that mass of stars due to the repulsive effect of the singular rim of the universe being blanketed off or at least diluted, by the concentration of stars in the flat spiral, and they would then each exhibit much the same velocities. I cannot be sure that this would be the result but it seems to me that there would be much less inverse square law involved, and if so then there would be no need for a halo of dark matter to encircle the galaxy in a sphere. Having said that, the stars on the outer edges of the galaxy would presumably tend to rotate at lesser velocities according to Newton-Kepler predictions their being seriously blanketed only to one side by the central bulk of the galaxy.

This was speculative enough for me to be interested but not too excited by such a possibility, until I read further from a Wikipedia summary on dark matter that globular clusters of stars within galaxies show little evidence that they contain dark matter. From which I conclude that the inverse square law of gravitation as we understand it acts as we might ordinarily anticipate with the outer stars circulating at appropriately lower velocities. Since globular clusters are spherical rather than spiral and less densely distributed in one plane, then by the same reasoning as above, this is what might be expected and would not be inconsistent with my explanation of the nature of gravitation.

If so then here was a simple conclusion to explain why the halo of dark matter around the galaxies was probably a non-starter, and reinforce the possibility that gravitation might be regarded as an emergent force. I understand that dark matter has to be cold, which would also fit very well with my proposals. Such an explanation for dark matter would hold good for both attractive and repulsive gravitation.

December 2013

Appendix 11 – On the Nature of Time

I attended a lecture by physicist Carlo Rovelli on 'The order of time' at the Royal Institution in summer 2018, and was reminded of something about which I had not previously considered seriously. German physicist Rudolf Clausius invented as the concept of increasing disorder and which he defined as the irreversible progress of heat in any one direction. He stipulated that in an isolated process, entropy could be measured and that it could increase or remain the same but it could never decrease. In other words, heat passes only from hot bodies to cold, and never the other way around. Rovelli emphasised that this is the only equation of fundamental physics that knows any difference between past and future, which is crucial for any discussion on the nature of time, and indeed the only one that speaks of the flowing of time. I had not appreciated this crucial last point before hearing him speak and then reading his book. The growth of entropy is nothing more than the familiar and natural increase of disorder over time: very good. Carlo makes the important point that entropy of increasing disorder is the only way we can know that there is a past and a future time, and it can only flow in that direction at a fundamental level.

This fits in very well with my definition of the nature of time. We know that the entropy of the universe is increasing as it expands, but I take things further. Very succinctly I define the passage of time to be directly proportional to and governed by the rate of expansion of the universe. You might ask that if so, how would we ever know that the rate of expansion slowed down, or accelerated? How we would be able to know that was happening? Well that is a point although currently it seems that since Hubble discovered in

1930 the universe was definitely expanding and later, after his death, its rate was calculated, and so could be measured. Having said that, if time was also variable as a result that acceleration then I am not convinced we would be aware of that. We do now know since 1999 from the supernova project headed by Saul Perlmutter (Nobel Laureate) that not only is the universe expanding but also that from observations of supernovae, the rate of expansion is accelerating. However, what does occur to me is that if the universe started to contract, time would start to reverse and I assume we could not avoid becoming aware of that.

So now to the rationale of my hypothesis of the way in which the universe expands. This is explained in a paper I drafted in 2010 with the title 'Mach's Principle, Gravitation and Matter distribution' (see Appendix 10) which in turn was developed from earlier papers on my main interest and attempts to explain Duplication Theory, a mechanism for memory to show how similar structures resonate through time. DT also accounts in a consistent manner for the radiation of electromagnetic action in a non-local quantum manner as a corollary effect to the way that information is transferred across time by entanglement. However, for this scenario to be consistent, the universe would have to be closed, bounded and finite. Furthermore, it would be necessary for the expansion rate of this singular and spherical rim of the universe to be expanding out at light speed. This outer edge, this rim beyond which there is presumably some other continuum, would have to be the most singular concept in the universe. A further implication of this is that all similar EM radiation within would be drawn out to duplicate the outwards action of this expanding singular rim, and what is more, in exactly the same direction and speed. This would be via a quantum resonance system of similar non local action through time as proposed by DT. This hypothesis is surprisingly similar to the Absorber theory on which I comment below. Diagrams produced of such a universe and the way in which EM radiation is thus drawn out give a very simple to grasp illustration of the special theory of relatively if viewed from outside the bounded universe.

The strongest point of reinforcement for such a hypothesis is that it is supported by the Absorber theory of Feynman and Wheeler (1945) which is well known enough to most physicists but not yet taken seriously by many. It is a theory which I use as evidence in support of part of DT which uses a quantum entanglement rationale to the same effect. The interesting thing about the Absorber theory is that it can only work on the assumption that the whole system has to be enclosed within an opaque box, but that was exactly how my universe within the singular rim also has to be arranged. The latter has to be not only opaque but absolutely impenetrable and impassable. The excellent book of mathematician P.C.W. Davies describing the theory does not consider the possibility of a bounded and finite universe, but then things have moved on since 1977 when his book was published.

There can be no better description of the opaqueness intended by the authors, as a finite and bounded universe, although I have no idea of whether Wheeler or Feynman considered that such an opaque universe exactly matches one which is bounded and finite. I am also not sure how the cosmologists saw the shape of the observable universe forty years ago, but today still nothing is at all certain. A number of assumptions have to be made initially about the shape and structure universe: that it is isotropic (uniform in all directions), and homogeneous (uniform in composition) and then this allows General Relativity to explain that mass and energy bend the curvature of space-time and is then used to determine what curvature the universe might possess. It turns out it can either be flat, or have positive curvature or negative curvature. If it is flat then everything is measured in Euclidean terms where triangles have 180 degrees. Or it can have positive curvature which results in the universe being a sphere, very easy to visualize, whereas if it had negative curvature then the universe would be hyperbolically shaped and not so easy visually. The FLRW metric instituted by Alexander Friedman in 1925, and endorsed by physicists Lemaitre, and then later Robertson and Walker, is the most commonly used model for describing various alternative ways of describing the universe, all using an exact solution of Einstein's field equations of general relativity.

The positive curvature version of the sphere is not the most favoured currently, but then the cosmologists, more than in any other area of physics, seem to be least able to agree on anything, despite the millions be spent on huge new telescopes and satellites, and the simplest version seems the most likely to me. This is now especially so for me since it supports my conjecture being in line with the Absorber theory which in turn adds credibility to the second part of DT which does away with the need for photons or particles which is non local and force at a distance, and therefore presumably is a quantum effect. From Carlo Rovelli's excellent book 'Reality is not what it seems' I note he does not favour the alternative of a closed and finite bounded sphere. The fundamental problem is whether the universe was infinite, or had a limit. Both hypotheses entail thorny problems. He states that an infinite universe does not seem to stand to reason, with which I agree, but neither does he approve of a limit to the universe. He suggests instead the concept of the 3 sphere which I find hard to visualise although I understand the rationale, which I do not find that convincing. It seems to me that not knowing what is the other side of a bounded universe is no less problematical than not knowing what is inside a black hole and yet we do know that black holes exist, and that they have very singular boundaries.

The singular rim of our universe is going to be the largest singularity imaginable and its effect would presumably be felt throughout the interior which I propose is in the form not only of the mediation of light speed but also of inertia and gravitation. The latter is still a subject of which we know little as to how it interacts with the other three forces and why indeed it exists, and ditto for light speed for that matter, other than it just does. Why is it such an important constant and why it is a constant at all, when it could be variable? And why is it at that one speed of c.186,000 miles per second? There have to be specific answers to all this, and my proposal offers one in principle, conjectural as it is. Not only does my proposal fit in with the intent of two very perceptive physicists to justify the possibility of nonlocal force at a distance, but we now know that teleportation by entanglement exists, via the work of John Bell's inequality theorem and two decades of successful experimental work.

We also now know that an event on the sun could be detected instantly as soon as it occurs via quantum entanglement effects instead of having to wait for 8 minutes for it to reach us by the limitation of light speed. In short it is possible in theory for the whole of the universe to be connected up with every other part of it in the same one instant. This has to change our perception of the notion of passing time, currently ruled only by light speed. Can such considerations cause us to have to destroy our current understanding of time, such as it nebulously is? No I do not think that but instead there is what I call classical time governed by light speed and the expansion rate of the universe, and then there is also quantum time where everything is engaged and can be interconnected whenever the moment becomes right for this to happen (as per the last chapter of this book). But my conjecture now, with assistance from Carlo's insight on entropy, is that the passage of time is directly proportional to the rate of expansion of the singular rim of the closed universe, which also governs and mediates the velocity of EM radiation within.

Meanwhile the two effects have to be better understood so that they might be correlated to work together to clarify time which can presumably happen only when we have a much-improved grasp of quantum entanglement. One final quotation on the subject of constants, variable or not, which is relevant to the above and is worth quoting from Paul Dirac is as follows:

"One field of work in which there has been too much speculation is cosmology. There are very few hard facts to go on, but theoretical workers have been busy constructing various models for the universe based on any assumptions that they fancy. These models are probably all wrong. It is usually assumed that the laws of nature have always been the same as they are now. There is no justification for this. The laws may be changing, and in particular quantities which are considered to be constants of nature may be varying with cosmological time. Such variations would completely upset the model makers."

References

Davies, PCW.*Space and Time in the Modern University* Cambridge, Univ Press 1977.

Dirac, Paul. "On Methods in Theoretical Physics", June 1968,

Greaves, N. *Mach's Principle, Gravitation & Inertia 2010. RG*

Milne, E.A. Relativity, gravitation and world-structure, S 1932

Wheeler, J & Feynman, R. "Interaction with the Absorber as the Mechanism of Radiation," *Reviews of Modern Physics*, 17, 157–161 (1945).

BIBLIOGRAPHY

Baddely A. D. — The Psychology of Memory. Harper & Row New York, 1976 Bell, Review Modern Physics, vol 38, p.47, 1966

Bohm D. — Wholeness & the Implicate Order. Routledge Kegan Paul, 1980

Brans C. & Dicke R. — Mach's Principle and a Relativistic Theory of Gravitation, Physical Review, 1921

Brooks, M----- Free Radicals, The Overlook Press, 2011

Capra, F.---- The Tao of Physics. Shambal Publications, 1975

Chester A. N. — A Physical Theory of Psi based on Similarity, Psychoenergetics. Vol. 4. nu. 2, P. 89- 111 1981

Clark S. *The Unknown Universe. Pegasus Books* , 2016

Crease R & Mann C---- The Second Creation, Macmillan, 1986

Davies C.P.W. — The Physics of Time Asymmetry. Surrey University Press, 1974

Davies C.P.W. — Space and time in the modern Universe, Cambridge Univ Press, 1972

Davies C.P.W.---- The Origin of Life, 1998
Davies C.P.W. — The Goldilocks Enigma, Allen Lane, 2006

Dirac P. —Scientific American, May. 1963
Dirac P. — On methods in Theoretical Physics, Trieste, June 1968

Eddington A.S. — The nature of the Physical World. P262-272, Cam. Univ. Press. 1929

Einstein A, — Berlin Academy of Sciences, 1921

Einstein A. Rosen N, Podolsky B. — Physics Review, Vol 47. 1966

Feynman R.--- The Character of Physical Law, 1965

Feynman R.--- QED The Strange Theory of Light and Matter 1985

Friston K.J.---The mathematics of mind-time, Aeon, May 2017

Greaves N.G- Duplication Theory, A synopsis: Journal of Scientific & Medical Network December 1988

Greaves N.G- Do the Laws of Nature Evolve? Review of SPR 1999

Greaves N.G. Website: www.mindandmemory.net

Hadamard J. — The Psychology of Invention in the Mathematical Field, Princeton U P 1949
Jung C.G. — Synchronicity. Routledge Kegan Paul. 1955

Joye S.R. *Tuning the Mind*, Viola Institute, 2017.

Joye S.R. *Ten Electromagnetic Field Theories of Consciousness*, Viola Institute, 2018.

Kauffman S. ---- At Home in the Universe, 1995

Koestler A. — The Act of Creation. Hutchison, 1964

Koestler A.--- The Sleep Walkers, Hutchinson 1959

Koestler A. — The Ghost in the Machine. Hutchison, 1967

Koestler A. — The Case of the Midwife Toad Hutchison 1971

Leibniz G.W. — Monadology. Morris edition. 1934

Leibniz G.W. — The philosophical Works of Leibniz. (trans:G.M.Duncan) New Haven, 1890

Marshall N. — ESP and Memory: a Physical Theory, British Journal for the Philosophy of Science, vol X. 1960

Mach E. — The Science of Mechanics, The Open Court Publishing Company, 1893

Mach E. — History and the root of the Conservation of Energy, The Open Court Publishing Company, 1910

Megidish E. et al ---Entanglement swapping between photons that have never co-existed, Phys Rev Lett. 110, May 2013

Milne E.A. — Relativity, Gravitation & World Structure, Oxford, Clarendon Press, 1932

Montmasson J.M. — Invention of the Unconsciousness. Routledge Kegan Paul London p.77, 1931

Nicolis G. Prigogine — Self Organisation in Non-equilibrium Systems, Wiley-Interscience, New York, 1977

Pizzi R. et al---University of Milan, Naval Postgraduate School Monterey: Anomalous Findings in Cultured Neurons in the presence of Laser Pulses, 2007

Pribram K.M. — Languages of the Brain. G. Globus et al: eds. p56. Plenum, New York, 1971

Rovelli C. Reality is not What it seems, Allen & Lane 2016

Rovelli C. The Order of Time, Allen & Lane 2018

Rucker R. — Infinity and the Mind. Harvester Press. 1982
Salisbury F.B. — Nature. Vol 224. P.342, 1969

Sheldrake R. — A new science of Life. Blond and Briggs,1981
Sheldrake R. — The Presence of the Past. William Collins, 1988

Sheldrake R. — The Science Delusion. Hodder & Stoughton, 2012

Schrodinger E.} — My view of the World.
Schrodinger E.} — What is Life? Cam. Univ. Press. 1944

Schopenhauer A. — Panerga und Paralipomena. On the Apparent design in the Fate of the individual. Ed: R.von Koeber, Berlin 1891. Trans: D.Irvine. London, 1913

Smythies J.R.— Science and ESP. P.3. Routledge Kegan Paul, 1967

Smolin, L ----- The Life of the Cosmos. Weidenfeld and Nicholson , 1997

Smolin, L ----- The Trouble with Physics. Houghton Mifflin, 2006

Smolin, L.---- Time Reborn, 2013

Stapp H.P.---- The Mindful Universe. Springer Heidelberg, 2011

Taylor J. — Transfer in Space Time: Journal Society Psychical Research 2000, 1998, 1995

Verlinde E. — On the Origin of Gravity & the Laws of Newton, Institute of Theoretical Physics, Amsterdam, January 2010

Zeilinger, A--- Dance of the Photons. Farrar Straus Giroux, 2010

Printed in Poland
by Amazon Fulfillment
Poland Sp. z o.o., Wrocław

54022884R00174